CRITICAL INSIGHTS

Technology
and Humanity

Editor
Carol Colatrella
Georgia Institute of Technology

SALEM PRESS
A Division of EBSCO Publishing
Ipswich, Massachusetts

Cover Photo: Male figure and circuit board © Rolffimage/dreamstime

Editor's text © 2013 by Carol Colatrella

∞ The paper used in these volumes conforms to the American National Standard for Permanence of Paper for Printed Library Materials, Z39.48-1992 (R1997).

Library of Congress Cataloging-in-Publication Data
Technology and humanity / editor Carol Colatrella.
   p. cm. -- (Critical insights)
 Includes bibliographical references and index.
 ISBN 978-1-4298-3739-2 (hardcover) -- ISBN 978-1-4298-3787-3 (ebook) 1. Technology in literature. 2. Literature and technology. 3. Technological innovations--Social aspects. I. Colatrella, Carol.
 PN56.T37T43 2013
 809'.93356--dc23
                2012023906

PRINTED IN THE UNITED STATES OF AMERICA

Contents

Resources

About This Volume

This volume investigates the diverse ways in which technology and literature meet and influence each other. Human creative expression in literature has long been bound up with technological products and processes. As the introduction "On Technology and Humanity" explains, the relationship between these entities is compelling and mutually constitutive. Interactions of technology and human thought and culture change over time, as cultural values and discourses shape the design, development, and dissemination of technological products and processes. Similarly, literary depictions of technologies and technical processes perform cultural work in illustrating or suggesting how technologies affect people and their prospects. Media theorists recognize that technologies, including the printing press, the factory, the automobile, and the computer, characterize certain historical eras, while socioeconomic circumstances enable or constrain particular inventions, applications, and systems.

Recognizing that it is impossible to construct a comprehensive survey of the national literatures, periods, and genres that reflect humanity's engagement with technology, these scholars instead analyze diverse appearances of technology in literature. Chapters by Narin Hassan, and Melissa Littlefield and Mike Black, describe historical and critical approaches. Looking more closely at particular technologies, Tanfer Emin Tunc considers the appearances of the automobile in early twentieth-century fiction, and Madeleine Monson-Rosen analyzes the representation of digital culture in Thomas Pynchon's *The Crying of Lot 49* (1966). Abigail Glogower, Melissa Dinsman, Claire Menck, Robert Blaskiewicz, Mike Griffith, and Aaron Barlow examine representations of tools, machines, and technical processes in a number of fictional and cinematic narratives that appeared after 1800 and hail from the United Kingdom and the United States, places where the Industrial Revolution emerged. Kevin LaGrandeur and Inger Dalsgaard

About This Volume **vii**

look at classical invention and mythology, while Luis Arata compares references to technology in Jean-Paul Sartre's *Nausea* (1938) and Julio Cortázar's "Treasure of Youth" (published in *Último round*, 1969). Annie van den Oever discusses formalist theory and early cinema, and Jaime Weida compares and contrasts the ways in which two works of Japanese anime reference technology and gender stereotypes. Although these writers cover different ground, they share a concern with how technology and culture influence each other in literature and often create new literary forms.

Narin Hassan's essay on cultural and historical context connects the Industrial Revolution and British Empire with development of the novel genre, emphasizing intersections of professional and personal interests in technology. Mentioning Charles Dickens's *Hard Times* (1854), Elizabeth Gaskell's *Mary Barton* (1848), and nonfiction by Friedrich Engels and Henry Mayhew, Hassan considers the increasing use of tools and technologies in the Victorian era, the development of professionalization in medicine, and the rise of the woman doctor. The chapter traces fictional references to the railway, the telegraph, and new modes of communication. These technologies helped to create new subgenres such as sensation fiction, which became more available due to cheaper means of publishing and the development of the circulating library. Hassan connects ideologies of domesticity to technologies of infant feeding, bottles, and pumps, explaining how novels connect architectural innovations in the home with the politics of women's rights.

In their essay on critical reception, Melissa Littlefield and Michael Black provide an overview of major scholarly works that explore technology and canonical and noncanonical literature, including science fiction and speculative fiction. Their discussion analyzes arguments by C. P. Snow, Cecelia Tichi, Leo Marx, Susan Squier, Colin Milburn, and N. Katherine Hayles to explore three scholarly trajectories: traditional and foundational works concerning American literature and technology (Tichi and Marx); feminist science and technology studies of literature (Squier); and informatics and nanotechnology (Hayles and Milburn). Although the chapter cannot comprehensively account for the volume and variety of scholarship on technology and literature, it delineates significant themes and readings in critical works.

Chapters 4 and 5, respectively, offer a comparative analysis of early twentieth-century American novels representing the automobile and a close reading of a postmodern novel that invents and critiques human engagement with media, surveillance, and computing technologies. Tanfer Emin Tunc's "The Model T and the Roaring Twenties: The Automobile, Social Change, and Cultural Critique in American Literature" examines the impact of the Model T and other automobiles on American culture in the 1920s. Works of fiction by Booth Tarkington, F. Scott Fitzgerald, and Sinclair Lewis offer intriguing analyses of Fordism, mechanization, standardization, and conformity (via the assembly line), and present biting commentaries on the destructive nature of consumer culture and the dangers inherent in sudden, turbulent changes in social values. Madeleine Monson-Rosen's essay "'An Intent to Communicate': Technology and Digital Culture in *The Crying of Lot 49*," explains how Thomas Pynchon's work adapts metaphors from science and technology to literary language. *Crying* marks the first appearance of computer network technologies, technologies that eventually became the Internet, in literature. The novel's focus on networks, its allusions to defense contractors such as RAND, and its use of terms found in media and communications theory and the work of the network developers identify a historically specific engagement with computer communications. Monson-Rosen's discussion relies on work by scholars Alan Liu, N. Katherine Hayles, and media theorist Friedrich Kittler, connecting digital culture and print culture.

Kevin LaGrandeur and Inger Dalsgaard define classical attitudes toward technology and technologists. LaGrandeur's "Technology in Cross-Cultural Mythology: Western and Non-Western" argues that ancient technology is not limited to references in classical mythology. He considers accounts such as quasi-mythological tales such as

Homer's *Iliad*, stories from ancient cultures in India and China, and nonfictional accounts of real instances of technological innovation by ancient inventors. Ancient Greek engineers made devices such as the Antikythera mechanism. Also noteworthy are the devices of Ctesibius and Hero of Alexandria and Philon of Byzantium because they reflect, and are reflected by, various fictional accounts. Chiefly important among technological innovations that appear in stories, myths, and historical events are automata, especially humanoid automata that symbolize how the machine represents the human. Dalsgaard's "The Technologist in Classical Mythology and American Literature" builds on mythological narratives mentioned in LaGrandeur's chapter and looks at myth from a fictional rather than a historical angle. She compares classical attitudes toward the emerging use of technology with works of nineteenth- and twentieth-century fiction that find the rapid progress of science and technology both frightening and promising. Antiquity did not imagine these artisans and engineers as heroic, tragic, or even socially useful, but rather as flawed, irresponsible and, to some degree, dangerous social outcasts. Dalsgaard compares images of classical inventors with literary heirs in Mary Shelley, Herman Melville, and Thomas Pynchon, who update mythological "technologists" such as Hephaestus, Prometheus, and Daedalus to provide a new critical focus.

Abigail Glogower's "'Now Let Us Meet the World': Being, Appearing, and Seeing in Hawthorne's *The House of the Seven Gables*" discusses two nineteenth-century technologies, photography and the railroad, which appear in Nathaniel Hawthorne's second novel. *The House of the Seven Gables* (1851) revolves around the poor, unfortunate siblings Clifford and Hepzibah Pyncheon, whose first railroad journey opens their eyes to the possibility of life beyond their home and present station. Holgrave, their tenant and a young daguerreotypist, helps clear Clifford's name and break the curse upon the Pyncheons. The novel is not a wholesale endorsement of technological progress, but rather a nuanced consideration of past, present, and future. Glogower investigates how Hawthorne incorporates rail travel and photography to make sense of shifting orientations towards public and private life, and the meaning of home in a period of dizzying technological innovation and social change.

In "Opposing Perspectives: Technology in Modernist Literature," Melissa Dinsman describes modernist ambivalence and enthusiasm for technology after radical transformations in manufacturing processes and the horrific outcome of World War I. She contrasts texts embracing technological power and potentials with those rejecting negative outcomes. For the avant-garde futurists, transportation, especially the car, was a welcome technological advancement for its speed and power. Yet these technical advantages lead to human destruction in F. Scott Fitzgerald's *The Great Gatsby* (1925). Linking works by other modern authors who highlight inventions to illustrate the constraining and enabling features of technology, Dinsman analyzes texts by Henry James, T. S. Eliot, and Bertolt Brecht to show how ambivalence toward technology coincides with modernist disaffection and alienation.

Imagined technologies are the subject of Claire Menck's "Inventions in Literature: Time Travel in Works by H. G. Wells, Mark Twain, and Douglas Adams." Time travel has a rich lineage in classic and modern popular literature. Twain's *A Connecticut Yankee in King Arthur's Court* (1889) and Wells's *The Time Machine* (1895) use time travel as a literary device that shifts the paradigms of characters and readers. Developments in space travel and other areas in the later part of the twentieth century initiated a subgenre of fiction that blends technological invention and pop culture. Science fiction narratives, including Douglas Adams's *Life, the Universe, and Everything* (1982) and the long-running BBC television program *Doctor Who*, map an evolution in representations of humanity and technology in elaborating conversations about time travel. The technology gives rise to the most fundamental human question: what is the meaning of life? Menck traces time travel as a literary tool that reflects our modern adaptation to, and relationship with, increased technology.

Luis Arata's chapter also explores synergies of humanity and technology in discussing the role technology plays in contemporary society. "Literary Models of Technological Mediation: Jean-Paul Sartre's *Nausea* and Cortázar's 'Treasure of Youth'" focuses on selected literary works by French philosopher Jean-Paul Sartre and Argentine writer Julio Cortázar, works that explain how technology enhances or diminishes our interaction with the world. Cortázar's short story "The Treasure of Youth" refers to the name of a popular encyclopedia for young readers and offers a hilarious reverse history of technological progress. His deliberately absurd chronology underlines the function of desire in technological progress. This humorous history caricatures the relentless human appetite for safer, simpler, and more intimate forms of transportation. Sartre's novel *Nausea* illustrates a historian's gradual revulsion that history does not rescue individual existence from oblivion; existence is inevitably indifferent to human desire for transcendence. Arata considers the convergence of ideas in these texts alongside contemporary theories, which acknowledge that it is through technology that humanity must mediate existence in the world.

Annie van den Oever's "'Art as Technique': Technology, the Avant-Gardes, and the Birth of the Cinema" uses formalist theory to explicate the relationship between technology and the history of early cinema. Early avant-garde movements, active from about 1905 to 1910, created a form of poetry intended to provoke audiences. Futurist poets, including Vladimir Mayakovsky and Filippo Marinetti, recited their poetry in innovative early avant-garde performances. Russian and Italian futurist poets issued manifestos attacking respected masters of literature, from Alexander Pushkin to Leo Tolstoy. Victor Shklovsky's famous manifesto "Art as Technique" states that we do not really hear or see things once we have become used to seeing and hearing them. Art (poetry, prose, film), according to Shklovsky, should "defamiliarize"—that is, make strange the most familiar things. Texts strike us as "strange" due to the use of techniques that "make [the seen or heard] strange." Van den Oever considers the strong perceptual impact of estranging techniques in poetry in relation to the birth of the cinema, analyzing the first confrontations between poetic technology and the techniques of early cinema. She argues that the emergence of technology—in this case, cinema—has had a lasting impact on modernist art from the 1910s onward, as well as on the "birth" of modern consciousness.

Robert Blaskiewicz asserts, in "Humanity and Technology at War," that a number of American writers who served in the military during World War II detected a change in the status of humanity, especially in one's capacity to shape his or her own destiny. While the phrase "war machine" is now used to describe the deployment of national power and resources to prepare for and wage war, the metaphor came into popular use only in the twentieth century. Authors drew on the metaphor of the machine to explore what it meant for a human to be subject to immense, impersonal forces, and to be both a part and a product of that war machine. Three important American novels that emerged from World War II—Kurt Vonnegut's *Slaughterhouse-Five* (1969), James Jones's *The Thin Red Line* (1962), and Joseph Heller's *Catch-22* (1961)—argue that the individual loses autonomy and free will in the vast machinations of war; however, each novel comes to different conclusions about the capacity of the individual to reclaim humanity in the context of those forces.

In "Android Dreams and Human Imaginings," Aaron Barlow looks at how literary representations of androids reconfigure what it means to be human or machine. Alfred Bester's "Fondly Fahrenheit" (1954) and Robby the Robot in *Forbidden Planet* (1956) build on Isaac Asimov's stories in *I, Robot* (1950) and Mary Shelley's *Frankenstein* (1818) to illustrate interactions between human beings and constructed beings that have intrigued subsequent writers and filmmakers. Humans take pride in a special ability to build, flattering themselves when they construct an artificial being that looks exactly like one found in the natural world. Considering questions of humanity raised in *Blade Runner*

(1982) and *Do Androids Dream of Electric Sheep?* (1968), Barlow also analyzes fiction by Stanisław Lem and William Gibson, and such film as *The Matrix* trilogy (1999; 2003; 2003).

Considering the complexity of technical information and the effects of this complexity on people, Mike Griffith's "Death of the Digital Messiah: Increased Complexity in Virtual Narratives" explores a shifting trend in recent popular science fiction from exploration of the real cosmos to exploration of the digital microcosm. The vast emptiness of space is filled with the density of digital information, and the question of humanity is explored through character development in a highly connected digital environment. Recent coming-of-digital-age stories offer examples of the bildungsroman that are centered on exploration and occasional mastery of digital environments. Examining differences between the exploration and mastery narratives of cyberpunk narratives such as *The Matrix* (1999), *Tron* (1982), and *Neuromancer* (1984), and the exploration, discovery, and growth narratives of *Tron: Legacy* and Gibson's recently completed Bigend trilogy (2003–10), Griffith analyzes the relationship between characters and the environments they adapt to, operate in, and explore. In the nearly twenty years since *Terminator 2* (1991), a series of cultural shifts have taken place, first from overcoming the computer to looking outward, and then from looking inward to an exploration of the digital space that surrounds us.

Jaime Weida's "Ghosts and Girls in the Machine: Technology and the Human in Japanese Visual Popular Culture" compares the representation of the feminine in two Japanese films, *Ghost in the Shell* (1995) and *Armitage III* (1995). Both films became classics of their genre for representing the symbols and tropes of the cyborg commonly observed in Japanese animation. Despite the diversity of the anime medium, there are several common elements of the animated Japanese cyborg that reveal overarching tropes. In anime, the cyborg is more often than not female and contains common gender and sexual markers. The cyborg in anime replicates existing objectification of women, by reenacting the patriarchal creation myths and the general commodification of the female body.

Throughout history, technological achievements in print and digital media have developed and disseminated texts, literary and otherwise. Depictions of technological devices and processes in literature reflect on the relationship between technology and humanity, indicating the possibilities and constraints of how machines, systems, and processes shape and are influenced by human conditions. Essays in this volume explain the connections between technology and culture, surveying political and historical conditions and analyzing features in literary texts that reveal human ingenuity, appreciation, and anxiety with regards to technology. Detailing features of products and processes, representations of technology in literature explore aspects of human character and understanding. The following chapters document how literature continues to offer innovative and speculative views on technologies imagined and otherwise, and to inform inventors, theorists, builders, and consumers. Given the growing relationship between these roles, it is inevitable that over time the interaction of culture and technology will produce new forms of creative expression.

On Technology and Humanity ——————————

Now and Then

Given that each day we encounter technological innovations in scientific fields such as medicine, robotics, nanotechnology, and computing, the project of connecting issues of humanity with issues of technology might seem a strictly contemporary concern. We view Internet and cable television at any time, choose among a variety of social media, and have continuous access to a wide range of text and images. We easily communicate in real time with individuals around the world using cameras in computers or portable devices. Broadcast and print media inform us about emerging events almost immediately and demonstrate how technology—particularly cameras or broadband cell phones—affect outcomes in social and political realms. In 2011, people around the world could watch photos and videos of battles between government forces and insurgents working to overthrow authoritarian regimes and create democracy in a number of Middle Eastern countries (Weingarten et al.). In some cases, protestors organized or at least disseminated information about demonstrations via cell phones and social media networks such as Twitter. Despite the constraints that we associate with the use of technology, ranging from technical failure to intrusive surveillance, the pervasiveness and robustness of its use alert us to the capacity of technology to empower individuals and groups and to create and implement social change.

Yet it would be a mistake to assume that a discussion of technology's benefits and costs in everyday life describes only our own age. Human engagement with technology has a deep history; social progress and creative expression have long been connected with the development, deployment, and representation of what we recognize as technologies. Anthropologists identify early humans as toolmakers and tool users whose inventions enabled hunting, gathering, and other forms of sustenance, including building shelters and cooking food (Stanley). Cave explorations in Lascaux and Chauvet, France, and Altamira, Spain, have uncovered bones that were likely used as tools, paintings from the Paleolithic period that depict animals and indicate that early humans hunted, and diagrams that scholars now regard as sky maps representing constellations. More than 17,000 years old, these cave paintings document how humans made sense of the natural world, using technological means to illustrate it. Likely produced with torches that lit the inside of the caves (fire is one of the earliest technologies), cave paintings reveal the artistic, spiritual, scientific, and technological interests of our ancestors. Thus, the paintings are both technological achievements and aesthetic artifacts, as professor of art Peter Giscombe notes.

Technology and humanity share a relationship of mutual influence. Historical accounts of the Western world's development of communication technologies, and literary representations of technology in diverse contexts, exemplify two modes of interaction. These narratives investigate the ways in which technology constrains and enables cultural representation, notably by depicting how human beings use and reconfigure technology.

Terms and History

The word "technology" signifies more than technological processes and material artifacts (machines, tools). Scholars investigating the historical and social aspects of technology's development and deployment argue that the tool, the toolmaker, and the tool user should be understood in the term "technology." Professor Rosalind Williams's university website explains that she is "a historian who uses imaginative literature as a source of evidence and insight into the history of technology." In "The Political and Feminist Dimensions of Technological Determinism," an essay about feminism and technology, Williams asserts that "knowledge and ideology are inherently part of the meaning of 'technology'" (218). Similarly, for Richard Guy Wilson, "The machine in all its manifestations—as an object, a process, and ultimately as symbol—became the fundamental fact of modernism" (23).

According to Liddell and Scott's Greek lexicon, the etymology of the word "technology" reveals associations of craft, creativity, and culture. The Greek term *techne* signifies art, skill, and craft in work, including references to shipbuilding and offering prophecies. Essays in this volume by Kevin LaGrandeur and Inger Dalsgaard document classical Greek interest in and ambivalence about inventors and inventions. Plato's fifth-century BCE dialogues—*The Republic*, *Gorgias*, and *Phaedrus*—explore why the debating philosophers prefer craft to art. Their argument centers on how art works unpredictably, even dangerously, to stimulate human subjects, as demonstrated in dramatic performances and recitations of Homer's *Odyssey*. In contrast to art that appears to incite without purpose, household objects (e.g., containers, dishware) and tools employed in agriculture, shipping, and other labor were appreciated by these thinkers as functional works of craftsmanship. Hearing about Odysseus's travels and his slaying of the suitors who took over his household may thrill the bard's audience, but what listeners might learn from the epic is not predictable. The power of fiction, poetry, and drama to excite an audience worried those philosophers concerned with moral education; a similar debate occurs today when we discuss the influence of mass media (sound recordings, television shows, films, video games, YouTube videos) or social media on unethical and illegal acts.

The cultural dimensions of the word *techne* point to its meaning as a system or method of making or doing—resonances that contemporary theories of science and technology incorporate when describing the interface of technology and social organization. Historians of science and technology identify texts by inventors and patrons that acknowledge ideological motivations and influences. Religious inspiration also motivated achievements in science and technology, which developed in the contexts of culture and society (Noble; McKenzie and Wajcman). The history of millenarian ideologies, which stipulate a future following the Second Coming of Christ in which he will reign on earth in peace, reveals how religious figures promoted interest in mechanical arts and technology throughout Western history.

Historian of technology David Noble explains how medieval thinkers "formulated . . . a perception of the advancing useful arts as at once an approximate anticipation of, an apocalyptic sign of, and practical preparation for the prophesied restoration of perfection" (29). Noble quotes literary historian Perry Miller, to describe the Second Great Awakening in America: "the advance of the arts was at once the work of man and God, the useful human development of the earth and the reign of heaven on earth. As Miller suggested, 'it was not only in the Revival that a doctrine of *perfectionism* emerged; the revivalistic mentality was sibling to the technological'" (90–91). Educator Amos Eaton and statesman Stephen Van Rensselaer's founding in 1824 of the first civilian engineering school in the United States (now Rensselaer Polytechnic Institute) put "preaching into practice" (93). Noble draws attention to American author Henry David Thoreau's 1843 review of John Adolphus Etzler's *The Paradise within the Reach of All Men, Without Labor, by Powers of Nature and Machinery* (1833), which points out "that there is a transcendentalism in mechanics" (qtd. in Noble 92).

American medical professor Jacob Bigelow used the word "technology" in the title to his published lectures *Elements of Technology* (1829), identifying the term as "the principle, processes, and nomenclatures of the more conspicuous arts, particularly those which involve applications of science" (v). Borrowing the term from German Johann Beckman, Bigelow celebrated technology's powers: "we have acquired a dominion over the physical and moral world, which nothing but the aid of philosophy could have enabled us to establish" (qtd. in Noble 93). Bigelow's speech at the opening of the Massachusetts Institute of Technology admitted that "[technology] has had a leading sway in promoting the progress and happiness of our race" (Noble 93). Our understanding of technology as useful tools and inventions aiding in the progress of civilization has expanded over time.

Contemporary historians of technology recover and regain meanings of the word "technology" to reference systems, including systems of communication. In this way, language is understood as a technology. In *The Legacies of Literacy* (1991), scholar Harvey Graff defines literacy as "above all *a technology or set of techniques for communications and for decoding and reproducing written or printed materials*" (4). He understands the connections between literacy and systematizing as organic and not linear:

> Literacy is for the most part an enabling rather than a causal factor, making possible the development of complex political structures, syllogistic reasoning, scientific enquiry, linear conceptions of reality, scholarly specialization, artistic elaboration, and perhaps certain kinds of individualism and of alienation. Whether, and to what extent, these will in fact develop depends apparently on concomitant factors of ecology, intersocial relations, and internal ideology and social structural responses to these. (2)

The domains of language and literature thus qualify as technologies, as they constitute systems of human knowledge. Literature is shaped and disseminated by technology, and as a form of creative expression in turn influences the development and reception of technologies.

Technologies of Printing and Publishing

Writers and readers depend on publication technologies for the development and distribution of texts, processes that help shape the conventions of literary genres and structures of specific works. Historians of technology, including Jacob Bigelow in his chapter "The Arts of Writing and Printing," document the transmission of texts, literature included, which has appeared at different times and places on Sumerian tablets, Egyptian papyrus, Chinese paper, and parchment and cotton paper. Context matters: the circumstances of the production and dissemination of texts identify literature's critical engagement with technology.

Print and digital publishing initiate and respond to the development of a reading public. Audience demands spur innovations in writing, producing, and disseminating literature and other media that have profound cultural outcomes (Watt). After Johannes Gutenberg's development of the printing press with movable type around 1440, the Bible was more readily available in Europe. This allowed a greater portion of the populace to read without clerical intervention, as was formerly necessary; reading individually encouraged the rise of Protestantism. Successive eighteenth- and nineteenth-century innovations in printing and distribution enabled cheaper book and newspaper production, and a larger readership in Great Britain and Europe for many literary genres, particularly the novel (Watt). Booksellers and printing companies dispersed a selection of works formulating ideas of national identity in colonial and revolutionary America (Brown).

In the twenty-first century, we witness the fast-paced, innovative development of information technologies and their deployment around the world. Instead of consulting printed books, journals, and newspapers available by subscription or in libraries, we read breaking news, electronic mail, literature, and more on networked portable devices that also show films and play music. The ubiquity of social and civic media reinforces the need for more scholarly work concerning social interactions with technology, particularly since its products, processes, and systems have pervasive, powerful effects around the world and not all populations enjoy equal access or authority (Colatrella, 2011).

Information technology enabled the creation of portals and free databases of electronic text, as users of Alan Liu's Voice of the Shuttle and Google Books recognize, giving rise to new modes of analyzing and discussing literature. Digital humanities scholars such as Franco Moretti employ technology to search texts and to quantify their role in the history of publishing. Theorist Friedrich Kittler declares that literature is a media technology, one capable of expressing, guiding, and resisting cultural values. New forms of text on personal digital devices and social media reconfigure literary structure and content (Murray).

In 2008, a number of young women wrote cell phone novels that dominated the publishing market in Japan, and today poets practice their craft using Twitter, creating genres that would be unavailable without the technology involved (Onishi). Technology and literature continue to evolve in tandem with each other in productive yet unpredictable ways.

The Interaction of Technology and Humanity

Scholars from various disciplines and interdisciplinary fields have devised different conceptual models to generalize about the relations of humanity and technology. For example, media theorist Marshall McLuhan's *The Gutenberg Galaxy* (1962) considers that "technological environments are not merely passive containers of people but are active processes that reshape people and other technologies alike" (ixii). Thus, the interaction of technology and humanity occurs as two-way traffic. Social scientists Donald McKenzie and Judy Wajcman note their objections "to a simplistic technological determinism"—that is, to a view wherein technology decides social structure and cultural values: "Politically, it seemed to us to encourage a passive attitude to an enormously important part of our lives. It discouraged creative engagement with technology. . . . [and] it neglected the ways in which the relations between people affect the things they make" (xiv). We encode our cultural values in building and using things and processes. Such two-way traffic of social change and technology is illustrated by a number of essays in this volume.

Individuals and social groups do not always engage with a technology in the same way. As Ronald Kline and Trevor Pinch describe it, the theory known as "social construction of technology (SCOT) emphasizes the 'interpretive flexibility' of an artifact. The same artifact can mean different things to different social groups of users" (113). For example, the telephone was initially marketed to facilitate business activity, but women using it from their homes contributed to "changing the social practices of telephone use" (Martin 50). As historian

Michèle Martin documents, women used the telephone for informal conversations and to arrange social engagements. The telephone became a device that promoted personal relationships and broke down social barriers separating young men and women, whose interactions had previously been constrained.

Some frameworks for understanding the relationship of technology and humanity emphasize their recursive interactions (i.e., that they influence and shape each other). Political scientist and philosopher Langdon Winner argues "technologies are not merely aids to human activity, but also powerful forces acting to reshape that activity and its meaning. . . . When a sophisticated new technique or instrument is adopted in medical practice, it transforms not only what doctors do, but also the ways people think about health, sickness, and medical care" (6). Technology transforms social organizations and the individuals participating in them, as the texts discussed in the second half of this chapter assert.

Classicist and computer scientist Jay David Bolter writes in *Turing's Man* (1984) that each historical era of Western civilization has had its "defining technology," which "develops links, metaphorical or otherwise, with a culture's science, philosophy, or literature; it is always available to serve as a metaphor, example, model, or symbol" (11). Tanfer Emin Tunc's chapter tracks the Model T's development and its influence on a number of American modernist novels. The key relationship parsed by technology is that which stands between humanity and nature, for as Bolter explains, "A defining technology defines or redefines man's role in relation to nature" (13). Philosophers Asle Kiran and Peter-Paul Verbeek agree: "Technologies co-shape the appearance of the world; we do not just see a world, the world appears to us in certain ways; technologies structure and organize the world" (417). They also consider the effects of technological interaction on humanity: "every technological development puts at stake what it means to be a human being" (409). Following French philosopher Bernard Stiegler,

Kiran, and Verbeek argue, "Technologies do not extend human beings, but rather help to constitute them" (419).

Some scholars point to how creativity and imagination affect development and reception of technology. Dutch social scientist Wiebe Bijker claims that "stories we tell about technology reflect and can also affect our understanding of the place of technology in our lives and our society" (1), a stipulation noted in this volume by Narin Hassan, Madeleine Monson-Rosen, Abigail Glogower, and Melissa Dinsman. Arnold Pacey, who writes and lectures on the history of technology and policy, points out that "studies of social construction and the political economy of technology have led to important insights," adding that "personal or imaginative responses to technology" are also useful (4). Pacey acknowledges that gender is "a very significant factor in attitudes toward technology (and to related ethical problems)" (5). Similar issues are noted by feminist scholars, as the chapter by Melissa Littlefield and Michael Black acknowledges. The last part of this introduction considers how race, ethnicity, hierarchical rank, and nationality also affect the deployment and reception of technology.

Literary Conventions about Technology

Printing, publication, transportation, and other technologies shape the conventions of literary genres and the structures of particular works. Many literary texts describe, celebrate, and criticize technology on the basis of humanist concerns related to social organization, politics, or psychology. Human curiosity and ambition to exercise power over nature appear in narratives that have become touchstones in modern culture for their delineations of how the human and the technological meet. The classical myths of Pandora and Prometheus demonstrate anxiety about human overreaching, a topic also touched on in Mary Shelley's novel *Frankenstein*, which expresses caution about what happens when an ambitious scientist seeks to reproduce the human in technological form (Colatrella, *Toys and Tools*).

A cinematic example of human aspirations and anxieties regarding technology, Stanley Kubrick's *2001: A Space Odyssey* (1968) references compelling episodes of humanity's interaction with technology across different historical periods. Based on a science-fiction story by Arthur C. Clarke, the film is both a document detailing future technologies and a new kind of film technology. One celebrated scene illustrates a primate descendant picking up a bone as an early example of a tool deployed for violent purposes. Another episode depicts the dependence of twentieth-first-century astronauts on the HAL 9000, a computer with deadly aims to supplant them. Film scholar Robert Kolker explains the film's invention of modern ideas of space: "*2001* is not only a narrative of space travel, but a way of seeing what space travel *should* look like. The film is a design for our imagination and a notion of modernity, creating the lineaments of a modern environment and enunciating the metamorphosis of human into machine" (108). *2001* tests viewers' capacities by presenting a series of scenes that do not share settings or characters; the audience must meditate on what each scene means and how it relates to other scenes, finding that the connections among the episodes are thematic, representing various intersections of technology and humanity.

Contemporary writer Brian Selznick similarly reconfigures genres to produce an innovative novel exploring the invention and deployment of several technologies, including automata, card tricks, clocks, locks and keys, trains, and movies. Selznick's *The Invention of Hugo Cabret: A Novel in Words and Pictures* (2007) melds conventions of magic, film, children's books, and graphic novels to create a cinematic book that tells the story of the work and rediscovery of the French filmmaker Georges Méliès (1861–1938). The protagonist Hugo is a twelve-year-old boy secretly living and working in a Paris train station in 1931, where he takes up his uncle's position as the winder of the station clocks. A gifted mechanic who can put together wind-up toys, Hugo learns magic from a grouchy toy seller in the station, works to finish his deceased father's robotics project, and fortunately meets up with a young girl who holds the key to the mechanical man. Putting the key in the robot produces a drawing, and Hugo and his new friend Isabelle work to find out what the mysterious drawing means and why it includes the signature of Isabelle's godfather, Georges Méliès. The narrative details the rediscovery of Méliès and a trove of his films, a number depicting human engagement with technology. The French Film Academy helps to subsidize Hugo's moving into the Méliès household. The novel, as written and drawn by Selznick, becomes an innovative technological artifact, bringing together image and word and celebrating cinema.

Technology in Literature, Literature as Technology

Many literary works from the United States and Europe represent technology and its interaction with individuals and social groups. Works written during and after the Industrial Revolution reference technology as a force behind cultural change; for example, Elizabeth Gaskell's *Cranford* (1851–53) and Stendhal's *Le rouge et noir* (*The Red and the Black*; 1830) acknowledge the railroad and the factory as intrusions that upset traditional ways of life in small villages.

Herman Melville's *Moby-Dick* (1851) is a celebrated American literary depiction of the cultural dimensions of a nearly outmoded technology. In addition to Captain Ahab's obsession with the white whale who "dismasted" him, and the making of Ishmael as a writer, the novel documents the tools and technical processes employed by nineteenth-century whaling crews to hunt, kill, and process the animal. Whaling was an industry on the decline when Melville wrote the novel; the number of whales had decreased and petroleum has become a preferred energy source. Acknowledging the anachronistic status of whaling, the *Pequod* appears in Chapter 16 as "a rare old craft," "a ship of the old school, rather small if anything; with an old-fashioned claw-footed look about her" (69).

The *Pequod*'s mission to conquer and lay claim to a natural species for profit exemplifies the political philosophy of Manifest Destiny, first mentioned in John L. O'Sullivan's 1845 article supporting the U.S. annexation of Mexico in the *United States Magazine and Democratic Review*. Emphasizing Ahab's mission and identifying the virtues of first mate Starbuck and chief harpooner Queequeg, the novel shows the ship's diverse crew as representing the United States. Technically proficient and rapacious, the multiethnic crew exert their advantages over their competitors and their prey. *Moby-Dick* documents the deployment of whaling technologies and suggests the dangers of the enterprise. At the same time, the novel revels in the brotherhood of men who, while splashed with the creature's blood, use whaling tools and techniques to capture, murder, and dismember the whale. Only Ishmael—whose narrative identifies Ahab's obsessive quest to kill the white whale with American political and technological ambitions—survives the three-day battle with Moby-Dick. Ishmael survives to tell of these adventures because his tolerance, rationality, and hard-won technical skill persist despite the whale's brute force and Ahab's revenge scheme (Colatrella, *Literature*).

We can identify similar embeddings of technology in other literary periods, as the chapters in this volume illustrate. Building on Bolter's ideas about technology defining a historical era, literary scholar Cecelia Tichi argues that "the machine-age text does not contain *representations* of the machine—it too *is* the machine" (16). Tichi looks at how fiction and poetry in the age of modernism "became recognizable as designed assemblies of component parts, including prefabricated parts." She argues that writers such as John Dos Passos, Ernest Hemingway, and William Carlos Williams "exploited" "the creative potential of the dominant technology." "Their work [creates] . . . the culture of the gear-and-girder technology" and "demonstrates that a technological revolution is a revolution not only of science and technology but of language, of fiction, and ultimately of poetry" (16).

Technologies of Dissent

Literary scholar Sacvan Bercovitch considers that in American culture, helped by persuasion and the human desire for change over time, dissent becomes consensus. His phrase "transcendentalizing the subversive" inspires analysis of American texts in which technology becomes an important means of dissent, enabling individual empowerment in society (*Rites of Assent*, 24). Frederick Douglass's *Narrative of the Life of Frederick Douglass* (1845) and Charlotte Perkins Gilman's *What Diantha Did* (1909–10) illustrate human engagement with technology as the protagonists overcome social barriers. Depicting a similar recuperation, Margaret Edson's *Wit* (1999) highlights the ways in which medical technology must consider the human dimension of medical care. Richard Powers's *Gain* (1998) more critically connects individual medical prospects with those of a corporation producing a range of consumer products that affect human health. These texts focus on questions of identity, cultural authority, individual and corporate achievement, and social relationships central to the development of society and politics in United States. These issues become important in other places as technical innovations spread around the world, impacting individuals and societies.

Frederick Douglass's nonfiction account in his 1845 narrative acknowledges the inequity of slavery and the cruelty of slave owners as reasons to abolish the practice. The thematic conjunction of unjust punishment, inherent human value, and yearning for equity becomes the essential dynamic of Douglass's memoir. Incorporating historically authentic information, the narrative is both a story of how one man escaped the bonds of slavery and a parable inspiring readers to pursue literacy and education. Douglass describes his subordination by owners at each stage of life: fathered by his master, deprived of mother and siblings, treated as an animal and as chattel, and eventually maturing to adulthood and freedom. He does so despite his various owners' adherence to slaveholding ideology, for he understands that words can initiate the process of setting him free.

Douglass's work describes three types of technology: bonds, shackles, and whips used to hobble or torture slaves; tools for working on plantations and in shipyards; and finally literacy, the key technology that allows slaves to aspire to freedom. Horrific scenes—such as young Frederick's observing his aunt being whipped, and his violent battle with Mr. Covey, which makes the slave a man—point to the abuse that forms Douglass's resistance to bondage. His experience as a slave includes being unfairly accused of damaging the master's tools, being whipped, and obtaining a root that serves as a protective tool. As an instrumental technology, literacy helps Douglass recognize and reduce his dependence on his owners; it enables his escape from slavery. He describes his move from a state of oppression under the technology of slavery to one of literacy and, eventually, proficiency as a teacher, writer, and public speaker.

The wife of one of Frederick's owners, Mrs. Auld, teaches him to read until her husband points out that reading and writing will help Frederick understand the hypocritical ideology of slavery and overcome his bondage. Acknowledging literacy as empowering, Douglass recognizes that physical abuse and torture employ technologies to punish (and, in certain cases, murder) African American slaves. Technology appears in the text as both problem and solution. The narrative's abolitionist argument documents technologies (the lash and literacy) to persuade readers of the horrible conditions endured by slaves, their intelligence and competence while working for slave owners, and the slaves' desire for freedom. Later writers followed Douglass, reporting how technology could benefit socially marginal and powerless groups.

Many women invented and deployed tools and technologies throughout history (Stanley), although these achievements were not always recognized during their lifetimes. Historians of domestic technology, notably Dolores Hayden, relate numerous innovative housekeeping schemes intended to improve efficiency and reduce workload for the individual housekeeper (most often the wife and mother). Sociologist Ruth Schwartz Cowan's study, based on early twentieth-century time diaries kept by urban and rural housewives, finds that greater availability of improved domestic technologies, such as refrigerators, washing machines, electric irons, and vacuums, counter-intuitively made more work because of elevated norms in housekeeping and childcare standards.

Gilman's novella *What Diantha Did* tells how one young woman creates a career as a successful entrepreneur, employing technologies and implementing systems to improve housekeeping and elevate the quality of domestic work. After an unsatisfactory stint as a schoolteacher, Diantha Bell thinks up a way to systematize housework that allows her to earn a living as a manager of domestic servants. She establishes herself first as a domestic servant for a couple, then ramps up her scheme by becoming the manager of servants in a large wealthy household. With her millionaire employer as her partner, Diantha develops an agency for domestic servants, a cafeteria, and a food delivery service before designing and establishing a restaurant and hotel.

Diantha aims to earn enough to marry her fiancé Ross, a young man burdened by family debt and obligations (a widowed mother and four unmarried sisters disinclined to work). Although Diantha's plan to professionalize housekeeping shocks Ross's family as well as her own, by sticking to it she creates businesses that help employers, domestic laborers, and families. Domestic servants' self-esteem and professionalism increase, while housewives are able to work outside the home as cooking and cleaning are entrusted to professional workers. Families are happier because domestic employees do quality work for reasonable pay. The maids are not live-in servants, so families have more room in their homes. There is less anxiety about inappropriate relations between family and servants. Eventually, Diantha's earned money and an anonymous benefactor encourage Ross to sell his family grocery store, which enables the couple to marry. Her husband quietly resents Diantha's choice to continue working at her various business operations when they marry. But after he travels abroad and learns how the world praises his wife, he finally recognizes the social value of Diantha's achievements and tells her that he is proud.

Gilman's didactic fiction illustrates how women should take inventory of their assets and skills to create entrepreneurial schemes satisfying individual and social needs and goals. Like Gilman's many short stories, her novel represents the value of work and the importance of technical systems designed to improve home and society. Within her father's household, Diantha uses financial accounting to figure revenue and expenses, to detail her labor and its value, and to convince him that he undervalues her contributions. She applies the same methods to her employers and, eventually, to assess her own business practices. Applying this technical system enables Diantha to move toward financial independence, and enables readers to understand the benefits of establishing organizational systems to manage domestic work.

Douglass and Gilman write generically different works (autobiographical memoir and novel) that share an interest in representing how technologies constrain and enable individual labor and socioeconomic prospects in an entrepreneurial world. These texts acknowledge the costs and benefits of their characters, who have both accessed or become subjects of technological tools and techniques. Each work highlights tools and processes that shape plot, characterization, and setting. Characters' notions of self and society are transformed through their engagement with technological systems (literacy and housekeeping). Yet, as Edson's play and Powers's novel demonstrate, sentiment and empathy are important supplements to technology.

Medicine, Gender, and Technology

As historian of technology Melvin Kransberg reminds us, technology is not good, bad, or neutral. Appreciation of technology's value shifts depending on the circumstances of development and employment. A compelling play that focuses on medical technology and care, Edson's *Wit* depicts the last months of Vivian Bearing, a professor of English literature who is a terminal cancer patient. Vivian receives state-of-the art treatment through an experimental clinical trial and endures extreme doses of chemotherapy to eradicate her stage-four metastatic ovarian cancer. Accustomed to being in control of her research and teaching, Vivian, during her hospital stays, transforms from a demanding professor to a frustrated patient. She endures frequent tests, painful procedures, and the ubiquitous question, "How are you feeling today?" even when she is violently ill or "emerging from a four-hour operation with a tube in every orifice" (5).

Her vulnerabilities are not recognized by every character in the play. Dr. Jason Posner, Vivian's former student and clinical fellow, regards her as tough and able to withstand intense treatment, while senior specialist Dr. Harvey Kelekian treats his patient as a machine when he tells her "to keep pushing the fluids" (Rimmon-Kenan). In contrast, the women in the play (Vivian's nurse Susie and her former professor, the great E. M. Ashford) treat Miss Bearing as a human being in need of physical care and emotional comfort.

In a childhood flashback, Vivian reveals her pride in first learning to love a word ("soporific" in Beatrix Potter's *Flopsy Bunnies*), and other flashbacks reveal her most distinguished scholarly achievements of analyzing and teaching John Donne's poems. Vivian's sense of self depends on this intellectual work, her careful, highly regarded scholarly research, and related teaching. Engaging the attention of hospital employees, she reports, is "flattering. . . . for the first five minutes" (16). The rest of the time Vivian endures indignities, many related to technical procedures. Hurried from her hospital bed for a test, Vivian must wait for the procedure while the technician takes a break. She has a pelvic exam administered by her former student, whose bedside manner is so underdeveloped he leaves Vivian's feet in the stirrups while he looks for a "girl" to be present during the exam. Without acknowledging Vivian as a person, the residents discuss her case in front of her during "Grand Rounds" conducted by Dr. Kelekian.

During her hospital treatment, Vivian comes to realize that, like her, Jason loves research more than people. He deeply resents clinical training as a waste of time, for he would rather analyze data than treat patients. Observing Jason's cold, technical efficiency, Vivian concludes near the end of her life that her technical brilliance and scholarly absorption prevented her from connecting with others. Appreciating the popsicles Susie brings and chats over, and the affection that Professor Ashford shares during a brief visit, Vivian transforms from a stuffy pedagogue absorbed by poetry into a suffering, lonely woman who eventually finds some relief from her disease in human companionship.

The play parallels Professor Bearing's technical expertise with words and Donne's complex language with the doctors' medical abilities and technical vocabulary. Shlomith Rimmon-Kenan acknowledges, "Language in *Wit* is thus perceived both as offering an alternative to the world of the hospital and as similar to the very space it tries to transcend, gradually shrinking and ultimately helpless against pain and death" (352). Both technologies—language and chemotherapy—prove insufficient in keeping Vivian alive. Yet, by valuing human contact and communication at the end of her life, Vivian achieves the grace of humanity (Purcell). Human sentiment, characterized as feminine in this play, appears as a necessary supplement to cutting-edge technology in meeting the patient's needs. Without humanity, technological interventions in medicine treat the patient as a machine-like body to be fixed. The audience, like Vivian, resists accepting the formulation of patients as machines and recognizes value in responding to each patient's emotional and mental concerns.

Richard Powers's 1998 novel *Gain* tracks a similar transformation of a female protagonist with ovarian cancer, Laura Bodey, and "braids" her personal story, treatment, and death into a larger story of capitalist ingenuity and technical innovation. Laura's family—including her ex-husband, daughter, and son—learn to recognize her illness as an outcome of environmental pollution in their community. Lacewood, Illinois, is the midwestern home of Clare, a company that begins as a soap factory and becomes a global corporation with thousands of consumer products.

The history of Clare's development becomes an allegory of American capitalism, describing technical and social circumstances affecting research and development, emerging governmental regulations, and consumers' changing preferences for products. Powers adopts the heterogeneous narrative style of Melville's *Moby-Dick* to present a modern tale detailing how a corporation and its changing cast of officers profit from technically improved products, while consumers bear the medical costs of treating cancers that result from their use of these products. The book contains a variety of documents related to the corporation: a number of adages and advertisements, scripts for television commercials (106–8, 336–37), the pamphlet "Good business makes good neighbors" (157–58), a chart detailing material inputs and outputs of the manufacturing process (194), a president's notes for a speech, an excerpt from Henry Adams extolling the benefits of technology (282), and a 1909 organizational chart (312). The company grows large enough to create "a new managerial class," which the narrator describes as "a vast man-of-war, if not a small armada" (312).

Like the varied accounts of the gold doubloon in *Moby-Dick*, *Gain* incorporates different characters' perspectives on Laura's illness and treatment. These include her gradual realization that while her gardening has exposed her to carcinogenic pesticides, she could scarcely avoid coming into contact with dangerous chemicals. Two scenes in the novel describe the terminally ill Laura meditating over objects associated with Clare. She reviews Clare advertising items and confronts the products found in her own home. In a historical museum, Laura views the origin of Clare soap and sees the root discovered in the South Seas by a founder's brother; the root has an odd smell and a "native name" that "meant either *strength* or *use*" (335). She half-expects to see the class-action lawsuit against Clare as the last exhibit. A late effort at a consumer boycott of Clare proves impossible, as her house and its maintenance, along with her medical care, rely on the corporation's technologies (345).

The final pages of the novel detail how the infertility of Laura's daughter Ellen leads to her early treatment for ovarian cancer, allowing her to avoid death. Laura's son Tim grows up to become a computer scientist collaborating with "an interdisciplinary research group working on a computing solution to the protein folding problem" (404). They design a computer program that

> told how a given protein sequence would fold up and behave. . . . The team found itself staring at a universal chemical assembly plant at the level of the human cell. Together with a score of other machines just then coming into existence, their program promised to make anything the damaged cell called out for. And no one needed to name the first cure that would roll off their production line. (405)

Tim contributes the settlement money from Clare, his mother's legacy, toward the effort to find a cure for cancer.

Instead of an unambiguously happy ending, the final sentence of the book—"Tim suggested that it might be time for the little group of them to incorporate" (405)—offers a warning. The historical narrative describes benefits and risks associated with the ambitious, greedy corporate expansion of Clare, and the last sentence suggests Tim's research could devolve into a similarly harmful development. Powers's and Edson's texts point to women as victims of experimental medical technologies used to treat ovarian cancer. Because Vivian and Laura die from cancer, and because Vivian and Ellen are childless, the technological innovations that derive from greed appear destructive to human life. The accounts of technology and technical innovation discussed here acknowledge many ingenious achievements as progressive and dangerous, exciting and risky, but the question of whether there are technologies that might be beneficial without requiring human sacrifices remains unanswered.

Conclusion
Many literary depictions of technological tools and procedures celebrate how advances reduce labor and increase productivity, or decry how humanity is diminished when technologies dominate individuals

and society. These texts represent technology's costs and benefits and advance the case that slaves, women, and patients should be treated as humans, not as interchangeable parts. In similar ways, the chapters by Claire Menck and Annie van den Oever show how technological imaginings and inventions inspire new narrative conventions and genres. Contemporary science fictions such as *Blade Runner* and *Neuromancer*, as discussed in chapters by Aaron Barlow, Mike Griffith, and Jaime Weida, consider ambivalent attractions of how the human and the machine mix in a genre centered on the future.

Intersections of technology and humanity encompass a large field of study, touching on the history of craft and invention and the dissemination of text via mechanical means. Media theorists recognize the capacities of technology to define the historical age. The intersections of humanity and technology also involve the literary and cultural depictions of technology, which in turn reveal technology's capacity to enable or constrain humanity. Educators acknowledge the future promise of increasing the use of technology in humanities research and teaching. William Paulson notes that if "literary culture is worth continuing, if it is to have a dynamic role in the future, then its institutions need to be adapted to the media environment of today's transformed world, a world radically different from the one in which modern literary culture took shape" (149). The Wit Film Project has become part of medical school curricula to educate scientists and technicians regarding the experience of the terminal patient. Electronic editions, online journals, and databases of print texts have increased the availability of a wide range of texts. Social media and listserv communication enable scholars to communicate with others interested in the same topics. Mark Bauerlein's criticism of the digital generation notwithstanding, the future for the humanities will be more invested in technology. Technology's capacities fascinate us even as its costs annoy us. Our future engagement with it will continue to shape both humanity and the humanities in unpredictable ways that innovators have not yet envisioned.

Works Cited

Bauerlein, Mark. *The Dumbest Generation: How the Digital Age Stupefies Young Americans and Jeopardizes Our Future (Or, Don't Trust Anyone Under 30)*. New York: Tarcher, 2008.

Bercovitch, Sacvan. *The Rites of Assent: Transformations in the Symbolic Construction of America*. New York: Routledge, 1993.

Bigelow, Jacob. *Elements of Technology: Taken Chiefly from a Course of Lectures Delivered at Cambridge, on the Application of the Sciences to the Useful Arts*. Boston: Hilliard, 1829.

Bijker, Wiebe. *Of Bicycles, Bakelites, and Bulbs: Toward a Theory of Sociotechnical Change*. Cambridge, MA: MIT P, 1995.

Bolter, J. David. *Turing's Man: Western Culture in the Computer Age*. Chapel Hill: U of North Carolina P, 1984.

Brown, Richard. *Knowledge Is Power: The Diffusion of Information in Early America, 1700-1865*. New York: Oxford UP, 1991.

Colatrella, Carol. *Literature and Moral Reform: Melville and the Discipline of Reading*. Gainesville: UP of Florida, 2002.

_____. *Toys and Tools in Pink: Cultural Narratives of Gender, Science, and Technology*. Columbus: Ohio State UP, 2011.

Cowan, Ruth Schwartz. *More Work for Mother*. New York: Basic, 1985.

Douglass, Frederick. *The Narrative of the Life of Frederick Douglass. Classic Slave Narratives*. Ed. Henry Louis Gates, Jr. New York: New American Library, 1997.

Edson, Margaret. *Wit*. New York: Faber, 1999.

Gilman, Charlotte Perkins. *What Diantha Did*. Middlesex: Echo Library, 1999.

Giscombe, Peter. "The Arts & Humanities/Science & Technology." *Forum on Public Policy*, 2010. Web. 6 May 2011.

Graff, Harvey J. *The Legacies of Literacy: Continuities and Contradictions in Western Culture*. Bloomington: Indiana UP, 1991.

Hayden, Dolores. *The Grand Domestic Revolution*. Cambridge, MA: MIT P, 1982.

Kiran, Asle H., and Peter-Paul Verbeek. "Trusting Ourselves to Technology." *Knowledge, Technology, and Policy* 23.3–4 (2010): 409–27.

Kittler, Friedrich. *Gramophone, Film, Typewriter*. Stanford: Stanford P, 1999.

Kline, Ronald, and Trevor Pinch. "The Social Construction of Technology." *The Social Shaping of Technology*. Philadelphia: Open UP, 1999. 113–15.

Kolker, Robert. *A Cinema of Loneliness*. New York: Oxford UP, 2000.

Liddell, H. G., and Robert Scott. *An Intermediate Greek-English Lexicon*. Oxford: Clarendon, 1975.

Martin, Michèle. "The Culture of the Telephone." *Sex/Machine: Readings in Culture, Gender, and Technology*. Ed. Patrick Hopkins. Bloomington: Indiana UP, 1998.

McKenzie, Donald, and Judy Wajcman, eds. *The Social Shaping of Technology*. 2nd ed. Buckingham: Open UP, 1999.

Melville, Herman. *Moby-Dick, or the White Whale*. Ed. Hershel Parker. New York: Norton, 2002.

Murray, Janet. *Hamlet on the Holodeck: The Future of Narrative in Cyberspace*. New York: Free Press, 1997.

Noble, David. *The Religion of Technology: The Divinity of Man and the Spirit of Invention*. Penguin, 1999.

Onishi, Norimitsu. "Thumbs Race as Japan's Best Sellers Go Cellular." *New York Times*. New York Times Company, 20 Jan. 2008. Web. 3 Apr. 2012.

Pacey, Arnold. *Meaning in Technology*. Cambridge, MA: MIT P, 1999.

Paulson, William. *Literary Culture in a World Transformed: A Future for the Humanities*. Ithaca: Cornell UP, 2001.

Powers, Richard. *Gain*. New York: Farrar, 1998.

Purcell, Kim. "Margaret Edson." *New Georgia Encyclopedia*. Georgia Humanities Council, 12 Aug. 2005. Web. 13 May 2011.

Rimmon-Kenan, Shlomith. "Margaret Edson's *Wit* and the Art of Analogy." *Style* 40.4 (2006): 346–56.

Selznick, Brian. *The Invention of Hugo Cabret*. New York: Scholastic, 2007.

Stanley, Autumn. "Women Hold up Two Thirds of the Sky." 1983. *Sex/Machine*. Ed. Patrick Hopkins. Bloomington: Indiana UP, 1998.

Tichi, Cecelia. *Shifting Gears: Technology, Literature, Culture in Modernist America*. U of North Carolina P, 1987.

Wajcman, Judy. *Feminism Confronts Technology*. Pennsylvania State UP, 1991.

Watt, Ian. *The Rise of the Novel: Studies in Defoe, Richardson, and Fielding*. Los Angeles: U of California P, 1957.

Weingarten, Elizabeth, and Chris Wilson. "The Arab Powder Keg." *Slate*. Slate Group, 23 Mar. 2011.Web. 11 Apr. 2012.

Williams, Rosalind. "The Political and Feminist Dimensions of Technological Determinism." *Does Technology Drive History?* Ed. Leo Marx and Merritt Roe Smith. Cambridge, MA: MIT P, 1994:217–36.

_____. *Rosalind Williams' Website*. Massachusetts Institute of Technology, 20 Mar. 2009. Web. 30Aug. 2011.

Wilson, Richard Guy. "America and the Machine Age." *The Machine Age in America: 1918-1941*. New York: Abrams, 1986.

Winner, Langdon. *The Whale and the Reactor: A Search for Limits in an Age of High Technology*. Chicago: U of Chicago P, 1986.

CRITICAL
CONTEXTS

Industrial Revolution, Empire, and the Novel _____

Narin Hassan

During the nineteenth century, humans interacted with technology with unsurpassed intensity and frequency. The Industrial Revolution, a major historical, economic, and political landmark, brought immense changes to the social and cultural climate of the period. This era marks the shift toward what we would term the "modern" age of machines and technology, an age marked by invention and rapid growth in numerous areas of industry. During this period, the discovery of steam power placed Great Britain at the center of industrial progress. The impact of this shift toward a modern, industrial society resulted in major changes in the way of life for individuals—concepts of time and space rapidly changed, and the effects of the Industrial Revolution impacted both life at home and in Britain's widely expanding colonies overseas. Thus, at this moment, industrial and technological progress expanded across the globe and created notions of what it meant to be a civilized and productive society. Further, while the expansion of technologies produced big cultural shifts and new objects of human and machine interaction, they also became more visible in fictions and narratives of the period, as many nineteenth-century texts were inspired by and addressed technological change.

One of the major shifts in this period was the transition from a rural or agrarian society toward growing cities and industrial centers. Populations that were scattered across rural areas and small townships prior to the nineteenth century began to centralize within growing industrial and city centers. The Industrial Revolution created new opportunities for growth in these regions, and large numbers of people flocked there seeking work. In Britain, where the steam engine was invented, these areas included Manchester, Liverpool, and Birmingham—locations that quickly became congested and overpopulated. New technological advances in transportation, such as the development of railway and subway systems and the growth of steamships, facilitated the ability to travel quickly from one location to the other, and supported both industrial growth and the timely transportation of both people and things from one location to another, thus increasing the circulation of new goods to new markets, and the movement of people toward growing urban centers. Concepts of both time and space were rapidly changing, and technological innovations visibly shifted the view of the landscape as well as the pace of life within it. The first steam-powered public railway line, the Liverpool Manchester Railway, emerged in 1830. By 1850, at least 6,000 miles of railway line had dramatically reconstituted the landscape. In 1863, the world's first subway line was built in London. Thus the vision of a picturesque English landscape that had been recorded and idealized by romantic poets such as William Wordsworth and William Blake earlier in the nineteenth century was literally remapped and demarcated by thousands of miles of track, which visibly changed the landscape, and by the sound of trains, which symbolized the shift toward an increasingly industrial and mechanical moment in time. Charles Dickens noted the development of the railway with dramatic and destructive images in his novel *Dombey and Son* (1848):

> The first shock of a great earthquake had, just at that period, rent the whole neighborhood to its center. Traces of its course were visible on every side. Houses were knocked down; streets broken through and stopped; deep pits and trenches dug in the ground; enormous heaps of earth and clay thrown up; buildings that were undermined and shaking, propped by great beams of wood. . . . Everywhere were bridges that led nowhere; thoroughfares that were wholly impassable. (60–61)

Space became reorganized by the railway, as Wolfgang Schivelbusch has noted (54–58), and this reorganization of space marked in turn the birth of modern concepts of standardization.

Industrialization brought a sense of progress and "newness" to Britain, and many early inventors and engineers seized this moment as one of boundless opportunity and possibility. Figures such as Isambard Kingdom Brunel, an ambitious and innovative engineer who built bridges, railways, and steamships, and Joseph Paxton, who designed the Crystal Palace, were monumental forces shaping the energetic and enterprising mood of the age; however, these rapid changes brought both opportunity and struggle for the millions of people who flocked to growing towns and cities. While industrial expansion provided opportunities for many, and while the increased engagement with technology allowed for greater economic and social exchange, this era was also marked by devastating poverty, illness, and social unease. Many writers of the era attempted to capture the mixed effects of industrialization within their writing, and a range of cultural forms, such as novels, paintings, and philosophical essays, responded to technological progress and industrial innovation.

Industry, Technology, and the Realist Mode in the Nineteenth Century

One of the big literary shifts visible from the early to the late nineteenth century marks a transition toward realism of representation. Artists and writers tried to capture the mood of the period and the socioeconomic struggles—psychological, social, and cultural—of individuals through the narrative and realistic qualities of their work. The push toward social reform was supported by their vivid and detailed depictions of industrial and urban life. Visual representations such as Ford Madox Brown's *Work* (1852–65) captured the numerous forms of labor that became more and more a part of individual lives, and depicted the increasingly visible class differences that emerged as the physical labor of the working classes was distinguished from the leisurely life of the upper classes and the more intellectual and managerial work of the growing middle class. Other paintings, such as *Found Drowned* (1848–50) by George Frederick Watts and *The Outcast* (1851) by Richard Redgrave, captured newly visible "social evils" such as prostitution and narrated the fate of so-called fallen women who had been

---

banished to life on the streets. Some of the powerful prose writers of the period, such as Thomas Carlyle, Henry Mayhew, and Friedrich Engels, took as their focus the struggles of the lower classes and the new challenges that an industrial society had placed upon individuals. While Engels focused on the larger landscape of industrial change, noting the ways that building and progress shifted lifestyles and living conditions, other writers including Henry Mayhew and Thomas Carlyle commented on the ways that industrialization impacted the poor and created new class distinctions; they also emphasized how industrialization and new technologies created an emerging fusion between humans and machines. For example, in *Signs of the Times*, Carlyle's famous critique of industrial expansion, he notes that "men are grown mechanical in head and heart, as well as in hand" (67).

Just as much of the prose writing of the period addressed the impact of industrial expansion and technological growth, a number of nineteenth-century fictional works took as their focus the rise of industry and technology and its intersections with humanity. In one of the most sustained and compelling examples, *Hard Times* (1854), Charles Dickens creates a fictional industrial town, Coketown, as the setting for his narrative. The novel is filled with vivid descriptions of the industrial landscape of Coketown:

> It was a town of red brick, or of brick that would have been red if the smoke and ashes had allowed it; but as matters stood, it was a town of unnatural red and black, like the painted face of a savage. It was a town of machinery and tall chimneys, out of which interminable serpents of black smoke trailed themselves forever and ever, and never got uncoiled. It had a black canal in it, and a river that ran purple with ill-smelling dye, and vast piles of building full of windows where there was a rattling and trembling all day long, and where the piston of the steam engine worked monotonously up and down, like the head of an elephant in a state of melancholy madness. It contained several large streets all very like one another, and many small streets still more like one another inhabited by people

equally like one another, who all went in and out at the same hours . . . and to whom every day was the same as yesterday and tomorrow, and every year the counterpart of the last and the next. (19)

In this passage, Dickens references the blackened, industrial landscape of Coketown through repetitive language, highlighting the drudgery of factory work, and the monotony of the buildings and the lives of people who live and work there. While he posits the stark imagery of blackened brick and a foul-smelling, darkened river to emphasize the inhospitable landscape of Coketown and the harshness of the "rattling" windows, he also juxtaposes images of the natural world within his industrial scene. The rattling windows are also "trembling" as if they themselves are alive, the smoke coils like a serpent, and the steam engine works monotonously, "like the head of an elephant in a state of melancholy madness." Tamara Ketabgian has discussed such imagery in the novel through the concept of the "animal machine." She notes:

> the concept is twofold: on the one hand, it envisions machines as bestial and instinctive organisms; on the other hand, it refers to animal bodies fueled by powerful mechanical drives that reproduce the hydraulic energetics of steam. Spanning a number of disciplines, this figure was commonly invoked by Victorian industrial critics, philosophers, and medical writers. (651)

Dickens presents his readers with exotic creatures that inhabit worlds far from the industrial center of Coketown, fusing the monotony of the industrial scene with wild, savage, and animalistic scenes of nature. This fusion mirrors the oppositional forces in the novel, forces of "fact," "fancy," "factory," and "circus." While the Gradgrind family and their cold, dreary home of Stone Lodge (note Dickens's use of names) is at the plot's center, the novel is framed, both at the beginning and at the end, with characters and scenes from the circus. Along with emphasizing the oppositional worlds of the circus and the factory, Dickens presents his readers with a sympathetic portrait of the lives of workers through Stephen Blackpool—who suffers not only because of the monotony of the life he leads as a "Hand," or worker in the factory, but also because of his inability to seek a divorce from his alcoholic wife. Through the scenes surrounding a labor strike, Dickens also narrates the tensions between workers and factory owners and depicts the conditions in industrial towns. While the novel paints a realistic, albeit occasionally sentimental, portrait of the working classes, it also suggests that the rigidity and monotony of the factory model has entered middle-class, respectable homes. Stone Lodge is

> a great square house, with a heavy portico darkening the principal windows, as its master's heavy brows overshadowed his eyes. A calculated, cast up, balanced, and proved house. Six windows on this side of the door, six on that side, a total of twelve in this wing a total of twelve in the other wing; four-and-twenty carried over to the back wings. A lawn and garden and an infant avenue, all ruled straight like a botanical account-book. (8–9)

This square, balanced, and practical home mirrors the staid, monotonous model of the factory. Even the children within the home are surrounded by scientific and technological tools that enhance the teaching of "fact" and standardized notions of knowledge: "the little Gradgrinds had cabinets in various departments of science too. They had a little conchological cabinet, and a little metallurgical cabinet, and a little mineralogical cabinet, and the specimens were all arranged and labeled" (9).

The mid-nineteenth century spawned a number of novels that contributed to this sociological and realist mode of writing. Other notable examples include Elizabeth Gaskell's *Mary Barton* (1848) and *North and South* (1855), as well as Charlotte Brontë's *Shirley* (1849). Major novelists of the period such as George Eliot alluded to the impact of technology and industry even if their novels were set in preindustrial England or in agricultural settings. Although Eliot's novels *Adam Bede* (1859) and *The Mill on the Floss* (1860) were written in the mid-Victorian period, their earlier historical and geographical settings allow the author to provide commentary upon the ways that life has changed. In *The Mill on the Floss*, her narrator often pauses and provides nostalgic references to the past, reminding readers that their own age is one of rapid technological change. Describing the town of St. Ogg's and the early-nineteenth-century era, Eliot notes:

> It was a time when ignorance was much more comfortable than at present, and was received with all the honors in very good society, without being obliged to dress itself in an elaborate costume of knowledge; a time when cheap periodicals were not, and when country surgeons never thought of asking their female patients if they were fond of reading, but simply took it for granted that they preferred gossip; a time when ladies in rich silk gowns wore large pockets in which they carried a mutton bone to secure them against cramp. Mrs. Glegg carried such a bone, which she had inherited from her grandmother with a brocaded gown that would stand up empty, like a suit of armor, and a silver headed walking stick; for the Dodson family had been respectable for many generations. (185)

Eliot's references to the "cheap periodicals" and notions of family history and respectability allude to the rapid changes within society that created anxieties about both reading and the mixing of social classes and families. Her readers confronted such concerns within the modern age of technological change. Eliot's novel was published when new technologies allowed for a boom in publishing and in the distribution of written matter, and when new "sensation" novels—often categorized in contrast to the intellectually and psychologically realistic novels that Eliot wrote—began to dominate the literary marketplace.

Technological advances in printing and transportation supported the rise of the novel as a major literary form in the nineteenth century. This was the era in which "triple decker" (three-volume) novels flooded the marketplace and were made available to a widening audience through various forums, including new circulating libraries, popular journals, and magazines, which published many of these novels in serialized versions. Reading became a primary source of entertainment for families, and also a greater source of circulating information. Newspapers, magazines, household guides, pamphlets, and numerous other textual forms could be easily reproduced and distributed, and printed matter thus became a part of the household. While novels such as Dickens's *Hard Times* and Gaskell's *Mary Barton* attempted to provide realistic and psychological portraits of characters living in an age of industry, other narrative forms also became popular. Of these, the sensation novel was a genre that caused controversy and that aptly represents the technological and industrial growth of the age, and the birth of mass media.

Sensational and Gothic Texts and the Rise of Technology and Mass Media

The publication of three popular novels between 1860 and 1862 contributed to the term *sensation fiction*, which would characterize much of Britain's fiction in the 1860s. The term was assigned to Wilkie Collins's *The Woman in White* (1859–60), Mary Elizabeth Braddon's *Lady Audley's Secret* (1861–62), and Ellen Wood's *East Lynne* (1860–61). The almost instant popularity of these works, along with their utilization of the dangers of home to create page-turning plots, marked their leadership on the path toward an era of sensationalism. All of these novels were initially serialized in popular journals, which meant they were read in installments over a long period of time. Thus, like popular serialized television shows in the twentieth and twenty-first centuries, these novels provided sustained entertainment, and installments often ended with dramatic plot twists that kept readers engaged and enticed. They also attracted vast audiences of varying social and economic classes—as Susan Balee notes, "*East Lynne* has the honor of being *the* best-selling novel of nineteenth century England" (143). Critics read these novels as being potentially dangerous to readers because of their bold plots—which often included adultery, bigamy, mistaken identities, and murder—and also because of their association with a new, fast-paced, industrial society. Such novels were sometimes called "railway novels" because they were associated with the fast pace of railway culture, and because they were sold cheaply at railway stations. David Allen notes that "the first railway bookstall opened at Euston Station in 1848 and publishers rose to the challenge with great numbers of special cheap editions the equivalent to today's paperbacks—expressly aimed at this new market. Technical improvements in printing and illustration also helpfully coincided" (123).

The plots of sensation novels often depended on technologies that had emerged by the mid-nineteenth century, and the narratives often included references to scandalous crimes, real events, and tabloid stories that could now be distributed to hungry audiences more widely. Critics of the genre such as H. L. Mansel implied that the novels were consuming and addictive, and often noted that "a commercial atmosphere floats around works of this class, redolent of the manufactory and the shop" (573). An anonymous critic of *Lady Audley's Secret*, writing in 1863 argued that "the 'sensation novel' of our time, however extravagant and unnatural, yet is a sign of the times—the evidence of a certain turn of thought and action, of an impatience of old restraints, and a craving from some fundamental change in the working of society. . . . sensation writing is an appeal to the nerves rather than to the heart" (qtd. in Braddon 485–86). Such examples increasingly associated sensation novels and the process of reading them with the dangers of a new and uncertain technological and industrial age. The novels themselves also alluded to the relationship between their characters and new technologies and mass media. In *Lady Audley's Secret*, a novel filled with depictions of household commodities and technologies, such as telegrams and trains, Braddon describes the deterioration of an "old" and "noble" home, Audley Court, under the intrusion of a young, poor governess with an unstable past who marries Sir Audley and quickly gains control of the household.

Lady Audley's Secret and *The Woman in White* have plots that address the question of madness and, like *East Lynne*, the use of new technologies. Connecting characters' morality with technology, they raised new concerns about identity, family lineage, and respectability by incorporating such topics as mistaken identities, madness, and hereditary disease.

These novels also emphasized the newness of a modern, industrial, consumerist, and global society. Lady Audley, a beautiful but dangerous heroine whose crimes rely upon telegrams and trains, surrounds herself with the luxurious commodities of Audley Court, her new aristocratic home: "Beautiful in herself, but made more bewilderingly beautiful by the gorgeous surroundings which adorn the shrine of her loveliness. Drinking cups of gold and ivory . . . cabinets of buhl and porcelain . . . gilded baskets of hothouse flowers, fantastical caskets of Indian filagree work; fragile teacups of turquoise china" (308). Throughout the text, Braddon emphasizes the "newness" and complexity of modern society in contrast to the past, her references to "hothouse flowers" implying that even nature has become technologized. Further, her emphasis on the foreign commodities cluttering the home reveals the ways that the mid-century English home is tied to British empire's trade of exotic goods, and the consumption and display of these objects by British women. With such authors as Braddon, Wood, Rhoda Broughton, and Ouida (also known as Maria Louise Ramé) producing some of the major fictions, women writers dominated the marketplace of sensation fiction. The genre was also associated with women readers, as many of the novels focused on middle-class families and domestic spaces.

While sensation fiction alluded directly to the technological and industrial innovations within mid-nineteenth-century culture, novels published later in the period continued to emphasize scientific and technological ideas. Late-nineteenth-century texts linked technological innovation with scientific and medical progress and addressed the broader cross-cultural interconnectedness that technology produced. If Mary Shelley's early gothic novel *Frankenstein* (1818) and later works such as *The Last Man* (1826) suggested how medical and scientific ideas could capture the attention of readers, later Victorian texts such as Robert Louis Stevenson's *The Strange Case of Dr. Jekyll and Mr. Hyde* (1886), H. G. Wells's *The Island of Dr. Moreau* (1896), Henry Rider Haggard's *She* (1887), and Bram Stoker's *Dracula* (1897) deeply relied on scientific ideas and technological innovations. *Dracula* engages with technology, medicine, and industry throughout. The structure of the novel—a palimpsest of journal entries, newspaper articles, medical records, and personal letters—reflects a modernist narrative approach, in which the story itself relies on technologies (typewriters, stenographs, cable messages) and offers the reader multiple shifts in time and perspective, creating a sense of repetition and emphasizing the rapidly changing interconnectedness of a global world. Jennifer Wicke's influential article "Vampiric Typewriting: *Dracula* and Its Media" addresses this important aspect of the novel. She notes:

> A narrative patchwork made up out of the combined journal entries, letters, professional records, and newspaper clippings that the doughty band of vampire hunters had separately written or collected, it is then collated and typed by the industrious Mina. . . . *Dracula*, draped in all its feudalism and medieval gore, is textually completely *au courant*. Nineteenth-century diaristic and epistolary effusion is invaded by cutting edge technology, in a transformation of the generic materials of the text into a motley fusion of speech and writing, recording and transcribing, image and typography. (469–70)

Just as the construction of the text itself is inscribed by technology and the intermingling of different media forms, the narrative of *Dracula* expresses late-nineteenth-century anxieties about the vulnerabilities of the British Empire and industrial prowess, and tensions between "old" and "new" technology. In the early pages of the novel, Jonathan Harker prepares for his journey to Transylvania with his camera, with which he can record "Kodak views," as well as his journal, in which he records the primitive qualities of natives and their lack of modern technology: "I had to sit in the carriage for more than an hour before we began to move. It seems to me that the further east you go, the more unpunctual are the trains. What ought they to be in China?" (33). The novel contrasts these observations with the new technologies of the modern world—transfusions, telegraphs and gramophones, trains and ships—but also implies that these advances cannot protect England from the dangers of a primitive and powerful enemy. Van Helsing's traditional approaches—the use of garlic and crucifixes—become crucial in the struggle against the vampire, and Stoker suggests early in the novel that England's technological advancements and wide influence actually make the nation more vulnerable to the threat of foreign enemies. Dracula has access to English books, magazines, and newspapers; the sweep of English texts has made maps of London, law journals, and Army and Navy lists available (50). These publications expose the city and allow Dracula to successfully plan his journey and secure real estate in London. *Dracula* is thus a novel about journeys from east to west, and the technologies that enabled such journeys in the late nineteenth century. Exposing an increasingly interconnected global world, Stoker presents what Stephen Arata has termed "reverse colonization"—a late-nineteenth-century reversal of the colonial model in which an ancient figure from the so-called primitive world travels to the imperial center, echoing the haunting violence of imperial expansion and evoking fears of degeneration, a decline in imperial power.

Technologizing Nature: Natural History, Scientific Travel, and Nineteenth-Century Global Expansion

Texts of the late nineteenth century, such as Stoker's portrait of the horrors and anxieties surrounding travel, reveal how far society had progressed in terms of technology, scientific inquiry, and global interconnectedness. Scholars have argued that these issues began as early as the eighteenth century. Travel and the proliferation of English texts suggested what Mary Louise Pratt terms "planetary consciousness." Pratt claims that, in the late eighteenth century, major European expeditions and the publication of texts (such as Carl Linneaus's *System of Nature* in 1735) helped to establish European superiority around the globe and connect a knowledge of nature with notions of civilization and progress. Pratt suggests that the development of natural history was closely tied to industrial and technological advancement, and she considers the advancements in print technology as crucial to planetary consciousness and the systematizing of nature. She writes:

> The systematizing of nature in the second half of the century was to assert even more powerfully the authority of print, and thus of the class which controlled it. It seems to crystallize global imaginings of a sort rather different from earlier navigational ones. Natural history maps out not the thin track of a route taken, nor the lines where land and water meet, but the internal "contents" of those land and water masses whose spread made up the surface of the planet. . . .
>
> Like the rise of interior exploration, the systematic surface mapping of the globe correlates with an expanding search for commercially exploitable resources, markets, and lands to colonize, just as navigational mapping is linked with the search for trade routes. . . . one by one, the planet's life forms were to be drawn out of the tangled threads of their life surroundings and rewoven into European based patterns of global unity and order. (30–31)

Indeed, the intersections of science and literature in the eighteenth century reveal the interest in natural history and its intersections with technology. Charles Darwin's ideas regarding evolution were influenced by his travels, and his *Voyage of the Beagle* (1838), which recorded his expeditions abroad, gave readers a sense of the lands, plants, and peoples in distant regions and enhanced a sense of the difference between so-called primitive societies and civilized, industrial nations. His later scientific writings, including *On the Origin of the Species* (1859) and *The Descent of Man* (1871), dramatically impacted and shaped ideas about evolution, raising questions about what it means to be human and where the boundaries between animals and humans lie.

Late-nineteenth-century novels raised such questions. Just as *Dracula* provided readers with a monster that could transform victims into a new breed of bloodthirsty and animalistic creatures, texts such as Wells's *The Island of Dr. Moreau* addressed the topic of vivisection and questioned the boundaries between animal and human. Like Shelley's Victor Frankenstein, Dr. Moreau crosses boundaries and performs grotesque and controversial experiments on "Beast People" on a tropical island. The novel suggests that the Beast People can be trained to behave as humans but also emphasizes that their wild, animalistic traits are tied to their closeness to nature. Similarly, Haggard's *She* presents readers with a primitive society lost in time and submerged in the depths of a tropical forest, far from civilization.

Such novels emphasized the ways European progress and industry contrasted with primitive cultures and their immersion in the natural world. These works consider the question of *nature*, and the question of how human and technological engagement with nature was being reconstituted through the literary and cultural advancements of the nineteenth century. If industrial and technological progress helped to mark the rise of Britain as a major superpower in this period, one of the most obvious expressions of that role was the Great Exhibition of 1851. The architectural structure of the Crystal Palace celebrated the fusion of industry and nature; incorporating new advances in the production of iron and glass, the Great Exhibition was housed in a gigantic glass structure modeled like a glasshouse or conservatory. Joseph Paxton, an ambitious gardener at Chatsworth Gardens who was known for his designs of massive fountains and garden spaces, had been inspired to build a large heated structure to house a giant water lily from Guyana. Just as conservatories housed tropical plants and natural life, the Crystal Palace, named for its dramatic glass architecture, also housed grand trees that framed Hyde Park in the middle of London. In this way, the building embraced the collaboration of industry and nature. The grand spectacle of the Crystal Palace and the massive industrial exhibition that it housed—including major inventions and accomplishments of British industry and manufacturing, as well as the work of other nations—drew huge crowds to London and also helped to establish Britain as the technological, imperial, and industrial center of the planet.

While the Crystal Palace reflected the technological innovations of the nineteenth century, it also influenced the design of middle-class homes and encouraged people to make use of technology to embrace the natural world. Interest in the botanical world and the development of household conservatories spread very quickly. John Loudon, a famous garden designer, was one of the first figures to promote the development of household conservatories and greenhouses, encouraging people to grow tropical plants in their own homes. His gardening guides provided readers with illustrations and designs for building economical and efficient conservatories, features that became popular in the Victorian home. New technological innovations allowed for the invention of "Wardian cases." These miniature cases, designed initially by Nathaniel Bagshaw Ward, allowed for the transportation of exotic plants and living things and encouraged widespread knowledge of plant life. Such innovations enhanced the sense of the world becoming a smaller, more connected space but also contributed to a sense of the European connection to distant lands and peoples. Furthermore, such innovations domesticated the culture of botany and gave women opportunities to study and tend to rare tropical plants and domestic fauna. Wardian cases became portable household accessories, and in middle- and upper-class homes, household conservatories became sites for ladies' tea parties and social functions. The numerous gardening and botanical guides published during this period reveal how women engaged with the scientific culture of botany, taking advantage of new garden design and technology. Jane Loudon, John Loudon's wife, wrote a number of botanical guides for women, including *Botany for Ladies* (1842) and *The Entertaining Naturalist* (1850). During the same period, figures such as Gertrude Jekyll became well-known female garden designers.

The popularity of the Crystal Palace and household conservatories led to representations of conservatories and "hothouses" in literary texts. As early as 1848, Dickens's *Dombey and Son* included a description of a "little glass breakfast room" connected to Dombey's dark study. During the 1860s, numerous texts, including Eliot's *The Mill on the Floss*, Gaskell's *Wives and Daughters* (1864–66), and Broughton's *Not Wisely but Too Well* (1867), incorporated extended descriptions of conservatory scenes. In many of these novels, conservatories provided lush, tropical settings for romantic interludes between characters and evoked a sense of the fluid boundaries between the inside and outside, the foreign and familiar. While these novels were set in England, scenes within conservatories alluded to the ways that technological and scientific expansion brought the tropics home and connected their characters with the exotic and the unfamiliar. Conservatory scenes depicted characters surrounded by glass (another technology that recently had been perfected and produced) and the lushness of plants, removed from their native lands and tended within an artificial space.

Bodies and Homes: Gender, the Expansion of Medicine, and the Development of Domestic Technologies

Just as natural history, botany, and biology emerged as major disciplines in this period, the nineteenth century also witnessed major developments in medicine and health care, developments that influenced novels, travel narratives, medical guides, and other works concerning the personal and household use of new technologies. Illness narratives were common in many texts of the period, and novels such as George Eliot's *Middlemarch* (1871–72), Elizabeth Phelps's *Doctor Zay* (1882), and Anthony Trollope's *Doctor Thorne* (1858) addressed the professionalization and shifting parameters of medicine, as well as the figure of the doctor. Technology increasingly intersected with medical practice, and simultaneously the hospital developed as a major administrative institution. The spread of major diseases such as cholera in industrial towns and overcrowded urban areas meant that life expectancy was short, but new advances in medicine chemistry, bacteriology, surgery, and anesthesiology also created new cures. Throughout the nineteenth century, the field of medicine was dominated by men, but through much struggle women began to practice medicine by mid-century. Florence Nightingale, famous for her nursing reforms, promoted popular ideas about ventilation and spatial organization for the maintenance of health. A significant female figure, Nightingale engaged in debates about public health at a time when such women as Elizabeth Blackwell, Elizabeth Garrett, and Sophia Jex Blake were emerging as pioneering women doctors. As efforts to educate women doctors and allow them into medical institutions were being waged within Europe and the United States, the technological advancements of the nineteenth century made communication and travel to foreign lands much easier, which meant that greater numbers of women could travel around the globe to study and work. Going overseas, women earned medical degrees and built their own practices. Mary Scharlieb and Edith Pechey Phipson built their medical practices in India during a time when it would have been almost impossible for them to do so at home. In India, both of these women were involved with the development of hospitals for women and children. They studied obstetrics and gynecology, and focused on the diseases of women and children. Mary Scharlieb wrote a number of popular medical guides for women.

Advancements in printing allowed for the mass publication of numerous domestic manuals, medical guides, and household magazines, all of which shaped notions of the healthy body and family and standardized the processes of childbirth and child-rearing. Scharlieb's medical guides included *A Woman's Words to Women* (1905), *The Mother's Guide* (1905), and *The Seven Ages of Women* (1915), among others. These guides contributed to a wider set of popular texts, such as Isabella Beeton's *Guide to Household Management* (1861), which provided advice on the management of children and the home—further securing women within the domestic realm and under the responsibilities of households and child care. Through their wide distribution and use as hard science, such texts also standardized notions of how a household should be managed. The domestic manuals and magazines of the period articulated technological and scientific approaches to child-rearing and household management, and established these methods as the norm for middle-class households. One of the great nineteenth-century technological shifts concerned infant feeding; the development of new infant formulas and baby bottle designs inaugurated an era of artificial feeding, in which mothers learned to become expert consumers and engage with new technologies in the realm of infant care.

Conclusion

In the nineteenth century, new technologies became readily available in the home, and industrialized models shifted domestic notions of time and space: examples include structured time for the meals and rest of babies; rooms that separated children from parents in middle-class households; nurseries as common spaces for children; and separate quarters for servants. Literary texts recorded the ways industry and technology revised the pace and patterns of the public world, as scientific works imagined greater possibilities of invention. Technology's domestic role reveals the ways in which the household was increasingly influenced by industrial change and, in a sense, modeled after the factory. The Industrial Revolution—described, debated, and sometimes derided by the authors and thinkers of the age—thus left its mark not only in the public world, but also in the most private of realms, and continues to impact the way we live today.

Works Cited

Allen, David Elliston. *The Naturalist in Britain: A Social History*. Princeton: Princeton UP, 1994.

Altick, Richard. *Victorian People and Ideas: A Companion for the Modern Reader of Victorian Literature*. New York: Norton, 1973.

Arata, Stephen. *Fictions of Loss in the Victorian Fin de Siècle: Identity and Empire*. Cambridge, England: Cambridge UP, 1996.

Armstrong, Isobel. *Victorian Glassworlds: Glass Culture and the Imagination*. Oxford: Oxford UP, 2008.

Balee, Susan. "Correcting the Historical Context: The Real Publication Dates of *East Lynne*." *Victorian Periodicals Review* 26.3 (1993): 143–43.

Braddon, Mary Elizabeth. *Lady Audley's Secret*. Ed. Natalie M. Houston. Peterbrough: Broadview, 2003.

Carlyle, Thomas. "Signs of the Times." 1828. *Selected Writings*. Ed. Alan Shelston. Harmondsworth: Penguin, 1971. 61–85.

Dickens, Charles. *Dombey and Son*. 1848. New York: Books Inc, n.d.

———. *Hard Times*. 1854. New York: Books Inc, n.d.

Eliot, George. *The Mill on the Floss*. 1860. Ed. A. S. Byatt. London: Penguin, 1979.

Gaskell, Elizabeth. *Mary Barton*. Ed. Jennifer Foster. Peterborough: Broadview, 1999.

Ketabgian, Tamara. "'Melancholy Mad Elephants': Affect and the Animal Machine in *Hard Times*." *Victorian Studies* 45.4 (Summer 2003): 649–76.

Mansel, H. L. "Sensation Novels." *Aurora Floyd*. Ed. Richard Nemesvari and Lisa Surride. Ontario: Broadview, 1998. 573.

Otis, Laura, ed. *Literature and Science in the Nineteenth Century*. New York: Penguin, 2002.

Pratt, Mary Louise. *Imperial Eyes: Travel Writing and Transculturation*. New York: Routledge, 1992.

Schivelbusch, Wolfgang. *The Railway Journey: The Industrialization of Time and Space in the Nineteenth Century*. Berkeley: U of California P, 1977.

Stoker, Bram. *Dracula*. Ed. Glennis Byron. Peterborough: Broadview, 1998.

Wicke, Jennifer. "Vampiric Typewriting: *Dracula* and Its Media." *ELH* 59.2 (Summer 1992): 467–93.

Reading Technology and Literature in the Twentieth Century _____

Melissa M. Littlefield and Michael Black

As the first chapter of this collection so aptly indicates, literature and technology are mutually reinforcing. Literature does not merely respond to technology; it helps to create and explore the cultural significances of technology. As a handful of essays in this volume indicate, technology and humanity have enjoyed a long history. But it is also important to remember that *technology* can be understood as a relatively new term, as Leo Marx notes in the essay "Technology: The Emergence of a Hazardous Concept": "As late as 1911, the *Encyclopedia Britannica* contained no entry on *technology*" (570).

This chapter focuses on a specific set of American scholarly criticism concerning the analysis of technology and literature. It takes as a starting point the new understanding of technology that emerged with the so-called " 'Second Industrial Revolution' (c. 1880–1910), [which] gave us the electric light, the phonograph, the radio, the telephone, the X ray, the airplane, the moving picture, and—arguably—the automobile" (571). As Marx's essay notes, "these radical turn-of-the-century developments in the mechanic arts mark the final stage in the formation of the semantic void that soon would be filled by the concept of *technology*" (573). As a twentieth-century term, technology has come to mean many things. While it often refers to an artifact (the automobile, for example), Marx reminds us that technology also implies larger sociotechnological systems and the humans who develop, deploy, and depend on them.

During the second half of the twentieth century, scholarly work on literature and technology has blossomed into several distinct areas. Before turning to specific examples of current theoretical approaches, this essay considers the context of twentieth-century scholarly conversation about literature and technology—namely, the "two cultures" debates that diagnosed a division between the sciences and the humanities. The argument then turns to criticism from American studies scholars Leo Marx and Cecelia Tichi; Marx's work, in particular, is foundational to the technological focus in American studies and American literature. Feminist science and technology studies, exemplified here by the work of Susan M. Squier, offered significant contributions. Scholarship in this area emerged toward the end of the twentieth century and provides important new contexts and questions about gender, race, disability, class, and sexuality. Finally, we turn to developments in informatics (a term for information science) by describing the work of N. Katherine Hayles. Working at the intersections of computers, information technologies, and literature, Hayles has brought studies of technology and literature into the twenty-first century.

The "Two Cultures": C. P. Snow Theorizes the Divide

C. P. Snow's 1959 lecture, published as *The Two Cultures and the Scientific Revolution*, begins with the simple premise that specialization in education has produced two distinct groups of scholars: intellectuals who study and debate "traditional culture," and scientists who investigate and document the natural world. Snow argued that this divide posed a problem for an increasingly technological society, as a basic grasp of scientific principles is necessary for understanding and correcting the social problems faced by industrial nations. While this assertion may seem acceptable from the perspective of the twenty-first century, in which the benefits of science and engineering are more immediate, Snow's lecture was delivered at a time when universities were largely structured around a general education model that emphasized the study of philosophy and literature over science and mathematics. This model "trained its young men for administration" but left them ill equipped to "understand the [scientific] revolution or take part in it" (Snow 24–25). Snow feared that this divide would come to define Western society: the educated elite would discuss and enact laws and other forms of social policy, while the scientists and engineers, in a separate culture, would reshape society through the products of their invention.

In a sense, Snow's lecture is a defense of science's role in Western culture and a critique of the perceived short-sightedness of an intellectual life centered solely on the humanities. Far from being coldly rational and devoid of feeling, scientists share many of the same social concerns as literary scholars. Many scientists, Snow explains, see their research as addressing problems in society and hope that it will be used to build beneficial technologies. In regards to ethics and morals, he notes that "there is a moral component right in the grain of science itself" (14). Research must be performed ethically and scientists must continually consider moral norms; scientists, Snow suggests, are "by and large the soundest group of [moral] intellectuals we have" (14). In short, Snow views scientists as practicing cultural values that intellectuals merely discuss; literary scholars try to define "culture" as something found in books, blinding them to "the scientific edifice of the physical world . . . the most beautiful and wonderful collective work of the mind of man" (15). Science cultivates one's appreciation of beauty, social awareness, and capacity for moral reasoning, a process that grants willing scientists the ability to reach outside of their specialized training and engage with classic texts of literature and philosophy.

Yet acknowledgment of science as a legitimate pursuit is not enough to close the cultural divide, because while literary culture focuses on and is shaped by the knowledge of history, scientific culture focuses on and looks toward the future. Over time this difference has produced an entrenched hostility between two cultures, which have developed increasingly distorted impressions of each other. Literary intellectuals have accused scientists of being "shallowly optimistic" and more concerned with the advance of research than the human condition (5). Scientists are accused of blindly pushing for progress, seeing innovation as the solution to all social problems. Literary intellectuals, in contrast, are viewed as so engrossed with the history of aesthetics that they are "totally lacking in foresight" and "peculiarly unconcerned" with improving the well-being of others (6). Literary intellectuals, at best, can discuss the present in terms of the past but are unable to propose real solutions to social realities. As a result, Snow concludes, those invested in the "traditional culture" of literature and philosophy are "Luddites," unwilling to appreciate or contribute to technological and scientific discovery.

Snow's lecture was widely read among educators and intellectuals, including those invested in the traditional, humanities-based mission of university culture. Literary critic F. R. Leavis, who was Snow's biggest detractor, saw Snow as grossly misunderstanding what is necessary to ensure social well-being. Leavis delivered his response, "Two Cultures? The Significance of C. P. Snow," as a Cambridge Downing Lecture (subsequently published in the *Statesman* in 1962), but it was initially dismissed for its many attacks on Snow's personal character and writing style. Nonetheless, when Leavis engages directly with Snow's argument, he demonstrates Snow's inadequate "sense of human nature and human need" (21–22). The "optimism" that Snow acknowledges and defends, for example, never questions what humans need or whether they might not want a particular technology. In short, Snow's lauding of scientific progress conflates wealth and well-being. Without a strong sense of historical context, scientific discovery is blind to the "cultural consequences of the kind of rapid change [Snow] wants to see accelerated to the utmost and assimilating the world, bringing . . . salvation and lasting felicity to all mankind" (25). Despite highlighting the limitations of Snow's argument, however, Leavis leaves open the divide between literary intellectuals and scientists.

Snow's lecture and Leavis's critical response show that a divide between the cultures of science and literary study could have disastrous consequences, for society and for both fields of inquiry. Snow's proposal that literary intellectuals are natural Luddites incapable of understanding and indifferent to science and technology suggests that any cultural study that does not adequately acknowledge the latter field is incomplete. Leavis's argument, conversely, implies that scientists and engineers should engage with the historical and cultural dimensions of their work, reflecting on their discoveries rather than pressing on to the next innovation.

These debates diagnosed a potential rift in the academy. As a result, and throughout the years that followed, divisions between the disciplines were solidified and challenged at the same time. By century's end, new interdisciplinary groups (such as the Society for Literature and Science), fields of study (science and technology studies, for example), and publications (*Configurations: A Journal of Literature, Science, and Technology*) were established. Each entity bridges the "two cultures" in an attempt to theorize and challenge divisions between the humanities, the sciences, various technologies, and epistemologies (ways of knowing). Given the volume of interdisciplinary scholarship on literature and technology, it would be impossible to provide a complete survey; however, several key texts provide important foundations.

Machines, Gardens, Gears: The Work of Leo Marx and Cecelia Tichi

For scholars and students interested in the relationship between literature and technology, the work of Leo Marx is "an undisputed starting point" (Meikle 160). A respected environmentalist critic and the Kenan Professor of American Cultural History at MIT, Marx published his first book, *The Machine in the Garden: Technology and the Pastoral Ideal in America*, in 1964. A significantly influential work on the interdisciplinary study of literature and technology, *Machine in the Garden* has never been out of print. Marx's arguments, both in this book and in *The Pilot and the Passenger* (1988), center on the complex relationship that connects an idyllic American landscape, the machines of the Industrial Revolution, and the resulting sociotechnological systems that have come to dominate American culture. He argues that nineteenth-century American authors tend to represent the American landscape as pastoral and ideal; the "garden" of the title that "brings together a universal Edenic myth and a particular set of American goals and aspirations" (164). The irony, Marx notes, is that these American "aspirations" include such things as Manifest Destiny and the opening of the West, which rely on mechanistic endeavors directed toward the natural landscape. The machines that enable American expansion (such as the steam engine and the electric light bulb) entail larger sociotechnological systems (the railroad and the electricity grid), infrastructures that fundamentally change America's landscapes.

For Marx, nature and machines, the idyllic pastoral and technological progress, coexist in a complex relationship:

> Americans, in other words, could proceed to carry out the expansionary project of Western capitalism, leveling forests, building roads and factories and cities in the wilderness, and still, at the very same time, they could with some justice see themselves as engaged in the recovery of a simpler, more natural way of life—simpler and more natural, at least, as compared with the prototypical advanced societies of Western Europe. (*Pilot* 187)

In this passage—quoted from "American Literary Culture and the Fatalistic View of Technology"—Marx sketches the paradox at the heart of American culture: the centrality of technology to a nation whose imagined idyllic pastoralism "coincided with the development of industry" (Meikle 155).

The Machine in the Garden explores the tension between technology and nature in American literature and culture. Marx finds that many popular representations of machines in the American landscape were "affirmative, even celebratory" (375). He points to the speeches of political economist Tench Coxe, assistant to Alexander Hamilton: "Coxe understands that it is wise to represent the machine to Americans as another *natural* 'means of happiness' decreed by the Creator in his design of the continent. So far from conceding that there might be anything alien or 'artificial' about mechanization, he insists that it is inherent in 'nature,' both geographic and human" (160–61, our emphasis). By way of contrast, Marx observes that, in canonical American literature, anything mechanistic often is seen as an intruder on the pastoral. Indeed, *Machine in the Garden* opens by cataloging such instances:

> We recall the scene in *Walden* where Thoreau is sitting rapt in a revery and then, penetrating his woods like the scream of a hawk, the whistle of the locomotive is heard; or the eerie passage in *Moby Dick* where Ishmael is exploring the innermost recesses of a beached whale and suddenly the image shifts and the leviathan's skeleton is a New England textile mill; or the dramatic moment in *Huckleberry Finn* when Huck and Jim are floating along peacefully and a monstrous steamboat suddenly bulges out of the night and smashes straight through their raft. (15–16)

These selections illustrate Marx's primary contention that technology is not merely an addition to American cultural and literary landscape; technology, in fact, introduces a fundamental tension at the center of America's national identity.

Following in the footsteps of Leo Marx's trailblazing readings of technology and literature are several notable scholars, including Cecelia Tichi. Her work addresses American television culture and what she refers to as the gear-and-girders culture of the twentieth century. Although she has not received as much acclaim as Marx (Nicholls), Tichi's book *Shifting Gears: Technology, Literature, Culture in Modernist America* (1987) remains a centerpiece of literature and technology scholarship. Her study is best known for its focus on an extensive array of photographs, advertisements, and other cultural artifacts from the early twentieth century. These images represent an American culture obsessed with mechanization and efficiency, a culture that values the progressive power of technologies. From these images, Tichi interprets an ideological shift away from a romantic vision of idealized and unified nature and toward a mechanistic understanding of the world and humanity.

Less appreciated are Tichi's arguments concerning the discursive and material power of twentieth-century gears-and-girders technol-

---

ogy. As does her work on American television culture ("Television and Recent American Fiction"), *Shifting Gears* proposes that technology has held a largely unidirectional influence on art and literature. In other words, literature reflects, but does not impact, technological developments. Authors may use the language of gears and girders, but this is because their fiction operates like a mirror of larger cultural and technological changes. Tichi argues, for example, that the "machine culture" had "pervaded novelists' imaginations just as it had captured journalists' energies" (31), the use of the verb "pervaded" implying that authors could not help but be influenced. According to Tichi, the influence was so persistent that even those resistant to technology (she cites Sherwood Anderson, Willa Cather, and Edith Wharton, among others) could not help but employ the language of gears and girders. The trouble with Tichi's assumption of a one-way influence is that she leaves the division between the cultures open, with technology in a dominant, controlling position. As other scholars have argued since, modernist authors and artists often used their works as a means to respond to the dominant culture of industrialization and modernization. Aside from this critique, Tichi's *Shifting Gears* offers important historical updates of Marx's initial forays into the relationships between technology and literature. As subsequent scholarship illustrates, it is useful to think about literary and cultural representations of technology as key influences on technology, with regards to development, use, and reception. The sections that follow discuss two examples in which literature is a key player in debates about technology.

Feminist Theories of Literature and Technology: Susan Squier

Feminist scholars have analyzed the production of scientific knowledge for several decades, but feminist theories focused on technology specifically are a more recent phenomenon. Both types of scholarship tend to fall under the title of feminist science and technology studies (FSTS) and have offered important insights into the definition and theorization of natural sciences and technological developments. Judy Wajcman's groundbreaking book *Feminism Confronts Technology* (1991) explores the masculinist assumptions underlying definitions, constructions, and epistemologies of technology. Wajcman discusses the sexual division of labor and analyzes how this division is built into technologies, considering the potential of domestic technologies, from washing machines to vacuum cleaners, to liberate and enslave; the discussion extends to kitchens, homes, and cityscapes, as well as such reproductive technologies as in vitro fertilization and forceps. Wajcman's project both builds on and departs from feminist critiques of science by advocating for the need to redefine technology as "more than an applied science" (ix).

In the years since Wajcman's book, and since related work by Donna Haraway and Emily Martin, FSTS scholarship has focused on several areas, including medical imaging technologies and the gendered body (Cartwright; Waldby), cyborg theory (Haraway), disability studies, and reproductive technologies. In this section, we focus on Susan M. Squier, who links feminist theories, literature, and biomedical science and technology. Squier comes out of a tradition that includes feminist scholars Sandra Harding, Evelyn Fox Keller, and Helen Longino. Squier's work distinctively explores the value of literature in the shaping of biomedical science and technology.

Squier's *Babies in Bottles: Twentieth-Century Visions of Reproductive Technology* (1994) and *Liminal Lives: Imagining the Human at the Frontiers of Biomedicine* (2004) helped to define key questions for feminist studies of technology and literature. In line with other FSTS scholars, Squire asks how metaphor and language affect the shaping of techno-scientific knowledge. For example, war metaphors appear in medical discourse ("battles" with viruses); similarly, passive language is used to describe human egg cells in biology textbooks, whereas active verbs are used to describe sperm cells (Martin). In each case, language not only determines how we understand techno-scientific knowledge, but also helps to shape that knowledge from the outset:

techno-science is not value neutral or objective, for it depends on the ideologies of the surrounding culture. Squier applies these ideas to literatures of all kinds, including poetry written by scientists, science-fiction narratives, and magazine articles.

Literature, Squier argues, is a crucial part of techno-scientific knowledge. It helps to shape subjects and objects, explore theories and desires that the sciences overlook, and provide ordered narratives for techno-scientific developments. *Babies in Bottles* investigates these claims through representations of reproductive technologies in historic and contemporary writing. Instead of separating the "two cultures" of science and humanities, Squier gives equal weight to scientists and novelists. She values each representation of "babies in bottles," as each representation informs her differently about the cultural and techno-scientific assumptions that led to its creation. Squier collects visual and textual images to reveal that "reproductive technologies" are "malleable, deployable differently and to different ends, depending on its context" (18). Like technology scholars, Squier asserts that reproductive technologies are not inherently good or bad, nor are they deterministic. Instead, technologies are shaped by social and political ideologies, by creators and users. In the case of reproduction, technologies such as in vitro fertilization can be both empowering and repressive. Through genetic testing, for example, a woman can learn more about the fetus growing in her body, but to do so she must submit to a larger medical system that determines the "health" and "fitness" of her child.

In *Liminal Lives*, Squier branches out from reproductive technologies to consider technologies that challenge our notions of life and personhood. In each chapter, Squier explores techno-scientific products and practices: growth hormones, organ and limb transplantation, xenogenesis (hybrid embryos, often made of human and animal parts), age extension, and regeneration. Each case study explores life-forms at the margins of our classificatory systems. The "liminal beings" (that is, life-forms between strict classifications or states of being) in Squier's study "are powerful and dangerous representations of a transformation we are all undergoing as we become initiates in a new biomedical personhood mingling existence and nonexistence, organic and inorganic matter, life and death" (5). Her examples from works of fiction allow readers to think about the ways in which scientific categories and knowledge are produced and maintained. Which kinds of "life" does science value, study, or see as productive? In fiction, liminal life-forms such as H. G. Wells's "Beast People" from *The Island of Dr. Moreau* (1896) challenge our assumptions about categorization. Wells's creatures would not fit our definition of man (human) or beast (nonhuman), given that they began life as leopards, apes, sows, and oxen, and have been surgically altered to look and act human. They are liminal creatures because they exist on the boundaries of known categories, informing us about our assumptions of what it means to be human. The creation of the Beast People also challenges us to reflect not only on the ethics of scientific studies but also on the limits and purpose of techno-science.

To identify literature's relationship with science, Squier borrows the term "biomedical imaginary" from Catherine Waldby. The biomedical imaginary became an important concept for FSTS at the turn of the twenty-first century because it provided a new way to talk about the division between science and humanities. Instead of thinking about the disciplines as separate, the biomedical imaginary recognizes their joint development; as Waldby explains, the biomedical imaginary "refers to the speculative, propositional fabric of medical thought, the generally disavowed dream work performed by biomedical theory and innovation" (136). In other words, the biomedical imaginary captures some of the imaginative thinking, language, and ideology that "objective" techno-science must pretend to ignore. As Waldby and Squier explain, technoscience appears objective *because* it defines itself against so-called subjective work (such as fiction and journalism). Despite this arbitrary division, both literary and scientific texts create and reflect the biomedical imaginary. To make her case, Squier combines examples from popular fiction and science writing. In her chapter "Giant Babies:

Graphing Growth in the Early Twentieth Century," she references H. G. Wells's *Food of the Gods* (1904), Frank Patton's lesser-known science-fiction pulp story "Test Tube Girl" (1942), and Dr. Hasting Gilford's *The Disorders of Post-Natal Growth and Development* (1911).

In concert with other FSTS scholars, Squier offers another possibility for technology and literature's integration. Her work reminds us to question our assumptions about technology's development and popularization. Literature provides one window into the processes that inform technological development and use.

Information Technology: N. Katherine Hayles

N. Katherine Hayles's *How We Became Posthuman: Virtual Bodies in Cybernetics, Literature, and Informatics* (1999) is by no means the first book to propose that literature can contribute to the study of information technology. In 1964, Marshall McLuhan's *Understanding Media: The Extensions of Man* famously proclaimed that "the medium is the message," a notion that urged scholars and students of media to compare how different technologies construct symbols to better understand the verbal, visual, and auditory strategies used to produce meaning. Following the proliferation of personal computers, critics with expertise in literary study and computer science, such as Jay David Bolter and Janet Murray, have sought to compare software to literature. Hayles, who trained and worked as a chemist before becoming a prominent literary scholar, established a precedent for the study of literature and information technology by illustrating that both fields will continue to influence and reshape each other.

Like many branches of computer science, *How We Became Posthuman* begins in the field of cybernetics. Today the word "cybernetics" calls up images of robotic bodies and technologically enhanced superheroes and villains; however, cybernetics began as a series of mathematical theories following World War II, particularly in the writings of Norbert Wiener and Claude Shannon. Wiener, who worked on missile and radar guidance systems during the war, saw that from a mathematical perspective, a machine and its operator formed a single information system. In *The Human Use of Human Beings: Cybernetics and Society* (1950), Wiener defines this concept as "feedback." When using a machine, the operator issues commands that the machine carries out, reporting back regarding the success or failure of the command and leading the operator to issue new commands accordingly. In this sense, the two form a single information loop, as data move back and forth between them. Wiener adds that feedback occurs when any two entities, human or nonhuman, are in communication with each other, allowing for the possibility that machines, mathematically at least, can be independent actors.

In *How We Became Posthuman*, Hayles engages directly with the writings of Wiener, Shannon, and other cybernetic theorists to trace the various ways that "feedback" changes our understanding about what it means to be human and how literature participates in feedback loops with other media. For humans and literary texts, feedback suggests that bodies and minds are constantly interacting with their surroundings—from the air we breathe to the substances we ingest, to the various kinds of knowledge we use to map, diagnose, and understand ourselves. While she draws upon many established medical, philosophical, and psychological frameworks to discuss feedback and human experience, Hayles develops the concept of "materiality" to describe how feedback functions in literature.

Materiality represents the ways, often taken for granted, in which a particular medium enables and constrains the reading or recording of information. From cybernetic theory, Hayles observes that "information derives its efficacy from the material infrastructures it appears to obscure" (28). While reading and writing, we often focus on the text itself: the words on the page are thought to exist independently of any particular copy of the book they appear in. This way of reading is the result of generations of standardization. Books are printed, bound, and distributed according to a set of conventions that readers and writers have internalized. These conventions make the use of books easy and intuitive, but they also can limit the sorts of information that books can contain.

Taking up McLuhan's call to study media comparatively, Hayles notes that the materiality of literature is most visible when books are compared to media that seem to function similarly. For Hayles, computer software often tries to emulate the way that text appears on a printed page. But unlike books, digital texts have a less stable materiality. You can, for example, read text from a word processor or a website much as you would as if that text were printed on a page. Because the text is composed of pixels of light rather than bits of ink, the signifiers are never permanent. As "flickering signifiers," the words on the screen are continuously reproduced by a chain of codes written in programming language (31). A single command can change their size, font, color, or erase them entirely. In terms of feedback, the exchange between book and reader is primarily centered on the act of interpreting new words in light of concepts developed out of previously read texts. Computerized media incorporate these acts as well, but the symbols stored in them can be manipulated easily by readers. The materiality of computerized texts is therefore less stable, and as a result the feedback between human and machine is much more complex and rich in information.

Furthermore, because feedback also can occur between machines, the materiality of one medium can influence that of another medium. Hayles's two follow-up studies, *Writing Machines* (2002) and *My Mother Was a Computer: Digital Subjects and Literary Texts* (2005) explore how literature has been used to emulate digital-information technologies. Novels such as Mark Danielewski's *House of Leaves* (2000) push the boundaries of the page by incorporating a variety of typefaces, alignments, orientations, colors, and footnotes that resemble computerized texts, making it impossible to read the novel in the way one would read a conventional book. Hayles also shows that programming languages draw upon many conventions of human language. Computer code could and should be studied as a language, provided that readers are able to familiarize themselves with the conventions of these new modes of expression.

Hayles's most noteworthy argument is that literature and information technology—like the "two cultures" of literature and science—are not wholly distinct cultural fields. Her work is itself a feedback loop, demonstrating that because these two technologies influence each other, scholars should be prepared to engage directly with both.

Conclusion

Leo Marx recognized that technology is a relatively new term, one that refers to both artifacts (for example, the telephone) and sociotechnologcal infrastructures (communication systems). Over the past century, technology has appeared as a key term in many scholarly debates, including those catalogued in this essay. Technologies do not function in a vacuum; they depend on human actors and are influenced by cultural and social developments. Scholarship on literature and technology pays attention to the human and machine actors, the philosophical debates, and the human costs of technology.

It is clear from the scholarship surveyed here and the scholarship from the field at large that there is more work to be done. More space and time would permit further discussion of the fields that connect literature and technology—such as disability studies (Davis), theoretical and philosophical scholarship on the posthuman (Wolfe), and historical and rhetorical scholarship on race and technology (Fouché; Sinclair; Banks). Additional references in the works cited follow Hayles's suggestion to analyze the links between literature and computer technology, exploring such areas as video games (Bogost), fiber optics (Chun), and electronic literature (Manovich). As technology and literature continue to develop and change in tandem, more occasions certainly will arise for further discussion and reflection.

Works Cited

Banks, Adam. *Race, Rhetoric, and Technology: Searching for Higher Ground*. Mahwah: Erlbaum, 2005.

Bogost, Ian. *Unit Operations: An Approach to Video Game Criticism*. Cambridge, MA: MIT P, 2006.

Bolter, Jay David. *Writing Space: The Computer, Hypertext, and the History of Writing*. Hillsdale: Erlbaum, 1991.

Cartwright, Lisa. *Screening the Body: Tracing Medicine's Visual Culture*. Minneapolis: U of Minnesota P, 1995.

Chun, Wendy Hui Kyong. *Control and Freedom: Power and Paranoia in the Age of Fiber Optics*. Cambridge, MA: MIT P, 2006.

Davis, Lennard, ed. *The Disability Studies Reader*. New York: Routledge, 2006.

Fouché, Rayvon, Granville T. Woods, Lewis H. Latimer, et al. *Black Inventors in the Age of Segregation*. Baltimore: Johns Hopkins UP, 2003.

Haraway, Donna. *Simians, Cyborgs, and Women: The Reinvention of Nature*. New York: Routledge, 1991.

Hayles, N. Katherine. *How We Became Posthuman: Virtual Bodies in Cybernetics, Literature, and Informatics*. Chicago: U Chicago P, 1999.

_____. *My Mother Was a Computer: Digital Subjects and Literary Texts*. Chicago: U Chicago P, 2005.

_____. *Writing Machines*. Cambridge, MA: MIT P, 2002.

Kasson, John F. *Civilizing the Machine: Technology and Republican Values in America, 1776–1900*. New York: Hill, 1999.

Leavis, F. R. *Two Cultures? The Significance of C. P. Snow*. London: Chatto, 1962.

Manovich, Lev. *The Language of New Media*. Cambridge, MA: MIT P, 2002.

Martin, Emily. "The Egg and the Sperm: How Science Has Constructed a Romance Based on Stereotypical Male-Female Roles." *Signs* 16.3 (1991): 485–501.

Marx, Leo. "The Idea of 'Technology' and Postmodern Pessimism." *Does Technology Drive History: The Dilemma of Technological Determinism*. Eds. Merritt Roe Smith and Leo Marx. Cambridge, MA: MIT Press, 1994.

_____. *The Machine in the Garden: Technology and the Pastoral Idea in America*. 1964. Oxford: Oxford UP, 2000.

_____. *The Pilot and the Passenger: Essays on Literature, Technology, and Culture in the United States* New York: Oxford UP, 1988.

_____. "Technology: The Emergence of a Hazardous Concept." *Technology and Culture* 51.3 (2010): 561–77.

McLuhan, Marshall. *Understanding Media: The Extensions of Man*. 1964. Cambridge, MA: MIT P, 1994.

Meikle, Jeffrey. "Classics Revisited: Leo Marx's *The Machine in the Garden*." *Technology and Culture* 44.1 (2003): 147-159.

Murray, Janet. *Hamlet on the Holodeck: The Future of Narrative in Cyberspace*. New York: Simon, 1997.

Nicholls, Peter. "Machines and Collages." *Journal of American Studies* 22.2 (1998): 275–80.

Nye, David E. *American Technological Sublime*. Cambridge, MA: MIT P, 1996.

Sinclair, Bruce, ed. *Technology and the African-American Experience: Needs and Opportunities for Study*. Cambridge, MA: MIT Press, 2004.

Snow, C. P. *The Two Cultures and the Scientific Revolution*. New York: Cambridge UP, 1959.

Squier, Susan M. *Babies in Bottles: Twentieth-Century Visions of Reproductive Technology*. Piscataway: Rutgers UP, 1994.

_____. *Liminal Lives: Imagining the Human at the Frontiers of Biomedicine*. Durham: Duke UP, 2004.

Tichi, Cecelia. *Shifting Gears: Technology, Literature, Culture in Modernist America*. Chapel Hill: U of North Carolina P, 1987.

_____. "Television and Recent American Fiction." *American Literary History* 1.1 (1989): 110–30.

Wajcman, Judy. *Feminism Confronts Technology*. University Park: Penn State UP, 1991.

Waldby, Catherine. *The Visible Human Project*. New York: Routledge, 2000.

Wiener, Norbert. *The Human Use of Human Beings: Cybernetics and Society*. 1954. New York: Da Capo, 1988.

Wolfe, Cary. *What Is Posthumanism?* Minneapolis: U of Minnesota P, 2009.

The Model T and the Roaring Twenties: The Automobile, Social Change, and Cultural Critique in American Literature_____

Tanfer Emin Tunc

At the beginning of the 1920s, the Ford Model T, the first mass-produced car aimed at the middle class, accounted for about half of all automobiles in the United States. By 1927, however, production was discontinued, and by the end of the decade and due to fierce competition from the Chrysler, Packard, and Buick automobiles, the Ford Model T commanded a declining portion of the American road. Nevertheless, this technological innovation—designed, marketed, and distributed by the Henry Ford Motor Company—revolutionized not only transportation but also social values.

The personal freedom and independence that came with the Model T permanently altered American social dynamics. While women and the emerging youth culture hailed this development as an advance in social mobility, more conservative Americans—such as the town of Muncie, Indiana, examined by sociologists Robert S. and Helen Merrell Lynd in *Middletown: A Study in Modern American Culture* (1929)—saw it as the beginning of the end. The technology of the car allowed individuals and families to travel anonymously across the United States and beyond the scrutiny of small-town life, and also altered the nature of courtship. No longer did men and women meet in front parlors with chaperones; the automobile provided young adults with the ability to escape the prying eyes of parents, grandparents, and extended family members. As a result, one local judge described the automobile as a "house of prostitution on wheels" due to the sexual freedom that it facilitated (114). The same judge cited "that of [the] thirty girls brought before the juvenile court in the twelve months preceding September 1, 1924, charged with 'sex crimes' for whom the place where the offense had occurred was given in the records, nineteen were listed as having committed the offense in an automobile" (258). A Muncie preacher expressed concern, or "moral panic," that the automobile would destroy the religious and social ties of the community. Instead of attending church on Sundays, families could now drive out of town on independent excursions—a phenomenon that came to be known as "Sunday driving."

As represented by the Ford Model T, the automobile completely reoriented the way in which Americans interacted with one another. It spawned its own popular culture through magazines and songs, brought together isolated communities, impacted urban planning, and served as the foundation for the growing consumer society of the 1920s.[1] While many Americans perceived these changes as progressive steps toward social improvement, members of the literary community—especially those belonging to the modernist movement of the interwar years—were disillusioned by the changes they witnessed. This chapter examines the impact of the Model T, and the automobile in general, on American culture in the 1920s, and considers how the advent of this technology was critiqued by some of the era's most widely read authors, including Booth Tarkington (*The Magnificent Ambersons*, 1918), Sinclair Lewis (*Free Air*, 1919), F. Scott Fitzgerald (*The Great Gatsby*, 1925), William Faulkner ("Country Mice," 1926), and E. B. White ("Farewell, My Lovely," 1936). Through their works, these writers not only offer intriguing analyses of the social and cultural impact of the automobile but also present biting yet relevant commentaries on the problematic nature of consumer culture and the turbulence that accompanies sudden changes in social values.

Although the Ford Model T was not the first car on the road, it was certainly the automobile that changed American society. It emerged in 1908 from the business model of industrialist Henry Ford (1863–1947), the first American entrepreneur to implement the moving assembly line technique in the factory setting. While Ford became a "Captain of Industry" for many, for others he resembled the "Robber Barons" of the Gilded Age of the late nineteenth century. His philosophy of efficient mass production came to be known as *Fordism*, and its reliance on mass consumption in turn fueled his lucrative business, his belief in the Protestant work ethic, and his advocacy of a paternalistic form of welfare capitalism, which granted him permission to interfere in his workers' lives (Gillham 441–42). Despite his critics, "numerous commentators past and present have lauded Ford for the 'democratization of the automobile,' [and] for transforming the car from a luxury item for the rich to a part of everyday American life" (Hakim 77).[2] As production increased, the price of the Model T decreased, thus guaranteeing sales: "In its first year of operation, the assembly line increased the production of Model Ts from 82,000 to 189,000. By 1916 the plant produced 585,000 units. In 1921, Ford made one million automobiles; by 1923, two million. . . . By 1920 every other automobile in the world was a Model T Ford" (Halvorsen 21). Americans were drawn to the Model T for numerous reasons. It was affordable (middle-class families, in particular, had the option of paying in an installment plan), and compared to other models it had a "rugged body, mounted high to enable it to negotiate country roads. . . . Its twenty horsepower, four-cylinder engine was simple, as was its transmission. . . . And it was simple to repair and modify" (Halvorsen 20). By the 1920s, thanks to Ford, the United States had become a "nation on wheels."

Fordism not only changed the way Americans lived their lives but also changed society. The Model T increased mobility in all its forms—social, class, business, and leisure—and opened up new horizons. The "Tin Lizzy," as the Model T was nicknamed (due to its tinny sound), ushered in a cultural revolution that impacted every aspect of life, from the American geography (Melder 470), to the American lexicon, which adopted such new words as "flivver"—because the Ford shook up the liver—and "jitney"—a cheap method of transportation. According to Jonathan Gillham, "widespread automobile ownership led to massive programs of road building, to the near-extinction of public transit in many cities, and to the universal phenomenon of urban sprawl as larger and larger suburbs developed with ever more poorly-planned patterns of land use, swallowing up vast swaths of the countryside" (443).

Arguably, moral and cultural values were most profoundly impacted. As previously mentioned, the automobile revolutionized sexual relations, allowing young adults to travel to "lovers' lanes" and across state lines, away from the prying eyes of elders and small-town gossips. As families played hooky from church and other local events by driving elsewhere, solidarity among families and neighborhoods began to suffer, with central streets and their small businesses meeting their demise as shopping choices began to expand. "With the ability to easily escape to more distant locales," Darin Halvorsen notes, "residents no longer had to make nice with their neighbors; they could motor some miles distant to the friends of their choice. As a result, neighbors spent fewer hours on the front porch visiting and comparing lawns" (44).

As anonymity increased, so did crime; automobiles, as thieves and bootleggers soon discovered, not only functioned as an efficient way to transport goods and people, but also could serve as "getaway cars." Consequently, violence became an increasing part of everyday life: "In 1905, the murder rate was five per 100,000; by 1930, the rate had jumped to 225 per 100,000" (Halvorsen 36–37). The automobile also promoted consumer culture, as there were always more parts to purchase. While all twenty-six families studied in *Middletown* owned automobiles, only five had bathtubs (256). A working-class mother of nine told the Lynds, "We'd rather do without clothes than give up the car" (255). Another woman remarked, "I'll go without food before I'll see us give up the car" (256), illustrating the extent to which the automobile had become a powerful "necessity," displacing such needs as food, clothing, and cleanliness. Very rapidly the automobile came to occupy a "unique position in American culture . . . when Americans purchased cars. . . . they purchased something beyond the utilitarian object; they [bought] luxury, glamour, identity, freedom, escape" (Smoak 3).

While small towns suffered socially and economically, others, especially those located along highways, flourished. Rural isolation ended as roads and the provision of medical care improved; schools were consolidated, increasing the quality of educational and recreational opportunities. Even though the development of suburbs contributed to urban decay and a decline in the value of city real estate, immigrants and former residents of ghettos benefited from the move out of polluted neighborhoods (Flink 460). Many uninhabited areas of the country soon began to welcome settlers as Americans explored new spaces. New towns emerged in the Midwest and the West in particular, and the car came to represent a new promise of American society. According to Roderick Nash, "it is possible to think of these years as the automobile age and Henry Ford as its czar. The flivver, along with the flask and the flapper, seemed to represent the 1920s in the minds of its people as well as its historians" (153).

Yet American writers, especially the literary modernists, were highly critical of the automobile, citing it as a "vehicle" of individual turmoil, social change, and a harbinger of both good and evil. Shelby Smoak explains:

> In fiction, between 1918 [and] 1939, cars are represented as violent. Cars antagonize, crash, wreck, and kill; cars also confuse a person's financial judgment. . . .
>
> The American novel communicates an automobile whose violence is psychological, physical, and metaphorical. Psychological violence permeates Tarkington's *The Magnificent Ambersons* as George Amberson resists the automobile; physical violence exists in Fitzgerald's *The Great Gatsby* via the several car wrecks narrated. . . . In each novel . . . the violence serves different ends. For example, in *The Magnificent Ambersons*, the car and its violence highlight George's resistance to change. (56)

Although the works of Booth Tarkington have been categorized as examples of late American realism, scholars also have positioned him as an early American modernist, as he shared many of the same concerns about technology, the deconstruction of cultural norms, and the responses to social change evident in the works of F. Scott Fitzgerald, Sinclair Lewis, and William Faulkner. As is evident in *Middletown*, not everyone accepted the automobile with open arms. While some herald-ed the machine as the dawn of a new technological era, others saw the "horseless carriage" as the end of civilization. According to Halvorsen:

> This wariness . . . did not necessarily translate into a rejection of auto-mobiles. [These authors] used automobiles as symbols of change in their novels. . . . This suggests that, like the modern intelligentsia's views about cyber technology and the Internet, these authors recognized many of the possible social dangers connected to an automobile-based society, while at the same time accepting [their] inevitability." (v)

Tarkington examines many reactions to the automobile in *The Magnificent Ambersons*, which is set around the turn of the twentieth century in Midland, a sizeable midwestern town modeled on Indianapolis, Indiana—a small city that shares many traits with Muncie, Indiana, in *Middletown*. Caught in the middle of industrialization and urban sprawl, and a laboratory for such new technologies as electricity, the telephone, and the automobile, Midland also is the home of the Ambersons, a formerly prominent upper-class family whose decline reflects that of the inner city itself. Tarkington's characters perceive the automobile as one of the most potent "vehicles" of change in Midland. Not only has it polluted the environment with foul air and noise, but it also has polluted the citizens of the city, and perhaps America as a whole. By the beginning of the 1920s, the so-called horseless age had become a reality, and the automobile was now an indelible part of life. The new vehicle had altered time, distance, space, human values, and social norms; as Tarkington predicted, "what alters our lives alters our thoughts; what alters our thoughts alters our characters; what alters our characters alters our ideals; and what alters our ideals alters our morals. . . . the quiet of the world is ending forever" (qtd. in Beer 10–11).

Tarkington depicts the conflict between new and old values through George Amberson Minafer and Eugene Morgan (the father of George's love interest, Lucy), two characters who embody the two sides of the automobile debate. While George attempts to live in the vanishing romantic past, an age of upper-class leisure and quiet, his foil Eugene, a middle-class automobile entrepreneur, embraces and attempts to profit from change, especially from the sterile, hurried world of technology. While George believes that "those things are never going to amount to anything" (52), bragging that a horseless carriage could never compare to a horse, Eugene sees automobiles as representing a future of change and new technology. This tension is most palpable when Eugene's car breaks down and passersby shout, "Git a hoss! Git a hoss! Git a hoss!" (62). In the same scene, however, George's own sleigh veers off track, causing him and Lucy to crash. In this way, Tarkington juxtaposes the imperfections of both technologies—the old horse-drawn carriage and the new automobile—highlighting his own ambivalence toward both. "More importantly," Smoak notes, "the passage foreshadows the horse-driven vehicle eventually being 'overturned' by the horseless carriage. While the accident does not result in a permanent injury, the scene yet suggests the automobile as a harbinger of change, one that is 'upsetting' to those who resist it such as George" (65).

No matter how much George may try to resist the impending rise of automation and automobiles, Tarkington suggests that it is impossible to stop the inevitable; to survive, one must adapt or face his or her own demise. Thus, an inverse relationship begins, as the more successful Eugene becomes as a technological innovator and automobile manufacturer, and the more pitiful George becomes an outdated relic. While Eugene, like Ford, succeeds in turning his ideas "into such a splendid, humming thing as that factory—all shiny steel, clicking and buzzing away, and with all those workmen, such muscled looking men" (155), George succeeds at nothing, suggesting that in the modern age, simply "being a gentleman" is no longer enough. The entrepreneurs like Eugene and Ford will build America, not the fops and dandies of upper-class nineteenth-century society. Yet Tarkington, George, and even Eugene cannot help but be nostalgic for the past, creating an ambivalence that undergirds the entire novel. As Eugene notes:

[Automobiles] will not add to the beauty of the world, nor to the life of men's souls. . . . They are going to alter war, and they are going to alter peace. I think men's minds are going to be changed in subtle ways because of automobiles. . . . it may be that George is right . . . Perhaps, ten or twenty years from now, if we can see the inward change in men by that time, I . . . would have to agree with him that automobiles had no business to be invented" (173–74).

Inevitably, the automobile proves to be the ruin of the Ambersons. As urban sprawl leads to the development of the suburbs, the value of the Ambersons' assets plummets, driving the family into destitution. While Eugene becomes rich due to investment in the "right" automotive business, the money that George's Aunt Fanny invests on the electric headlight is lost due to overspeculation in the wrong product. In this "inverse riches-to-rags narrative" (Smoak 217), George becomes an impoverished wagon driver, and his world collapses under the "weight of the automobile's progress" (Halvorsen 70). As a gentleman who resists change, he is haunted by the past, hopelessly searching for a bygone era that will never return. Crossing the street, he is struck by an automobile: "Fate had reserved for him the final insult of riding him down under the wheels of one of those juggernauts at which he had once shouted 'Git a hoss!'" (Tarkington 307). He is not hit by "a big and swift and momentous car such as Eugene manufactured," but rather "a specimen of the hustling little type that was flooding the country, the cheapest, commonest, hardiest little car ever made"—probably a Model T Ford (307). Unable to decide between moving forward or backward, he is struck and paralyzed by the oncoming car. Though he reunites with Lucy, George loses his "magnificence," becoming a victim of the very technology that he challenges throughout the novel.

Like Tarkington, whose novel won the Pulitzer Prize, Sinclair Lewis also incorporates the automobile into the plots of his most prominent novels to critique the technology's impact on American society.[3] For Milt Daggett and Claire Boltwood, the main characters of *Free Air*, the automobile symbolizes liberation. They find each other on the road during Claire's cross-country road trip from Minnesota to the Pacific Northwest—a trip that Lewis also made with his wife in their Model T in 1916 (Schwantes 117). A wealthy "new woman" from New York, Claire and her father Henry travel in her expensive Gomez-Deperdussin roadster, believing that the "free air" of rural America will be good for his health, which was ruined by urbanization.[4] Along the way they find adventure with Milt, a mechanic and owner of a repair shop. On the road, notes Jerry W. Passon, "the socialite and the mechanic meet as something like equals; the physical space of the West and the demands it places on ingenuity and personal character make the differences in social status inconsequential," thus highlighting the physical and social mobility that comes with car ownership (Passon 10).

According to Kathleen Franz, "*Free Air* bridged the transition between stories of female autonomy and those of the companionate couple by marrying the motor girl to the technological hero" (58). Although Claire is accompanied by her ailing father and Milt, who like a sidekick follows her in his Teal "bug," helps her out of "scrapes," and transforms her into a "real woman," *Free Air* is a novel of female empowerment. For most of the novel, Claire is behind the driver's seat and in control of their course. Driving gives her the strength and ability to challenge cultural norms by resisting conformity and creating her own "road" as one who rejects upper-class expectations. Like the American landscape itself, the road ahead is limitless, and individuals have the power to determine their destinies; Claire even calls her trip "a voyage into democracy" (Lewis 45, 47).

Milt and Claire are "brought together by the automobile and discover a world of possibilities, romantic and social, that the new technology has uncovered. Yet technology is not without a price; as human beings are not perfect creatures, neither are the cars that become our surrogates" (Passon 12). Despite its status as a luxury car, Claire's automobile is unreliable; it keeps breaking down, leading to new adventures while simultaneously suggesting a breakdown of social values. Smoak notes that along with "being critical of the general mechanical defects of the new automotive technology, *Free Air* also makes an equally critical comment upon the poor road conditions and an inability to keep up with the automobile's proliferation" (55). Like other novels, *Free Air* includes a violent car wreck, suggesting that everything, the notion of liberation through technology included, has a social and personal price.

F. Scott Fitzgerald's *The Great Gatsby* depicts life on Long Island during the so-called Roaring Twenties, a time period that has been described as " 'the most expensive orgy in history,' where waste is the rule, nobody trusts anybody, [and] everybody lies about everything" (Pardini 49). This world is full of "bad drivers" who represent the rotten people of Jay Gatsby's world—a world of empty consumerism, corrupt values, and selfish social climbing (Smoak 69). These characters include Daisy Buchanan (Gatsby's love interest); Jordan Baker, "whose name Fitzgerald drew from two popular automobiles of the era, the flashy Jordan Playboy and the Baker Electric" (Hakim 70); and a slew of other minor characters who, at Gatsby's lavish parties, carelessly get themselves into scrapes and car crashes.[5] While the automobile provides Daisy with physical mobility, for Jordan, another new woman, the car is a social and cultural statement of liberation, agency, and gender equality, as well as an expression of "such core 'American' ideals as individuality, freedom, and autonomy" (Hakim 71). For Gatsby, the yellow Rolls-Royce "is a personal, even intimate object, a . . . signifier of masculinity" (Passon 82). Gatsby's automobile—"a rich cream color, bright with nickel, swollen here and there in its monstrous length with triumphant hat-boxes and supper-boxes and tool-boxes, and terraced with a labyrinth of wind-shields that mirrored a dozen suns" (Fitzgerald 51)—functions as a symbol of "phallic" masculine power that allows him, as a *nouveau riche* bootlegger, to at least temporarily enter Daisy's world of inherited wealth and old money (Passon 83).

In the end, however, Gatsby's car proves to be his downfall. He uses his signs of wealth to attract Daisy, who then allows Gatsby to take the blame for the death of Myrtle Wilson, Tom Buchanan's mistress. Believing that Gatsby was the one both driving the "death car" and having an affair with Daisy, Myrtle's husband George murders Gatsby and commits suicide. As Nick Carraway comments, "They were careless people, Tom and Daisy—they smashed up things and creatures and then retreated back into their money or their vast carelessness or whatever it was that kept them together, and let other people clean up the mess they had made" (Fitzgerald 142). In the novel, the Model T is a "'dust-covered wreck' . . . an archeological find without a museum, a fragment of an old world long gone, invisible under its dust and thus forgotten" (Pardini 49), suggesting that in the modern world, old values have been lost forever, to be replaced by newer, faster, and even more destructive technologies. Rather than champion or passively reflect the culture that surrounds him and his characters, "Fitzgerald continually criticizes that culture and the changes that created it. . . . [He] uses images of technology, specifically the automobile, in his work as symbols of change, and often as a threat to humanity itself" (95).

As Deborah Clarke argues, the most prominent American novelists of the interwar years "took aim at the increasing dependence on automobility, exploring the potentials and dangers of a country determined to keep its cars moving. Nowhere was this scrutiny so pronounced as in the South, one of the last regions to be conquered by automobility" (143). Members of the conservative literary movement known as southern agrarianism were particularly wary of such "progress," accusing northern industrialization, urbanization, and mechanization of negatively impacting southern identity. Those who participated in the southern renaissance, such as William Faulkner, who examined the divide between the old and new South, were also ambivalent about this new technology. Faulkner's short story "Country Mice" focuses on the battle between tradition and modernity through the lens of the automobile, which ostensibly symbolizes the hollow, morally bereft values of the new South. In the process, as Randall Waldron maintains, he also draws on numerous elements from Fitzgerald's novel, which had been published "in April 1925, just four or five months prior to the composition of 'Country Mice.' Thus not only is it possible that Faulkner had read it, he could only have done so recently enough for it to be fresh in his mind" (281–82). The texts share undeniable parallels: both center on bootleggers with colorful and ambiguous pasts, expensive but vulgar tastes (flashy shirts, watches, and ruby jewelry), and narrators with "insight" into the protagonists' struggles (Waldron 282). Both Gatsby and Faulkner's bootleggers also have flamboyant cars, the latter's bearing a remarkable similarity to Gatsby's Rolls-Royce: "My friend the bootlegger's motor car is as long as a steamboat and the color of a chocolate ice cream soda. It is trimmed with silver from stem to stern like an expensive lavatory [and] is upholstered in maroon leather" (Faulkner 108).

"Country Mice" is told in flashback and begins with a ride in the southern countryside—described as an "airing off"—with the wind blowing through the narrator's hair and the open road in front of them (a description reminiscent of Lewis's *Free Air*). During the ride, the bootlegger recounts a "liquor run" he did with his brother Gus to New Haven to supply a Yale football game. As they continue their drive in the rural South, the bootlegger explains how one should never underestimate cunning "hick cops" (111). Despite being bribed, the "country hicks" near New Haven outwit the bootleggers by hijacking their liquor and making a quick getaway, thus inverting stereotypes about the naiveté and dimwittedness of rural folk compared to city folk. The technology that catalyzes the short story—from the "airing off" to the criminal activities—is the automobile. While Faulkner praises the liberation that the car provides, he posits the car as the root of social change, mobility, and evil in way that brings to mind the residents of Middletown —especially in the new South, where "southern aristocrats" (representatives of the old south) are being displaced by immigrants such as the bootlegger (who is Italian). Within the context of Prohibition, the impact of the automobile on the South was exponentially multiplied.

By the 1930s, it became clear that for better or worse the automobile had changed American society. For many, the Model T *was* the automobile and the ultimate symbol of the social transitions that surrounded it. When Ford discontinued its production in 1927, Americans reacted with relief (for it was not the most reliable car) and nostalgia. E. B. White addressed both these reactions in his 1936 essay "Farewell, My Lovely," an ode to the Model T. Like Lewis, White drove cross-country in a Model T in 1922 and was familiar with the everyday experiences of Model T ownership (Gillham 442). While White is nostalgic for the "primitivism" of the Model T, which reminds him of a simpler, happier time, he is also a realist, acknowledging that the loss of American "simplicity" was a by-product of the car itself. He underscores the fact that the Ford automobile, and Fordism in general, was not particularly admirable; it was, in fact, "conceived in madness." "White's remembrance of the Model T is," according to Gillham, "an homage only in jest. It is a litany of the car's quirks . . . presented in [a] humorous mood. . . . like a human being, the Ford was inscrutable, perverse, and unpredictable" (444). Nevertheless, White highlights the automobile's social significance: "The last Model T was built in 1927, and the car is fading from what scholars call the American scene— which is an understatement, because to a few million people who grew up with it, the old Ford practically was the American scene."

While contemporary readers are too young to remember the Model T, the emergence of new technologies in the twenty-first century allows us to relate to the underlying technological dilemma: "Gadget bred gadget," White wrote in 1936. "Owners not only bought ready-made gadgets, they invented gadgets to meet special needs." Ultimately, the automotive quirks that White describes resemble the "quirks of all things mechanical in the modern [age]. The Model T is merely an exaggerated exemplar of that type. . . . Familiarity with modern mechanisms of the type represented by the Ford is sufficient" (Gillham 447–48). Like White and the literary characters described in this chapter, we are still "trying to find our place in a world traveling at a frightening velocity toward an unknown destination" (Rogers 661).[6] Although White begins his essay on a pessimistic note, declaring the golden days of the automobile gone forever, he resigns himself to the possibility of new adventures and the exciting technologies of the future. These technologies may alter our lives forever—and not necessarily for the better— but we must deal with them as they arise.

Notes

1. Some popular "car songs" from the 1910s and 1920s include: "On the Old Back Seat of the Henry Ford," "Keep Away from the Fellow Who Owns an Automobile," "Take Me Out for a Joy Ride," "I Think I Oughn't Auto Anymore," "Out in an Automobile," "Tumble in a Rumble Seat," "Henry's Made a Lady Out of Lizzy," "He'd Have to Get Under, Get Out, and Get Under," and "In My Merry Oldsmobile." Many of these songs included sexually suggestive lyrics and were considered potentially scandalous at the time. According to Halvorsen, some of these songs, such as "Love in an Automobile," may be worth examining for their influence on the literature of the period (42).

2. In 1907, the number of cars registered for the entire United States was 140,300. "Only 157,000 cars had been produced and sold by the hundreds of producers of the American car industry. [By] 1926 . . . the majority of the 22,044,600 cars registered were Model T Fords" (Melder 467).

3. These novels include *Free Air* (1919), *Main Street* (1920), *Babbitt* (1922), and *Dodsworth* (1929). The latter three works are beyond the scope of this chapter but worth examining. In *Main Street*, Lewis critiques the ways in which the car inverts the traditions of Gopher Prairie, Minnesota, a Middletown-like example of small-town America. *Babbitt* is a satire of consumer culture that focuses on George Babbitt's obsession with possessions, especially his car, his favorite status symbol. *Dodsworth* tells the tale of Sam Dodsworth, vice president and manager of the Revelation Automobile Company.

4. "New women" of the late-nineteenth century represented self-actualization and liberation. They participated in the public sphere, were college-educated, and often advocated women's rights. They chose whom they wanted to marry, practiced birth control, and rejected restrictive clothing, such as corsets. By the 1920s, the flapper—a hedonistic version of the new woman, who bobbed her hair, wore cosmetics and short skirts, listened to jazz, smoke, drank, danced, drove automobiles, and engaged in casual sexual behavior—came to represent

young middle- and upper-class womanhood (Tunc, "Sin, Sex and Shopping" 82).

5. In 1925, the publication year of *The Great Gatsby*, there were "17,427 automobile related fatalities. . . . Thus, Fitzgerald's inclusion of automobile crashes in *This Side of Paradise* and *The Great Gatsby* reflect the public visibility of automobile accidents" (Smoak 70).

6. According to Aldous Huxley, this aspect of our "brave new world" began in 1908, or "1 A.F. (i.e., after Ford). Blessed is Our Ford," thus equating the creation of the Model T with God's creation of man (Halvorsen 23).

Works Cited

Beer, Jeremy. "What About Booth?: Newton Booth Tarkington, Neglected Hoosier." *University Bookman* 46.3 (2008): 7–11.

Clarke, Deborah. "Eudora Welty's Losing Battles: Cars and Family Values." *Mississippi Quarterly* 62.3 (2009): 143–57.

Faulkner, William. "Country Mice." *New Orleans Sketches*. 1958. Ed. Carvel Collins. Jackson: UP of Mississippi, 2002.

Fitzgerald, F. Scott. *The Great Gatsby*. 1925. New York: Oxford UP, 1998.

Flink, James J. "Three Stages of American Automobile Consciousness." *American Quarterly* 24.4 (1972): 451–73.

Franz, Kathleen. *Tinkering: Early Consumers Reinvent the Automobile*. Philadelphia: U of Pennsylvania P, 2011.

Gillham, Jonathan Brown. "The Laugh of the Oppressed Creature: Early Twentieth-Century American Magazine Humor as Affective Adaptation to Modernity." Diss. Wayne State U, 2009.

Hakim, Andrew Mark. "Fictions of Representation: Narrative and the Politics of Self-Making in the Interwar American Novel." Diss. U of Southern California, 2009. Web. 2 May 2012.

Halvorsen, Darin D. "Low-Swinging Chariots: The Automobile and Fateful Nostalgia in *The Magnificent Ambersons*, *One of Ours*, and *The Great Gatsby*." MA thesis. South Dakota State U, 2006.

Hugill, Peter J. "Good Roads and the Automobile in the United States 1880–1929." *Geographical Review* 72.3 (1982): 327–49.

Lewis, Sinclair. *Free Air*. 1919. Ithaca: Cornell U Lib., 2010.

Lynd, Robert S., and Helen Merrell Lynd. *Middletown: A Study in American Culture*. 1929. New York: Harcourt, 1957.

Melder, F. Eugene. "The 'Tin Lizzie's' Golden Anniversary." *American Quarterly* 12.4 (1960): 466–81.

Nash, Roderick. *The Nervous Generation: American Thought, 1917–1930*. Chicago: Rand, 1970.

Pardini, Samuele F. S. "The Engines of History: The Automobile in American and Italian Literary Cultures, 1908–1943." Diss. SUNY Buffalo, 2005.

Passon, Jerry Walter. "The Corvette in Literature and Culture: Material Object and Persistent Image." Diss. Southern Illinois U–Carbondale, 2010.

Rogers, Barbara J. "E(lwyn) B(rooks) White." *American Writers: A Collection of Literary Biographies, Supplement 1.* Ed. Leonard Unger. Vol. 2. New York: Scribner, 1979.

Schwantes, Carlos A. *Going Places: Transportation Redefines the Twentieth-Century West.* Bloomington: Indiana UP, 2003.

Smoak, Shelby. "Framing the Automobile in Twentieth Century American Literature: A Spatial Approach." Diss. U of North Carolina at Greensboro, 2007. Web. 2 May 2012.

Tarkington, Booth. *The Magnificent Ambersons.* 1918. San Diego: ICON, 2009.

Tunc, Tanfer Emin. "*The Great Gatsby*: The Tragedy of the American Dream on Long Island's Gold Coast." *Bloom's Literary Themes: The American Dream.* Eds. Harold Bloom and Blake G. Hobby. New York: Chelsea, 2009. 67–79.

_____. "Sin, Sex, and Shopping: Conspicuous Consumption and Modern Identity in F. Scott Fitzgerald's *The Great Gatsby* and *This Side of Paradise.*" *The Globetrotting Shopaholic: Consumer Spaces, Products, and their Cultural Places.* Eds. Tanfer Emin Tunc and Annessa Ann Babic. Newcastle-upon-Tyne: Cambridge Scholars, 2008. 77–90.

Waldron, Randall. "Faulkner's First Fictional Car—Borrowed from Scott Fitzgerald?" *American Literature* 60.2 (1988): 281–85.

White, E. B. "Farewell, My Lovely." *New Yorker* 16 May 1936: n. pag. *Wes Jones,* 2003. Web. 20 May 2011.

"An Intent to Communicate": Technology and Digital Culture in *The Crying of Lot 49*

Madeline Monson-Rosen

In Thomas Pynchon's *The Crying of Lot 49* (1965), protagonist Oedipa Maas finds herself drunk in a motel bathroom, where a can of hairspray propels itself around by its own pressure: "The can knew where it was going, she sensed, or something fast enough, God or a digital machine, might have computed in advance the complex web of its travel" (25). This image, the utterly absurd situation, and the incongruous metaphor—comparing a precise calculation with an event of dangerous randomness—signal an important historical shift: the arrival, in the literary imagination, of the digital communications network. Pynchon's short novel invokes the possibility of networked digital communication, linking it to a long, troubled history of communications technologies. The publication of *The Crying of Lot 49* in 1965 situates the work in the middle of the computer's emergence as an information technology.

The Crying of Lot 49 marked, for the first time in literary fiction, the appearance of images associated with computers, digital communications, and network and media theory. Even as *Lot 49* introduces these elements into literary studies, it links them to technologies that range from the advent of private mail in fourteenth-century Europe to the nascent technology of computer communication, first theorized in 1962, four years before the novel's publication. Material issues hold a significant influence in the novel as well; media technologies are never separate from the material circumstances of history, global politics, and capital and labor. An analysis of *Lot 49* reveals that the text is permeated with references to technology, and that Pynchon goes to considerable lengths to situate technology in terms of history and material issues.

In the novel, Oedipa finds herself mysteriously appointed coexecutor of the will of a former lover, Pierce Inverarity, a wealthy business magnate whose financial interests span the globe. The novel's title is derived from Inverarity's stamp collection, which is to be auctioned—or "cried," in auctioneer's jargon—as Lot 49. Attempting to bring to light Inverarity's numerous business interests, Oedipa discovers what she comes to call the Tristero System, a secret communications network with a three-hundred-year-old history. The Tristero now operates under the auspices of the interoffice mail of Yoyodyne, a defense contractor and "San Narciso's big source of employment . . . Yoyodyne Inc., one of the giants of the aerospace industry" (15).

Throughout the novel references to technology have a dual emphasis. The subject matter itself is often technology, but the novel's scope encompasses diverse types and histories. *Lot 49* considers the cutting edge of 1960s information technology (computers, radio, television) and new theories of global communication, but it considers writing, print, and mail as information technologies as well.

More than informing the plot, technology lends *Lot 49* metaphors and formal devices. One example is the image of the hairspray can, which can be likened to a digital message traveling through a network. Late in the novel, Oedipa imagines that her search for the Tristero is "like walking among matrices of a great digital computer, the zeroes and ones twinned above, hanging like balanced mobiles right and left, ahead, thick, maybe endless" (150). In a famous scene from the beginning, Oedipa looks from above a housing development, "a vast sprawl of houses which had all grown up together, like a well-tended crop," and remembers "the time she'd opened a transistor radio to replace a battery and seen her first printed circuit." The two structures merge in her memory: "The ordered swirl of houses and streets, from this high angle, sprang at her now with the same unexpected, astonishing clarity as the circuit card had. Though she knew even less about radios than about Southern Californians, there were to both outward patterns a hieroglyphic sense of concealed meaning, of an intent to communicate" (14).

Used as a storytelling device, the language of mechanical and digital processes carries particular resonance. The focus on images that are historical and technological in nature—images of the transistor, for example—allows the *Lot 49* to build a continuous history of information technology.

Throughout the novel, stylized scenes use images of science and technology as metaphors. The hidden "intent to communicate" characterizes the circuit as well as the highways of Southern California. Yet the information conveyed by these "hieroglyphic" technologies— the circuit, the mail, the manuscript—is less important than the structures themselves, which Pynchon's text represents on a formal level. Pynchon demonstrates that these structures endure over time and in many iterations. As these structures reappear, so do the attendant cultures of forgery, piracy, and miscommunication. Both the world of print and the world of digital networks are, Pynchon shows, unreliable. The culture of print is merely resituated within a digital space.

Pynchon's use of binary code as a formal structure transforms the reading of the novel into a kind of decryption, which highlights the way in which context determines meaning. Pynchon inspires the reader to wonder how exactly binary coding is different from the alphabet. Similarly, Oedipa imagines that her search for the Tristero is

> like walking among matrices of a great digital computer, the zeroes and ones twinned above, hanging like balanced mobiles right and left, ahead, thick, maybe endless. Behind the hieroglyphic streets there would either be a transcendent meaning, or only the earth. . . . the bones of the GI's at the bottom of Lake Inverarity were there either for a reason that mattered to the world, or for skin divers and cigarette smokers. Ones and zeroes. (150)

In the end, does *Lot 49* reveal the existence of the secret Tristero or the creation of Oedipa's paranoia?

Threats to the communications network speak to the limitations of any system. The participants in *Lot 49*'s secret postal system admit that they have to make an effort to keep the network functioning: "To keep it up to some kind of a reasonable volume, each member has to send at least one letter a week through the Yoyodyne system. If you don't, you get fined" (39).

In addition to the development of computers, *Lot 49* depicts the connections between technology and communication. It stages the paradoxical status of media, the intersection between communication and technology, and the ways in which media seem wholly implicated in major historical events, remaining so ordinary as to pass unnoticed. This interest in media, as such, emerges as a narrative emphasis on the development of the postal system in Europe and the United States. Forms of media, a multifarious technology, proliferate throughout this short novel—radio and television, even bathroom walls and tattooed skin function as technologies of communication.

The Tristero may be a secret network whose history stretches back to the fourteenth century, but it may also be a posthumous practical joke played by Inverarity. What Oedipa describes as the "languid, sinister blooming of The Tristero" (39) begins with a visit to the Scope, "a haunt for electronics assembly people from Yoyodyne. The green neon sign outside ingeniously depicted the face of an oscilloscope tube, over which flowed an ever-changing dance of Lissajous figures" (34). Inverarity is a Yoyodyne stockholder. Oedipa and her coexecutor, the lawyer Metzger, follow Inverarity's trail to this point. Pynchon's interest in technology emerges here, in Oedipa's first witnessing of a secret mail delivery. Yoyodyne's "electronics assembly people"—elsewhere described as the "Galactronics" division—evoke the image of the galaxy as a figure for communication enabled by computers, and indeed the image of the galaxy, as a planetarium projection, offers a different take on Pynchon's characterization of electronic media's beginnings.

Mike Fallopian, a spare-time mail historian, explains this first appearance of the Tristero after a late-night mail call "just like in the army" (37). Fallopian tells her, "We use Yoyodyne's inter-office delivery. On the sly" (38). Oedipa's pursuit of the Tristero begins with her inadvertent witnessing of the secret mail delivery. According to media theorist Friedrich Kittler, *Lot 49* is an accurate source for "the U.S. part of the story" pertaining to the rise of communications monopolies and the suppression of postal routes that had been operated privately by guilds and universities throughout Europe. Due to Gutenberg's innovations in print technology, and beginning in the sixteenth century, European states would constrain and eventually outlaw private mail carriers to enable more centralized state control of communication and media (247). This is the story Mike Fallopian tells, arguing that the American Civil War was caused by the postal reform movement: "He found it beyond simple coincidence that in of all years 1861 the federal government should have set out on a vigorous suppression of those independent mail routes still surviving the various Acts of '45, '47, '51, and '55, Acts all designed to drive any private competition into financial ruin" (39). According to Fallopian, the Civil War is a direct effect of the U.S. government's efforts to regulate the postal system.

The Tristero System, perhaps a mysterious conspiracy, brings together the plot of the novel. Oedipa's pursuit of the Tristero is also her pursuit of the Inverarity estate; however, this conspiracy creates continuity between the ancient origins of the Tristero—going back to the ancient origins of communications technology itself—and the growing global communications network formed by radio, television, and, eventually, computers. Pynchon's Galactronics engineers are participating in an ancient conspiracy, perpetuated by a global network determined to undermine the state monopoly on mail delivery. Oedipa learns to recognize the Tristero conspiracy by an ancient symbol that appears everywhere, in postage stamps especially: the acronym WASTE and the symbol of "a loop, triangle and trapezoid" (38), a horn with a muted bell.

The symbol and acronym appear throughout the novel, making themselves apparent through forged and faked postage stamp cancellations, and through textual corruptions in books and plays. Oedipa also begins to identify it in locations that seem random but "bloom" around her: "With her own eyes she had verified a WASTE system: seen two

WASTE postmen, a WASTE mailbox, WASTE stamps, WASTE cancellations. And the image of the muted post horn all but saturating the Bay Area" (107). Although Oedipa continues to doubt her sanity, she also recognizes the magnitude and meaning of the secret system. "For here were God knew how many citizens, deliberately choosing not to communicate by U.S. Mail. It was not an act of treason, nor possibly even of defiance. But it was a calculated withdrawal, from the life of the Republic, from its machinery" (101). These signs, the WASTE acronym, and the muted post horn initially appear as errors and forgeries. Oedipa's investigation, however, reveals them to be a system for encoding information.

The Tristero makes itself known through postage stamps containing printing errors. Even before Oedipa visits the Scope, she receives a letter from her husband, Wendell "Mucho" Maas, with a stamp that reads "REPORT ALL OBSCENE MAIL TO YOUR POTSMASTER." When Oedipa asks Metzger to define "potsmaster," he takes her question at face value, enacting the text's emphasis on legitimation over interpretation. He decodes the meaning but does not understand the context and so fails to read correctly: " 'Guy in the scullery,' replied Metzger authoritatively from the bathroom, 'in charge of all the heavy stuff, canner kettles, gunboats, Dutch ovens'" (33). Metzger hears and defines "potsmaster" as "master of the pots," not the word "postmaster" with two letters transposed. Stamp and manuscript printing errors are gradually revealed to Oedipa not as errors but as signs in an alternate system.

Codes and secret messages transmitted by apparent errors also appear in the play that Oedipa and Metzger attend, *The Courier's Tragedy*, after they are alerted to the play's uncanny similarity to events in Inverarity's life. These events include a lawsuit over human bones, which belonged to GIs killed in a lake in Italy during World War II and are eventually and illegally sold to the Beaconsfield cigarette company for use in cigarette filters. A beatnik teen, part of a group sharing Oedipa and Metzger's San Narciso motel, alerts them to the familiarity of the story: "'You know, blokes . . . this all has the most bizarre resemblance to that ill, ill Jacobean revenge play we went to last week'" (48). The play repeats many of the novel's concerns within a revenge tragedy formula and begins to suggest to Oedipa the uncanniness of the Tristero's ubiquitous emergence.

The Courier's Tragedy, by the fictional Richard Wharfinger, has as complex and graphic a plot as any tragedy by a real Jacobean dramatist, like John Webster or John Middleton. The play, the plot of which hinges on messages sent through couriers of varying reliability (and who are often princes or spies in disguise), features usurped inheritances and elaborate plots for vengeance. A brigade of soldiers suffers a similar fate to that of the GIs, but in this case charcoal made from human bones becomes not cigarette filters but ink, with which the villain Angelo first writes "what is blatantly a pack of lies" (56), but which later becomes transformed and "is no longer the lying document Niccolo read us excerpts from at all, but now, miraculously, a long confession by Angelo of all his crimes" (57). Eventually, both the performed and printed versions of *The Courier's Tragedy* become essential in Oedipa's pursuit of the Tristero.

The manuscript history of *The Courier's Tragedy* mirrors the play itself. Oedipa pursues the actor and director Randolph Driblette, who wonders why "everybody [is] so interested in texts?" (61). Insisting that the play's meaning cannot be found in a reading of the authentic manuscript, Driblette describes himself as "the projector at the planetarium" (62). The image of the projected galaxy haunts Oedipa throughout the novel and mirrors the field of Galactronics. The projector, human or not, is a medium, and the planetarium's star map is strikingly similar to a communications network in which each star or celestial body is a node. Oedipa pursues the text of the play, hoping to reveal a concrete source of the history of the Tristero, but she finds that the play has no authoritative source. Oedipa's attempt to trace the manuscript to an uncorrupted original foreshadows the text's interest in digital reproduction. Oedipa thinks that if she searches for an original manuscript, she will be granted access to the truth about the Tristero; however, there is no authoritative manuscript. The problem of corruption, which digital reproduction attempts to resolve, is not an effect of the broadcast technologies of television or radio; it is intrinsic to mediation itself.

This image of the planetarium projector is another instance of the way in which Pynchon invokes the galaxy as a figure for the network. Concerning the execution of Inverarity's will, Oedipa wonders, "it was part of her duty, wasn't it, to bestow life on what had persisted, to try to be what Driblette was, the dark machine at the center of the planetarium, to bring the estate into pulsing stelliferous Meaning, all in a soaring dome around her?" (64). But despite Oedipa's best efforts to discover the meaning, to project and interpret a world, no meaning is ever achieved. The text invokes the possibility of a "global village," a worldwide social network brought about by "speech, drum, and ear technologies"—media theorist Marshall McLuhan's description of the technologies of the radio and the phonograph (9). Yet this utopian network eventually is rejected, a rejection that is depicted in the figure of Oedipa's disc jockey, acid-tripping husband "Mucho" Maas, whose personality is erased by the multitudes whose frequencies he imagines he can channel. He tells her, "You're an antenna, sending your pattern out across a million lives a night, and they're your lives too" (118). Mucho's aural utopia is rendered as a complete loss of identity.

In an attempt to elude the conspiracy that follows her, Oedipa spends one night drifting through San Francisco, hoping that by suspending her investigation of the Tristero their signs will relax their increasingly frequent appearances. She finds, however, that San Francisco is an "infected city." This description joins the functions of network communication and the dispersal of information and disease. The Tristero network works to communicate this infection. Oedipa passes the rest of the night

finding the image of the Trystero post horn. In Chinatown, in the dark window of a herbalist, she thought she saw it on a sign among ideographs.

But the streetlight was dim. Later, on a sidewalk, she saw two of them in chalk, 20 feet apart. Between them a complicated array of boxes, some with letters, some with numbers. A kids game? Places on a map, dates from a secret history? She copied the diagram into her memo book. When she looked up, a man, perhaps a man, in a black suit, was standing in a doorway half a block away, watching her. (94–95)

Paranoia unites the two functions of the social network: the communication of information and infection. The network is both the focus of, and the distribution mechanism for, paranoia. Paranoia is a key feature of Pynchon's oeuvre and a significant characteristic of 1960s political discourse, most notably in Richard Hofstadter's 1964 essay "The Paranoid Style in American Politics," which centers on the John Birch Society and its ideology that the United Nations is, in fact, a front for socialist world domination. Fallopian pronounces himself a member of the Peter Pinguid Society, an exaggerated parody of the John Birch Society.

The Peter Pinguid Society identifies itself politically as far to the right, calling the Birchers "left-leaning" (36) because of their opposition to perceived Communist plots, not the industrial capitalism that produces Communism. The Pinguids, late capitalists ahead of their time, only support capital accumulation, not capital circulation of any kind. But, like their models, the Birchers, they see themselves as a minority resisting a force that has already taken control. Pynchon's Peter Pinguid is a hero to his followers because he was the first U.S. citizen to mount military opposition against Russia. In 1864, "Off the coast of either what is now Carmel-by-the-Sea, or what is now Pismo Beach," the confederate "man-of-war 'Disgruntled'" and a Russian ship traded useless, out-of-range cannon fire (35–36). Pinguid, himself disgruntled, sees no difference between industrial wage slavery and southern chattel slavery. He is opposed to industrial capitalism because it leads "to Marxism. Underneath both are part of the same creeping horror," so he settles in southern California and amasses wealth by "[s]peculating in

California real estate" (37). Later, Metzger berates Fallopian, "You're so right-wing you're left-wing" (70). This parallel case to Inverarity, whose own immense wealth derives from real estate speculation, is the first instance in which Oedipa feels herself to be witnessing history repeating itself. The Pinguids are one of many secret organizations that take advantage of the Tristero system to communicate in secret. Yet the very presence of such secret networks fuels their paranoia, suggesting perpetual surveillance and conspiracy.

Like the shifting meanings of *The Courier's Tragedy*, which seem to provide grounds for paranoia about an official system that has been infiltrated by malicious conspiracies, fakes and forgeries become valuable signs in an alternative postal system, a discovery that Oedipa's investigation reveals. After consulting Genghis Cohen, "the most eminent philatelist in the L.A. area," retained by the estate to "inventory and appraise Inverarity's stamp collection" (75), Oedipa learns of the Tristero's history of undermining the legitimate postal service. Cohen shows her a "U.S. commemorative stamp, the Pony Express issue of 1940, 3¢ henna brown. Cancelled" (77). When Oedipa examines the cancellation, she discovers the WASTE symbol, the muted horn. Oedipa learns from Cohen the story of the rise of the postal monopoly, and the antagonism between the holder of the monopoly and its competitor, driven underground. Cohen shows her an antique German stamp with the legend "*Thurn und Taxis*":

"They were," she remembered from the Wharfinger play, "some kind of private couriers, right?"

"From about 1300, until Bismarck bought them out in 1867, Miz Maas, they were *the* European mail service. This is one of their very few adhesive stamps. But look in the corners."

Decorating each corner of the stamp, Oedipa saw a horn with a single loop in it. Almost like the WASTE symbol. (77)

The WASTE symbol is the symbol of the Tristero's hostility to the state postal monopoly, representing "an 800 year tradition of postal fraud" (79).

Even the opposition between authenticity and simulacrum, implicit throughout the novel, is invoked in the landscape of communications networks. After her discovery of the fraudulent stamps, Cohen assures her:

> ". . . the hatching, number of perforations, way the paper has aged—it's obviously a counterfeit. Not just an error."
>
> "Then it isn't worth anything."
>
> Cohen smiled, blew his nose. "You'd be amazed how much you can sell an honest forgery for. Some collectors specialize in them. The question is, who did these? They're atrocious. . . . Why put in a deliberate mistake? (78).

The Tristero stamps are not frauds but signs. Like digital copies that can be produced and reproduced infinitely without degradation, these stamps are not degenerated simulacra but rather signs in an alternative medium.

The stamps and the play are repeating images that make Oedipa increasingly paranoid, for they are the precipitate signs of new systems of code. By referencing such signs as the "ones and zeroes" of Oedipa's fantasy of binary computation, Pynchon explicitly evokes a nascent computer communications technology. Images, such as the hairspray, can be directed through an invisible network, and, in another fantasy of digital encryption, the lawyer Metzger's childhood movie stardom and his subsequent legal career provide the subject for a new TV show: "They've done the pilot film of a TV series, in fact, based loosely on my career, starring my friend Manny Di Presso, a one-time lawyer who quit his firm to become an actor. Who in this pilot plays me, an actor becoming a lawyer reverting periodically to being an actor. The film is in an air-conditioned vault at one of the Hollywood studios, light can't fatigue it, it can be repeated endlessly" (22).

Of course, film does eventually become fatigued. Endless repetition of information stored in an analog device is impossible, but digital messages, messages such as the one represented by the hairspray can, can truly be repeated, stored, and transmitted infinitely. The measure of information loss is described as "information entropy," or "Shannon's entropy," after the early computer scientist Claude Shannon. Oedipa encounters Shannon's entropy again in the home of crackpot inventor John Nefastis, creator of the Nefastis machine. This episode of the novel literalizes a thought experiment by Scottish mathematician James Clerk Maxwell known as "Maxwell's demon," and uses information entropy—that is, the amount of information lost in the degradation of a message in transmission—to offset thermodynamic entropy, the waste heat created by any engine. The text plays with this dual definition of entropy. Heat entropy is evoked literally and as metaphor, as with the hairspray can in the bathroom, and Oedipa is introduced to information entropy and its tenuous connection to heat entropy when she visits John Nefastis:

> She did gather that there were two distinct kinds of entropy. One having to do with heat engines, the other to do with communication. The equation for one, back in the '30's, had looked very like the equation for the other. It was a coincidence. The two fields were entirely unconnected, except at one point: Maxwell's Demon. As the Demon sat and sorted his molecules into hot and cold, the system was said to lose entropy. But somehow the loss was offset by the information the Demon gained about what molecules were where (84).

While thermodynamic entropy is a measure of certainty about a system, information entropy is a measure of uncertainty; so in this sense, they appear as the inverse of each other. Digital communication, however, undoes even this apparent similarity, communicating a message with a very low rate of entropy. What makes computer communication and information storage powerful is that, unlike older media, in digital devices storage and replication are almost infinite.

It is investigation into computers as communications devices that is the province of Yoyodyne's Galactronics engineers. When Oedipa visits Yoyodyne on a stockholders' tour, the other visitors hold a "Yoyodyne songfest" (65). One of the anthems laments Yoyodyne's subordination to other big defense contractors: "Bendix guides the warheads in, / Avco builds them nice, / Douglas, North American." The anthem concludes:

> Yoyodyne, Yoyodyne
> Contracts flee thee yet.
> DOD has shafted Thee,
> Out of spite, I'll bet. (66)

The Galactronics workers and shareholders themselves feel dispossessed by bigger corporations, but the song connects the field of communications technology with the military-industrial complex. The Galactronics engineers represent the paradox of early computer network development. While early network developers were members of the counterculture, corporations such as RAND, a subsidiary of Douglas aircraft, produced and funded the technology for military command and control application. McLuhan's utopian global village collides with the realities of technological research and development.[1]

When Oedipa wanders through the ranks of Yoyodyne's Galactronics workers, these technical problems appear recast as issues of labor and intellectual property. One engineer, Stanley Koteks, laments Yoyodyne's policy toward intellectual property: "Koteks explained how every engineer, in signing the Yoyodyne contract, also signed away the patent rights to any inventions he might come up with." Oedipa, attempting to goad him, responds, "I didn't think people invented anymore. . . . Isn't it all teamwork now?" (67). The Galactronics engineers are occupied

---

precisely with the legitimation and interpretation of codes, increasingly the binary codes that provide the building blocks for computing and computer communication. But Koteks's response highlights an often overlooked impact of the rise of computer communications: the changing economics of intellectual property and labor. Global-village collectivity, "teamwork," does little to benefit these engineers, who remain alienated from the products of their intellectual labor.

As evidence of the Tristero's plot surrounds Oedipa, technological images and references do the same. Oedipa's first encounter with the Tristero occurs under the sign of the oscilloscope, an early computer interface. The fictional term "galactronics" echoes both the "Gutenberg galaxy"—Marshall McLuhan's term for the media environment created by print—as well as the "intergalactic network," one of the first computer-enabled social networks.[2] Mucho Maas's multiple lives suggest the risk of losing one's self in a virtual world with no "real" basis. The image of the projector at the planetarium (the human medium projecting a network) is a figure for the way in which Pynchon's writing embodies communications technology and anchors it in social and economic structures. As the Tristero "blooms" around Oedipa, so does evidence of technology's permeation of the world. While technology comes to seem meaningless except as metaphor, the text reminds us that, as computer memory and digital messages replace printing and stamps, human society always has been permeated with technologies of communication.

Oedipa's odyssean journey through the San Francisco night reveals multiple appearances of the Tristero and the post horn symbol, and a world in which technology seems less like a tool for humans and more like a force with a life of its own. A man wearing a post horn pin on his jacket lapel identifies himself as a member of IA, Inamorati Anonymous, a support group for those in love, "the worst addiction of all" (91). The post horn becomes their symbol when "[i]n the early '60's a Yoyodyne executive living near L.A. and located someplace in the corporate root-system above supervisor but below vice-president, found himself, at age 39, automated out of a job" (91). Replaced by a computer, the IBM 7094, the executive finds himself a failure even at suicide. "You know how long it would've taken the IBM 7094?" his efficiency-expert nemesis asks. "Twelve microseconds. No wonder you were replaced" (93). He adopts the Tristero symbol after seeing it in the letter his superiors construct to fire him.

In a skid-row rooming house, Oedipa encounters an old sailor with a post horn tattooed on the back of his hand. She imagines his bed filled with "the insatiable stuffing of a mattress that could keep vestiges of every nightmare sweat, helpless overflowing bladder, viciously, tearfully consummated wet dream, like the memory bank to a computer of the lost" (103). Later, the old man's episode of delirium tremens turns, in Oedipa's memory to "DT," an abbreviation that sends her back to college calculus:

> "dt," God help this old tattooed man, meant also a time differential, a vanishingly small instant in which change had to be confronted at last for what it was, where it could no longer disguise itself as something innocuous like an average rate, where velocity dwelled in the projectile though the projectile be frozen in midflight, where death dwelled in the cell though the cell be looked in on at its most quick. She knew that the sailor had seen worlds no other man had seen if only because there was that high magic to low puns, that DT's must give access to dt's of spectra beyond the known sun, music made purely of Antarctic loneliness and fright. (105)

Unlike the image of the hairspray can that becomes a digital message, these images—of the computer that could have chosen suicide in "twelve microseconds," the sailor's urine-soaked-memory-bank mattress, and his DTs changed to differential time—do little to realize Oedipa's quest. Instead of proving evocative, these representations of technology become mere "low puns," or nothing at all.

Finally, Oedipa's quest resolves itself into binary coding, the fundamental building block of computer communication: "For now it was like walking among matrices of a great digital computer, the zeroes and ones twinned above, hanging like balanced mobiles right and left, ahead, thick, maybe endless. Behind the hieroglyphic streets there would either be a transcendent meaning, or only the earth" (150). This final binary image may serve as an instruction to the reader; either there is meaning, or there is not. Technology originates as the sign of conspiracy but becomes the very substance of reality.

Each of these figures, images, and cultural references—the galaxy, the computer, the oscilloscope, Shannon's entropy, binary code, the infinitely reproducible digital image—represents *The Crying of Lot 49*'s connection to the media discourse of the mid-1960s, a discourse that includes the origin of media studies, the development of computer communications, and the discovery of human social networks. Yet Pynchon represents scientific "discovery" and theories in a nexus of military and industrial capitalism and geopolitics, situating media in the context of historical conflicts over labor, race, and gender. In *The Crying of Lot 49*, media are never separate from mediation.

Invoking a secret and nearly ubiquitous conspiratorial mail network, Pynchon depicts the ways in which media already surround us, and argues that the transition from print to digital technologies is part of a long history of technological shifts that have shaped human interaction. In marking the network's emergence in computer science and social organization, Pynchon's novel reveals how the separation between the literary and the technological is invented and illusory; instead, the novel demonstrates how the humanistic enterprise of literature is inseparable from technology. Incorporating textual variants of faux-Jacobean drama and images borrowed from science and technology, *The Crying of Lot 49* asserts continuity between the literary-textual tradition and the approaching era of new media.

Notes

1. For conflicting narratives of network development, see: Streeter, Thomas. *The Net Effect: Romanticism, Capitalism, and the Internet*. New York: New York UP, 2011.
2. For the history of the intergalactic network, see: Waldrop, M. Mitchell. *The Dream Machine: The Untold History of the Notorious V-22 Osprey*. New York: Penguin, 2010.

Works Cited

Hofstadter, Richard. *The Paranoid Style in American Politics and Other Essays*. Chicago: U of Chicago P, 1964.

Kittler, Friedrich. "Universities: Wet, Hard, Soft, and Harder." *Critical Inquiry* 31.1 (2004): 244–55.

McLuhan, Marshall. *The Gutenberg Galaxy*. Toronto: U of Toronto P, 1962.

Pynchon, Thomas *The Crying of Lot 49*. 1965. New York: Harper, 2006.

CRITICAL READINGS

Robots, Moving Statues, and Automata in Ancient Tales and History

Kevin LaGrandeur

The ancient world was more technologically advanced than most of us realize. Its denizens' engineering skills were particularly notable, as we know from myths, literature written by ancient engineers, and, in some cases, technical artifacts that, miraculously, have survived thousands of years. The idea of creating artificial humanoids is persistent in classical myths and tales, and speaks to a cultural anxiety of intellectual and scientific risks. In turn, those stories correspond to, and perhaps even derive from, the achievements of technical experts in the ancient world. This essay discusses ancient tales of various world cultures that concern the invention of artificial humanoids, and then it considers the inventions and inventors that may have inspired the development of robots and automata.

The idea of creating an artificial human, or what we would call an android, is surprisingly old and appears in a number of ancient cultures. In ancient China, for instance, there is a story from the *Lieh Tzu*—a book most likely written in the third century BCE by Lieh Yü-Khou—that tells of an ingenious artisan named Yen Shih, who appears before a king with a lifelike automaton. The king asks the artisan who it is that he has brought, and a strange story unfolds:

"That, Sir," replied Yen Shih, "is my own handiwork. He can sing and he can act." The king stared at the figure in astonishment. It walked with rapid strides, moving its head up and down, so that anyone would have taken it for a live human being. The artificer touched its chin, and it began singing, perfectly in tune. He touched its hand and it began posturing, keeping perfect time. . . . The king, looking on with his favourite concubine and other beauties, could hardly persuade himself that it was not real. As the performance was drawing to an end, the robot winked its eye and made advances to the ladies in attendance, whereupon the king became incensed and would have had Yen Shih executed on the spot had not the latter, in mortal fear, instantly taken the robot to pieces to let him see what it really was. And, indeed, it turned out to be only a construction of leather, wood, glue and lacquer, variously coloured white, black, red and blue. Examining it closely, the king found all the internal organs complete—liver, gall, heart, lungs, spleen, kidneys, stomach and intestines; and over these again, muscles, bones and limbs with their joints, skin, teeth and hair, all of them artificial. Not a part but was fashioned with the utmost nicety and skill; and when it was put together again, the figure presented the same appearance as when first brought in. The king tried the effect of taking away the heart, and found that the mouth could no longer speak; he took away the liver and the eyes could no longer see; he took away the kidneys and the legs lost their power of locomotion. The king was delighted. (Ronan 92)

A similar story from about the same time in ancient India tells of a female android. According to this account:

There was once a knowledgeable artisan in the North of India who was an ingenious woodworker. So it came to pass that he made a woman out of wood. She was a beauty without equal. With her silk clothing and sash, and her magnificent adornments she was not in any way different from a real woman; she could come and go under her own power, and could also serve wine and make eye contact with those she served. All she lacked was the power of speech. (Chapuis, *Les automates* 18–20; translation mine.)

This android's maker decides to test his creation by playing a joke on a fellow artist. He invites the painter to his house for dinner and has his lovely artificial woman serve them wine. The painter is immediately stricken with desire for what he thinks is a beautiful maiden. But when he tries to hold her hand, he realizes with great alarm that she is made of wood. Enraged at the joke, he tries to take revenge on his friend by painting a realistic portrait of himself lying murdered on his bed. After trading such tricks back and forth, the two men decide that

---

the entire world is deceitful, and they swear off worldly pursuits to become monks.

These tales most likely derive from older Greek and Egyptian accounts of living statues and artificial humans, transmitted via trade with the Far East during the Hellenistic period (Needham 157; Chapuis, *Automata* 18). Indeed, there are many Greek stories of androids that predate the previously noted Chinese and Indian stories. *The Iliad*, which dates from about one thousand years before the earliest Chinese account, contains the most ancient literary reference to the creation of artificial humans. In book 18, Homer tells us of artificial serving girls forged by Hephaestus from solid gold. These maidens are no mere mechanical devices: "In them is understanding in their hearts, and in them speech and strength, and they know cunning handiwork by gift of the immortal gods" (419–21). In addition to these attributes, they possess considerable strength, as one of their common duties is to help support the god Hephaestus when he walks. When Thetis visits Hephaestus, he takes up his staff to walk across the hall, and his maids "busily moved to support their lord, and he, limping nigh to where Thetis was, sat him down upon a shining chair" (422–23). This part of *The Iliad* is not only a precursor to Indian and Chinese tales, for it is reflected in a later report of Indian androids by the Greek traveler and philosopher Apollonius of Tyana, who lived in the first century CE. Philostratus recounts that Apollonius of Tyana attended a feast in India where he saw "cup-bearers of dark bronze resembling the figures of Ganymede or of Pelops among the Greeks," figures who "mixed wine and water in due proportion, and carried the goblets about as at a wine party" (78, 81).

The devices described in Philostratus's account strongly resemble those in other Greek stories, which predate similar stories from the Far East. Daedalus, for example—who famously made wings so that he and his son could escape imprisonment on the island of Crete—was believed widely to have created not only the labyrinth that held the half-man, half-bull creature the Minotaur but also self-moving human statues. Aristotle and Plato mention these moving statues in various works. Aristotle's reference is the most specific; he notes that Daedalus's wooden statue of Aphrodite purportedly was animated by mercury, which was thought at the time to be a living substance (*On the Soul*, 406b, 19–20). Aristotle also refers to Daedalus's moving statues in his *Politics* (1253b). In Plato's *Meno*, Socrates mentions that Daedalus's statues would "run away" unless they were fastened to the ground (97d), and in *Euthyphro* Plato has Socrates make an implicit comparison between these statues and the way his opponent's arguments wander (11b-d).

Legends concerning Talos, the giant metal man made by Hephaestus and given to Minos, the King of Crete, relate that the creature guards the king's land from invaders. Talos also appears in the work of various ancient Greek authors, most famously in the *The Library* (bk. 1, ch. 9, sec. 26) attributed to Apollodorus of Athens, and in the *Argonautica* by Apollonius of Rhodes, in which the giant metal man attacks Jason and his Argonauts, tossing huge boulders at their ships to keep them away from the shore (bk. 4, sec. 1638). Depending on the version of the myth, Talos defends Crete by throwing rocks, as in the *Argonautica,* or by picking ships out of the water, holding them to his chest, and heating up his metal frame until they burst into flames. Talos is made of brass and almost indestructible. His only vulnerability is his ankle, where a pipe carries life-giving fluid and runs close to his metal skin. In some versions, the metal man is destroyed when his ankle is punctured in some way and the fluid, called ichor, drains away. This legend is among the most enduring Greek legends about artificial men, and Talos reappears in such later tales as Edmund Spenser's Renaissance poem *The Faerie Queene* (1590, 1596) and Herman Melville's "The Bell Tower" (1855).

Ancient Greek poet Pindar explains that the artists of Rhodes were so skilled that their statues could be seen walking the streets of the city (*Olympian Odes* sec. 7, 53). Similar to Pindar's assertions, the myth of Pygmalion, as related in book 10 of Ovid's *Metamorphoses*, tells the story of an artist and the King of Crete who sculpted a statue of a woman so lifelike and beautiful that he fell in love with it. Aphrodite sees his unrequited yearning, takes pity on him, and animates the statue, which becomes the lady Galatea.

Finally, the major Greek accounts concerning artificial humans would not be complete without the myth of the Titan Prometheus's creation of humankind out of wet clay. There is evidence that Plato's student Heraklides was the first to have written about the Prometheus myth as a story of human origins, but by the fourth century BCE the myth was fairly common. Ovid's account of Prometheus is probably the most famous and appears in the first book of his *Metamorphoses*, three hundred years after Heraklides's account (Wutrich 49).

Many Greek stories feature gods or demigods making artificial androids, and such humans as Daedalus, who build similar creatures, are godlike in the power of their knowledge: Daedalus's moving statues are, with the exception of their material, much like the ones made by the god Hephaestus in *The Iliad*, and the invention of wings allows Daedalus the power of flight previously reserved for beings like the sun god Apollo. As is evident in the various works that follow, the theme of human ingenuity is repeated throughout history, in stories concerning artificial androids and their creators. In this way, the artificial servant that derives from ancient tales becomes an emblem of the fears surrounding intellectual and scientific risks.

Tales that connect godlike powers with androids also were present in ancient Egypt. Unlike ancient Greek myths, however, some Egyptian stories that originated before 300 BCE appear to be historical accounts of real artifacts, and this may have influenced the Greek engineers based in Alexandria, Egypt, who built actual androids. Philostratus, Pliny, Juvenal, Strabo, and Tacitus each mention a statue of Amenhotep III at Thebes (the Greeks later renamed the statue Memnon) that was widely thought to be able to talk. In fact, according to the sources mentioned above, this statue made a sharp sound after dawn that sounded like the breaking of a harp string (Cohen 16). The stone figure was one of two identical statues of the pharaoh built side by side, facing east, and carved from single blocks of stone. According to the ancient Greek historian Strabo, the northernmost statue of the pair, which still attracts tourists, was damaged in an earthquake, which caused the torso and head of the statue to topple. Though Strabo expressed some skepticism about where the sound originated from, there were many others who heard the sound emanate from the base of the broken figure (Strabo 123–24). A basic knowledge of modern physics makes this story credible, since the sudden heating of a broken stone in a hot, dry climate could produce sufficient pressure along small fissures to make a high-pitched sound. This explanation is supported by reports indicating that when Roman Emperor Septimius Severus had the two halves of the statue put back together in 199 CE, the sounds stopped (Platnauer 123).

Also at Thebes, the Egyptian priests created statues that could give the appearance of speech and movement. One modern archeologist's description of an ancient talking statue provides insight into how these devices worked:

> in 1936, Loukianoff published an article on his recent discovery of a fairly large bust in white chalk or limestone of the god Re-Harmakis, coming from Lower Egypt. This bust, which may be seen today in the Cairo museum, has an oval cavity hollowed out in the back of the neck. From this cavity on the right-hand side a narrow canal leads to a small oval-shaped opening just under the god's right ear. This cannot be seen when the statue is looked at from the front. 'If,' says Loukianoff, 'the priest who was behind the statue, hidden by the great halo crowning it, and by the body of the statue, and so invisible to everyone, approached the mouth of the cavity and spoke, his voice became modified in the tube (Loukianoff himself proved this) and resounded, giving the impression that it was the statue which spoke.'" (Chapuis and Droz 16)

Similar clever mechanical tricks, like those used to create the illusion of speech, were used to give the arms and head an appearance of independent motion. During the late Ramses dynasty, around 1100 BCE, the priests of the god Ammon had become so powerful that they chose the pharaohs. In the city of Napata, the priests created a statue of their god that had limited powers of movement and speech, and they used it as a key instrument in their ceremonies for making coronation decisions. To choose a new ruler, "All the males of the royal family were made to pass in front of it, and the statue would stretch out its arm to seize one of them, while at the same time delivering an exhortation to him" (Chapuis and Droz 14–15).

A fair number of Egyptian records and some material evidence of automata (nondigital robots run by mechanical means, such as clockwork gears or steam) reveal how Egyptian automata might have functioned. The most abundant evidence of human automata dates from the period in which the Greeks controlled Egypt. Starting with Ctesibius, a group of very talented engineers arose at Alexandria after Alexander the Great's conquest of Egypt. Ctesibius and his followers had great technical and engineering skills and left behind documents that detailed automata powered by hydraulics and steam. He is most famous for his use of hydraulics and pneumatics (forced air) in creating marvelous devices, such as the suction pump, a water clock (clepsydra), and a water-powered pipe organ (hydraulis). None of his written work survives, but Ctesibius, his writing, and his inventions are mentioned by other notable ancient engineers, including Vitruvius, Athenaeus, Philo of Byzantium, and Hero of Alexandria (Lahanas).

Additionally, remains of an organ made in the first century BCE using Ctesibius's earlier designs were discovered in Dion, Greece, by archeologists in 1992, and a team of scientists subsequently was able to reconstruct a working model. Ctesibius also built human automata. As in previous times, these devices often were connected with religious and civil ceremonies; because Egyptian rulers were regarded as deities, religious and civil ceremonies were typically synonymous.

For instance, Ctesibius made a moving statue for a famous ceremony called the Grand Procession of King Ptolemy Philadelphus. This automaton was operated by curved wheels (called cams) mounted on rotating shafts that cause variable movement in connected parts. These cams enabled the figure to alternately stand and sit when moved on a platform through the streets (White). Ctesibius also decorated his water clocks with small moving figurines operated by gears attached to the clock (Lahanas).

Philo of Byzantium, one of Ctesibius's students, not only continued his mentor's groundbreaking work on pneumatics and hydraulics but made human automata as well. One of his most famous mechanical devices is a figure of a small girl pouring water. In *Pneumatica*, Philo also describes how to make automated theaters that incorporate human automata (16). This kind of mechanism, which is described later by Hero of Alexandria, is essentially a puppet theater in which figurines and stage sets move by mechanical means. Hero—or Heron, the last of the great Alexandrian engineers—describes how to make the simplest type of this theater in his treatise *Pneumatics*. One fashions little figurines of dancers and puts them on a circular wooden platform. This platform is enclosed on all sides in a glass cylinder or transparent horn. On the top of the cylinder is a small receptacle where a fire can be built; a hollow metal tube runs from the bottom of this little altar to the middle of the platform. Hollow metal spokes connect from the base of this pipe outward and curve ninety degrees at their ends, pointing in the same direction so that each spoke-end acts like a jet for the hot air that is forced from the altar. In this way, the hot air is forced against the sides of the glass cylinder, propelling the platform and the dancers in a circle.

In *Automatopoietike*, Hero describes a number of more complex automatic theaters—run mostly by pulleys, weights, and rope. Such theaters have more variety of movement than the previous example, and their various moving parts convey a little tale. One, for instance, tells the tale of Nauplius in the aftermath of the Trojan War. This theater features doors that open and close by themselves, as well as a series of nine two-dimensional tableaus, including a scene with moving nymphs that saw wood to build ships. Then the completed model ships appear to be moving on the sea, and model dolphins jump out of the ocean around them (James and Thorpe 137).

The most interesting of Hero's human automata are those that combine hydraulics and the mechanical devices of the automatic theaters to create a closer resemblance of lifelike action. One hydraulic machine incorporates a statue of Hercules (Hero 62), in which a person lifts a miniature apple and the machine shoots an arrow at a dragon, which then hisses. This illusion operates partly by mechanics: when the little apple lifts off the pedestal to which the whole scene is attached, a chain attached to a trigger mechanism in Hercules' arm releases the taut bowstring, shooting the arrow at a dragon on the other end of the pedestal. The same chain is attached to a plug inside the pedestal that lifts with the apple and allows water to run from an upper chamber to a lower one. Next, flowing water forces air from the lower chamber into a narrow metal tube that extends into the dragon's mouth. This airflow produces a hissing sound until the apple is replaced, stopping the flow of water and air.

Although none of Hero's automata survive, a number have been recreated from his detailed written descriptions and work perfectly. One recreation of a self-moving stand would have been used for one of Hero's automatic theaters. Constructed by Sheila M. Kyte, a student at Smith College, this self-moving container is exhibited in the college's Museum of Ancient Inventions. Fashioned according to Hero's description, the stand operates by means of a heavy weight attached to wheels inside the stand. The weight rests in a box of sand that drains at a measured rate into a compartment underneath. As the sand-level goes down, the weight pulls the ropes that turn the wheels. The stand moves on its own for a period of time that depends on the amount of sand inside. In Hero's theaters, ropes also moved various gears, which would power the human figures and the scenery within.

Replicas of Hero's devices have been made using computer modeling or computer animation programs. One fascinating mechanism automatically opens a temple door when a fire is lit on a nearby altar (Hero 59). The whole temple and altar sit above a hollowed area, or pedestal, under which is an elaborate apparatus. The heat of the fire forces air down a metal tube attached to the bottom of the altar and into a sealed container that is partly filled with water. The hot air raises the pressure inside of this container, pushing water through a lower tube and into a bucket suspended by chains. The chains, connected to the two extra long cylindrical hinges that extend into the space underneath the temple doors, tighten and turn those hinges when the bucket fills with water. A weight is attached to other chains wrapped counter to those that are positioned around the hinges, and when the fire is extinguished, the natural vacuum causes the water to siphon back into it. This lightens the bucket and allows the weights to pull the doors closed.

Perhaps the oldest surviving example of ancient automata is a mysterious technical marvel called the Antikythera mechanism, which was found in the early twentieth century by Greek sponge divers. In 1900, just off the coast of the island Antikythera, Elias Stadiatos, one of nine sponge divers working about 100 feet off the coast of the island, stumbled upon the wreck of an ancient Greek merchant ship on the floor of the Mediterranean Sea. The vessel, which sank about 80 BCE, lay more than 140 feet under the surface and contained statues, wine vessels, and other cargo that gave a snapshot of Greek life at the time. Among the artifacts, divers found several metal gears encrusted in a rocky mass of barnacles and sea debris. The gears that remained visible sat within a wooden frame. The wood rapidly disintegrated after the artifact was brought to the surface, but the mysterious protruding gear survived and remained a puzzle for many years, as there was no way for early twentieth-century scientists to separate the rock from the old metal without destroying it.

In the early 1970s, Derek J. de Solla Price, a noted science historian, had a colleague use x-ray scans and metallurgical tests to examine more of the rock's interior. Through these tests, he determined that the whole was a complex mechanism comprising thirty-two interlocking gears, and posited a model for how the mechanism functioned (Price). After Price died in 1983, his studies were developed further by such successors as Michael Wright, the curator of mechanical engineering at the Science Museum of London. Using a newer form of x-ray technology called linear tomography, which can reveal views of an object layer by layer, he verified Price's theory and corrected some errors he had made (Marchant). The work pioneered by Price and Wright continues today, with researchers trying to determine from where the artifact came and for whom it was made. The most notable current investigators are those associated with the Antikythera Mechanism Research Project. Since Price's initial discoveries, researchers have agreed that the device was most likely an analog computer used by the Greeks to calculate the position of the sun and the planets. One simply had to turn a handle and the intricate clockwork gears would make the necessary calculations, producing a result on dials positioned on the front of the wooden box. This automatic device proved Greek technical expertise and demonstrated that references to similar devices by writers like Cicero (bk. 2, sec. 34) and Vitruvius (bk. 9, ch. 8, sec. 4–7) were not merely theory or rumor. Additionally, it shows that Hero could have made the automata he described.

Alexandrian scientists Ctesibius, Philo, and Hero are important not only because their devices provide clues to the workings of the moving statues of ancient Egypt, but also because their inventions reveal the two primary motivations for their creation. Automata were mainly toys for the wealthy and tools for the priests. Inventions such as Ctesibius's hydraulis or Hero's "Hercules Shooting a Dragon" were amusements for those wealthy enough to commission their construction. They were also symbols of power, their magnificent designs conveying the status of their owners. The operation of these inventions likely instilled in observers a reverence for their makers' command of nature, and in this way automata were important tools for Egypt's priests; the enhancement of power was the main aim of mechanisms devised for religious purposes. The early Egyptians' talking and moving statues, Hero's self-opening temple doors, and even a coin-operated holy water dispenser—which Hero designed for use in a temple—were not just toys. They were instruments meant to transfix the crowds and increase the priests' control of worshipers. Because the observers of these devices knew nothing of their hidden mechanisms, they assumed that their owners possessed godlike knowledge. In some examples, such as the moving statue of the priests of Ammon, the automata contributed a supernatural aspect to their role and augmented the power of the priestly elite. This relationship between automata and power would prove persistent over time, growing into a preoccupation with marvels (*mirabilia*) during the Middle Ages and Renaissance.

Works Cited

Antikythera Mechanism Research Project. National Hellenic Research Foundation, n.d. Web. 4 Apr. 2011.

Apollodorus. *The Library* (*Bibliotheca*). Trans. James George Frazer. *Theoi E-Texts Library*. Aaron Atsma, 2007. Web. 4 Apr. 2011.

Apollonius of Rhodes. *Argonautica*. Trans. R. C. Seaton. *Theoi E-Texts Library*. Aaron Atsma, 2007. Web. 4 Apr. 2011.

Aristotle. *The Complete Works*. 1984. Ed. Jonathan Barnes. 2 vols. Princeton: Princeton UP, 1995.

Chapuis, Alfred. *Les automates dans les oeuvres d'imagination*. Neuchatel: Editions du Griffon, 1947.

Chapuis, Alfred, and Edmond Droz. *Automata: A Historical and Technological Study*. Trans. Alec Reid. Neuchatel: Éditions du Griffon, 1958.

Cicero, Marcus Tullius. *The Nature of the Gods and on Divination*. Trans. Charles Duke Yonge. Amherst: Prometheus, 1997.

Cohen, John. *Human Robots in Myth and Science*. New York: Barnes, 1967.

Hero of Alexandria. *The Pneumatics of Hero of Alexandria*. Ed. and trans. Bennet Woodcroft. London: Taylor, 1851.

Homer. *The Iliad*. Trans. A. T. Murray. New York: Putnam, 1929.

James, Peter, and Nick Thorpe. *Ancient Inventions*. New York: Random, 1995.

Kyte, Sheila M. "Self-Moving Stand (Egypt, Greece) Date: 100 C.E." *Smith College History of Science Museum of Ancient Inventions*. Smith College Program in the History of the Sciences, 2000. Web. 25 Mar. 2011.

Lahanas, Michael. "Ctesibius of Alexandria." *Hellenica*. Hellenica World, n.d. Web. 11 Apr. 2011.

Marchant, Jo. "In Search of Lost Time." *Nature* 444 (2006): 534–38.

Needham, Joseph. *Science and Civilisation in China*. Vol. 4. *Physics and Physical Technology: Mechanical Engineering*. Cambridge, England: Cambridge UP, 1965.

Ovid. *Metamorphoses*. Trans. Rolfe Humphries. Bloomington: Indiana UP, 1960. 241–43.

Philo of Byzantium. *Pneumatica*. Ed. Frank D. Prager. Wiesbaden: Reichert, 1974.

Philostratus, Flavius. *Life and Times of Apollonius of Tyana*. Trans. Charles P. Eells. *University Series in Language and Literature 2*. Stanford: Stanford UP, 1923.

Pindar. *Odes*. Trans. Diane Svarlien. 1990. *Perseus Digital Library*. Tufts U, 14 Mar. 2011. Web. 3 Apr. 2011.

Platnauer, Maurice. *The Life and Reign of the Emperor Lucius Septimius Severus*. London: Oxford UP, 1918.

Plato. *Euthyphro*. Trans. Harold North Fowler. 1966. *Perseus Digital Library*. Tufts U, 14 Mar. 2011. Web. 3 Apr. 2011.

_____. *Meno*. Trans. W. R. M. Lamb. 1967. *Perseus Digital Library*. Tufts U, 14 Mar. 2011. Web. 3 Apr. 2011.

Price, Derek J. de Solla. "Gears from the Greeks. The Antikythera Mechanism: A Calendar Computer from ca. 80 B. C." *Transactions of the American Philosophical Society* ns 64.7 (1974): 1–70.

Rhodes, Julian. "The Organ in Classical Literature." *Julian Rhodes' Dream Organs*, 1999. Web. 24 Mar. 2011.

Ronan, Colin A. *The Shorter Science and Civilisation in China: An Abridgement of Joseph Needham's Original Text*. Vol. 1. Cambridge, England: Cambridge UP, 1981.

Strabo. *The Geography of Strabo*. Loeb Classical Library. Trans. Horace Leonard Jones. Vol. 8. New York: Putnam, 1932.

Vitruvius Pollio. *The Ten Books on Architecture*. Trans. Morris Hicky Morgan. Illus. Herbert Langford Warren. Cambridge, MA: Harvard UP, 1914.

White, K. D. " 'The Base Mechanic Arts?' Some Thoughts on the Contribution of Science (Pure and Applied) to the Culture of the Hellenistic Age." *Hellenistic History and Culture*. Ed. Peter Green. Berkeley: U of California P, 1993.

Wutrich, Timothy Richard. *Prometheus and Faust: The Promethean Revolt in Drama from Classical Antiquity to Goethe*. Westport: Greenwood, 1995.

The Technologist in Classical Mythology and American Literature _____

Introduction

The figures of classical mythology that can be identified as "technologists" live on in later works of literature. Such mythic characters as Daedalus, Hephaestus, and Prometheus have survived through the years by a process of adaptation. Either their significance changes when they reappear in later works (as is the case with Mary Shelley's 1818 novel *Frankenstein, or the Modern Prometheus*), or their characteristics inform later technologist figures, as is the case in the fiction of Herman Melville and Thomas Pynchon.

Technologists and Myths

It is impossible to find one term that spans the time from ancient Greece to the twenty-first century. "Technologist," however, can be used to describe a character that consistently exhibits certain skills, attitudes, or actions relating to technology, whether in the shape of beeswax wings or a ballistic missile, as created by inventors, engineers, or artisans. Our understanding of a specific term changes over time, and with the development of new terminologies terms adjust to better reflect our world.

Similarly, a myth is not a fixed text, even when recorded and passed on in ancient texts. The meanings of myths continue to change as we understand and interpret them from ever-changing standpoints. According to Hans Blumenberg, myths are "not like 'holy texts,'" which cannot be altered by one iota" but instead are "distinguished by a high degree of constancy in their narrative core and by an equally pronounced capacity for marginal variation" (34). On the one hand, certain constant aspects are what make a myth recognizable throughout time; on the other hand, it is a degree of flexibility around those aspects that keeps a myth relevant. Such flexible myths have long-term viability.

---

112   *Critical Insights*

Surviving into later time periods and cultures, myths both absorb and inform perceptions of reality. In other words, the mythic technologist is reworked in literature to embody cultural and technological changes and attitudes in the author's own time.

Greek mythology has provided us with several core technologists: Hephaestus, the physically disabled Olympian master-smith; Prometheus, a rebellious demigod who furthers the course of human civilization; and Daedalus, a mortal whose inventions play a part in many famous myths—in particular, one that involves his son Icarus and his failed attempt at flight. Their stories have continued to influence and be influenced by our cultural and literary heritage. We still know these technologists by their own names and through characters that retain variations on their characteristics. Subsequent technologists, such as Faust, Paracelsus, and Frankenstein, have turned earlier themes of the impotent craftsman and the artisan rebel to new ends. The popular image of the technologist has also been illustrated by both historical and literary figures, from Sir Isaac Newton to Dr. Jekyll. Not surprisingly, some historical figures have become constructed "fictions" in popular imagination—Thomas Edison and Albert Einstein most famously so—to live up to, develop, and exploit ideas about the role and nature of men of science and technology.

The Flight of Daedalus

The fact that a preexisting and recognizable narrative core remains with these mythic figures suggests that a certain direction is embedded in later adaptations. Daedalus's son Icarus always falls to his death, but whether this is grounds to satirize the father's overweening ambition, to label the father and the son as hubristic offenders, or to dwell on the tragedy implicit in a young man's death depends on the changing expectations and values of a given audience over the course of hundreds of years of retelling. Playwrights Sophocles and Aristophanes are thought to have contributed several tragedies and comedies, respectively, about Daedalus. He was connected with the design of an artificial cow for Queen Pasiphaë, who wanted to change her appearance to seduce a bull—a mystical union reduced to farce by literature. The Minotaur that emerged as a result and the subsequent need for a labyrinth to contain it became the material of tragedy. Later, in the Roman poetry and satires of Virgil, Ovid, Horace, Juvenal, and Martial, the failed flight of Icarus from their labyrinth prison became central to interpretations of Daedalus's character (Morris 68–69). This focus on Icarus remained intact during the Middle Ages, as did Daedalus's reputation for subtle labyrinth-architecture and a poetic admiration of the father's feat of flying. Renaissance poets lavished praise on Daedalus as a skilled technician and a daring "constructor of the impossible" (Brunel 267–70). The Enlightenment and early industrialization provided a sympathetic atmosphere for a risk-taking technologist. By the twentieth century, empathy had returned to Icarus. Writers were informed by other cautionary tales from myth and folklore (the Golem created by Rabbi Loew in Prague), from fiction (Mary Shelley's invention of Frankenstein's monster), and from historical fact (the nuclear "sun" invented by the creators of the atom bomb). In this light, Icarus is less the disobedient, foolish son who misuses technology and more the tragic victim of a reckless, genius father, whose invention is inherently dangerous. This reading reflects a modern distrust of technologists and their inventions.

Modern adaptations of ancient myths may suggest recurring concerns. The political, economic, and personal motivations of real and fictional rocket engineers, nuclear scientists, and weapons designers might be compared with those of a Daedalus who feels compelled to work for a tyrant (King Minos of Crete, who wants a prison) and is persuaded to do so to satisfy another's desire (in this case, Queen Pasiphaë, who wants a sexual aid). At the core of the narrative is a technologist who feels bound to use his skills when called upon but who is either ignorant of or unable to refuse the murderous uses to which his inventions are put. In Thomas Pynchon's *Gravity's Rainbow* (1973), rocket engineers such as Franz Pökler, Major Weissman/

Dominus Blicero, and Gottfried work with flight technology and are more or less trapped by the technological system in which they participate. Three actions are shared by Pynchon's flight engineers and the original flying man: flying, fleeing, and fighting.

Flying: The Price Paid for Progress

First of all, there is Daedalus's most remembered feat, human flight, which quickly came to be viewed as a positive and symbolic representation of humanity's soaring imagination. The story implied that, with the aid of technological ingenuity, humanity could not be harnessed by Mother Earth's oppressive gravity but would understand and defy "natural" laws to exploit the unused potential of the material world. This way of thinking resembles Victor Frankenstein's original attitude toward his own project, fusing aspects of the "engineer of flight" with the "scientist of (en)light(enment)"—a figure to which the Prometheus myth contributes.

Cultures for which Daedalus symbolizes a spirit of invention read the Icarus myth differently from those that view the son's fall as a sign of Daedalus's faults. In different adaptations of the myth, the error that causes such accidents is attributed alternately to the theorist, test pilot, or invention involved. For his part, Icarus can be seen as either a tragic character or a foolish show-off; one or the other depends on his father being perceived as presumptuous for attempting flight, unfortunate for having a disobedient son, or unlucky that his invention had limitations. The apportioning of responsibility tends to fall on those who put dangerous technology in our way or those who do not understand its proper use (and whom the technological fathers must therefore mourn). At a time when pioneering technology was in demand or approved of as so-called progress, users tended to be blamed instead of the technology itself (or its makers, owners, or promoters). In the nineteenth century, operators, not construction engineers, were held responsible for train wrecks. During the twentieth century, progress in aircraft flight testing and the space race was "marked by great smoking holes in the ground."

To some such costs were inevitable, while to others they were horrifying, the difference depending on whether anonymous test pilots or well-publicized schoolteacher-astronauts disappeared in the smoke (*US News* 20). Some eras more than others have welcomed flights of imagination and the (heroic) technologists who make them possible—often as much for the lack of failure as for any particular success. The former can be explained away through the adoption of a "learning-curve" logic intrinsic to the trial-and-error methods of scientific practice.

Fleeing: Technology as Escape Mechanism

The second symbolic association that springs directly from the flight of Daedalus, and that proves evident in later representations of the character, is the desire to use technology as a means of escape. If the achievement of flight was the product of the engineer's battle with technology, the motivation that turns flying into fleeing is the desire to avoid losing the battle. Technology becomes a means of escape, often an escape from the effects of specific technologies or a technological system perceived to be taking over, physically or psychologically. Technologists aspire to rise above those cases in which the mastery of technology is a goal in itself (as is the case for Frankenstein), or those cases in which mastery allows the engineer to exercise a form of suppression (as is the case for Ahab, using his "factory-ship" the *Pequod* to hunt for the White Whale in Melville's *Moby-Dick*, 1851). Thus, Daedalus invents wings to escape the prison maze he has constructed himself, and likewise Franz Pökler, in *Gravity's Rainbow*, dreams that rocket-based human flight can take him away from the totalitarian prison that supports and is supported by his own engineering. In both cases, technology is not an outside object or objective but is instead internalized as that which controls the surrounding world.

For both Daedalus and Pökler, technology sets up boundaries (labyrinthine or gravitational) so all-encompassing and all-powerful that only technology itself can provide the means to cross them. Old and new versions of this narrative reveal that a successful escape of this kind inevitably carries the seeds of its own doom, because technology itself is the vehicle of "liberation." Escaping from technology by means of technology cannot resist introducing its seed into previously "uncontaminated" areas. In this way, Daedalus's labyrinth now extends into his own mind, betraying him in the wake of his flight to Sicily. According to Apollodorus's version of the myth, Daedalus's own ingenuity exposes him when he is challenged to run a thread through the convoluted corridors of a snail's shell—a challenge that is reminiscent of his exit strategy from the original labyrinth (Apollodorus 141). Though outside the physical maze, Daedalus can never escape its shadow inside his mind. In Herman Melville's fiction as well, Ahab cannot escape his project of subjecting whale to iron—it returns to haunt him with embedded steel. Similarly, the society that harbors the inventor cannot escape his imprint. In Melville's "The Paradise of Bachelors and the Tartarus of Maids" (1855), for example, the seedsman advances the very industry of which he is horrified (supporting it financially and disseminating its products by envelope). In Pynchon's *Gravity's Rainbow*, finally, the terminal image is the rocket's contamination of other lands by way of Gottfried's infection of and infatuation with all that it stands for. The rocket is not the means of escape that Pökler wants but, as Blicero explains, a way of pushing back the barriers of technology's reign (722–23). Escaping the labyrinth is futile, for "they own everything: Ariadne, the Minotaur, even, Pointsman fears, himself" (88).

Fighting: The Heroic Technologist

The third recurring pattern associated with the Daedalus myth combines the two preceding themes—one expresses optimism, the other pessimism—by relating to both the courageous, mental determination and the fear-driven escapism of the heroic technologist. Such a hero dares to move into the realm of fear and desire while taking risks in the name of progress, victory, and glory. The technologist does this in the service and with the aid of technology. The collective term "technologist" reveals a certain division of labor that becomes increasingly clear within industrial and postindustrial settings. For the present purposes, the technologist figure appears in three forms: as theorists, scientists, or high priests; as pilots, engineers, or adepts; and, finally, as industrial operatives—a mass of lay "ministers" to technology. In conditions of warfare and rapid motion, the first two forms may be described as tool-making creators and thrill-seeking users. The earliest weapons designers—such as Hero, Philon, Epimachos, and Ktesibios, under the employment of generals and governors of ancient Rome or Greece (Heiberg 37, 69; Armytage 27; Gillispie 311)— belong to the first category of creators, along with real and fictional twentieth-century rocket scientists. The second category of users, the heroic technologist, includes Homeric warriors and contemporary test pilots.

Users and creators raise technology from the base material aspect to something almost magical. In ancient Greece, armour was more than a tool: the "theorist craftsmen imbued works of armor with special qualities to which the combatant (or test pilot) gained access. Homer and Hesiod scarcely mention Daidalos (Daedalus), but they use the term *daidala* about particularly ornate pieces of armour or weapons to connote "glamour, power, and danger" (Morris 35). Book 18 of Homer's *Iliad* describes the glory of Hephaestus's daidalic armor; book 19 refers to the armor's magic potency as Achilles dons it for battle, levitating as if borne by "buoyant wings" (bk. 19, 430–56). The job of the creative technologist during Homer's war was to provide a "man-made barrier between warrior and weapon" that was marginally fallible, allowing the user to gain the glory of a slight but not fatal wound.

Daedalus's creativity could be perceived as embodying rationality or necessity, but the tragic flight of his son Icarus points to the heroic, especially since he took an unnecessary risk (Brunel 270). What is and was heroic is the known risk of death, courted via war technology. The decision to expose oneself to recognized danger, and even to court death, remains a thrill sought out primarily by young men in a war culture. According to Tom Wolfe's *The Right Stuff* (1979), even Cold

War warriors in space, alone and separate from the enemy, talked of single combat. In *Gravity's Rainbow*, Gottfried flies and falls inside the special 00000 rocket. He thereby becomes an Icarus character to either Blicero's premeditated or Pökler's helpless Daedalus character (102–103). Human beings sacrificed in the labyrinth that Daedalus designed, meanwhile, resemble those forced laborers and concentration camp inmates—the third kind of technologist—who worked and died in the industrial underground Mittelwerke network that built "vengeance-rockets" to protect the Fatherland. Pynchon's text points to how chief rocket designer Wernher von Braun escapes to the United States to father another rocket program, successfully fleeing responsibility for the human cost of the rockets he invented for the Third Reich. As in the flight of Daedalus, von Braun leaves others, behind and below, to their fates.

The Cunning of Hephaestus

In *The Iliad*, the glorious hero is contrasted with the disabled smith who arms him. Hephaestus, the ugly master smith, also surrounds himself with mechanical women, imitations of beauty, as if making up for his own shortcomings. In Greek mythology, Hephaestus is "ill-tempered, antisocial, and slightly suspect, and his skill is tinged with sorcery. There is something plainly disreputable about him" (Katz 25). Possessing many skills (in the original sense of the word), mythical technologists were often described as "cunning." But the inherent untrustworthiness of technologists seems to have extended the term's semantics to denote deception or duplicity. The ambiguity between material ingenuity and deception is well supported in the English language: in addition to cunning, words such as "conceit" and pairings such as "art and artifice" and "craft and crafty," allude to the deception (of nature, of the consumer) involved in fabrication.

Hephaestus reportedly used his inventions to trap both his mother and his unfaithful wife, and even Prometheus is tied down by his "blacksmith's masterpiece" (Aeschylus 23). Creators of technology are suspicious characters with hidden agendas, and so are their almost magical products. Hesiod describes the seductive qualities of ornate creations, like the jewellery created by Hephaestus for Thetis, Hera, Helen, and Pandora—the latter herself the "most splendid and most destructive artifice in all of epic poetry" (Morris 32). Such crafted items transfer an occasional jinx to the wearer (as the glamorous but treacherous armor did to Achilles), whether as a direct objective or a means to facilitate seduction. The effectiveness of Hephaestus's designs often was predicated on the wearer-victim *not* possessing knowledge of their real nature; this ignorance was important to their success in ensnaring the user. The true daidala is therefore designed with intentions that go beyond the apparent aesthetic value of ornamentation and elaborately wrought nature. These designs can be directed against others because of the secret knowledge its maker (if not wearer) retains. Whether the deceptiveness implied in the word "daidalic" pertained to the creator (Hephaestus) or the created (Pandora)—both her built-in curiosity and the jar of evil she released (Hesiod 39)—is a question that literature continues to ask (Warner 213–40). In Melville's "The Bell-Tower," for instance, which references Hephaestus's handiwork, a creator is fatally unaware of the true potential of his "iron slave" (209).

By current standards, Hephaestus is a somewhat pathetic figure, not because of his physical disability but because of his social inferiority as a service god. Specifically, he is cast out by women who find him wanting (such as Hera, his mother, and Aphrodite, his wife) and used by them only to create supernatural weapons for their favorite warriors (Athena especially) and magic jewellery so they can seduce other men. Skilled but deficient, Hephaestus shuns real women, surrounding himself instead with mechanical females and three-legged chairs that serve him obediently. Both the element of simulation and the desire to rearrange Mother Nature to create artificial "female" objects have been reworked ever since. Many texts critical of technophilia (the love of technology) take up this engagement with living or lifelike statues, Karel Čapek's *R.U.R.* (1921) seminally so. Interestingly, Shelley, Melville, and Pynchon all cast light on problems associated with technology by portraying life-impersonators: reanimated monsters, mechanical bell-ringers, and incorporated legal bodies. Hephaestus, Frankenstein, Ahab, the bachelor in "The Tartarus of Maids," and Tyrone Slothrop (more insidiously than Pynchon's other characters) all surround themselves with automata, metallic or human, replacing sexuality with power or channeling it into violent obsession. The epic quest for the monster, the whale, the great machine, or the rocket, in which the pursued often becomes the pursuer, centers on an object of desire whose creation or provocation technology is intimately involved with.

A ridiculous character in antiquity, a subservient and emotionally pathetic one today, Hephaestus is reduced to insignificance as a technologist myth. In Aeschylus, the figure performs as a simple smith, almost an operative (the third kind of technologist) vis-à-vis Prometheus's first form, the dangerous thinker, or theorist figure. Hephaestus is reduced from the weaver of intricate nets and animator of artificial life described by Hesiod and Homer; his name is rarely used when describing misguided Pygmalion-like characters. Hephaestus's characteristics were absorbed by the Prometheus figure, which, in turn, is superseded by Frankenstein.

Prometheus: Stealth and Rebellion

The Prometheus myth has been reworked over time to include many of the qualities attributed to other mythic characters. He shares with Daedalus a high-flown imagination and practical contributions to technical knowledge, but it is Prometheus who became the preferred cultural hero of the Enlightenment. Because of his daring and transgression, for which he was punished, he shares a moral platform with Icarus; both have soared and plummeted through condemnation, forgiveness, and pity through the ages. His use of deception to control his fate and the fates of others (as Prometheus pyrphoros, he stole fire with a fennel stalk and produced mock sacrificial-animals) and his creative skills (as Prometheus plasticator, an Attic pottery god, he created human beings from clay) identify him partially with Hephaestus, another creative and deficient god who deceived even his peers. Deficiency of character is seen as Prometheus's motivation to steal and seek the adulation of the entire human race—as does Victor Frankenstein. A "dubious benefactor to the human race," Prometheus's theft and punishment are also rewritten in Melville's defiant Ahab, who steals fire in the form of whale oil and meets his end by a godlike white whale (Sweeney 36–37). More than the smith-god Hephaestus or the human inventor Daedalus, the demigod and cultural hero Prometheus has continued to be reworked as a model of scientific wisdom, social beneficence, and political consciousness, according to Hans Blumenberg's *Work on Myth*. This is not because the figures of Prometheus (or *Frankenstein*, later) inherently stay true to their origins, but because they allow creative variations that keep them authentic and relevant as models for contemporary perceptions of technologists.

Just as Daedalus's mythology has been read in various ways and in light of various values, understandings of Prometheus's nature, extrapolated from original sources, have changed over time, as additional materials have joined his wider mythology. *Frankenstein* and *Moby-Dick*, for instance, straddle a divide between the romantic and modern periods in their political use of Prometheus, and in doing so they draw on the myth's core qualities, which makes Prometheus consistently useful for the purpose of criticizing science and technology. A criminal rebel, the classical Prometheus pyrphoros justifies his use of pretence and disguise—from secreting fire in a fennel stalk to presenting skin and bones as a whole ox for religious sacrifice—as necessary for solving the problems that he claims plague humanity (hunger or extermination by the gods). Prometheus's defense of his actions resembles one used by practitioners of science and the "practical arts" ever since: arguing a benefit to humanity that necessitates the manipulation of natural or divine laws. As both Shelley and Melville demonstrate in their fiction, however, such benefits may come at an aggregate cost to humanity and to the hero himself; such was the case with Pandora's curse and the bird that pecked at the innards of the bound Prometheus in ancient sources.

While ancient texts present literal crimes and punishments, the Renaissance—a period that turned its gaze inward even as science looked outward—viewed these events as symbolic, and the powers that affected mythic characters were internalized. When Robert Burton, in *The Anatomy of Melancholy*, and Francis Bacon, in *The Wisdom of the Ancients*, worked with the Greek and Latin versions of the Prometheus myth, his crimes against the gods became crimes against his own nature, and the bird preying on his guts became an expression of his own tortured thinking. There is also a strong suggestion in Mary Shelley's novel that the obsession with the mind and thinking creates the monster. Herman Melville continues this criticism; in his version of Burton's words, Ahab's "thoughts have created a creature in thee; and he whose intense thinking thus makes him a Prometheus; a vulture feeds upon that heart for ever; that vulture the very creature he creates" (303). Victor Frankenstein and Captain Ahab both reflect a representation of Prometheus as Burton's melancholy student, suspected for "abstaining from all worldly pleasures" in the pursuit of forbidden knowledge, and as "one who would rape or aggressively penetrate the Divine Mind (Minerva)," according to Bacon (Sweeney 64–65). Ahab's mood swings appear almost bipolar, but his movement between an internal and external pursuit of Moby Dick contains elements of the theorist and heroic technologist. He not only contemplates his prey, excessively and in solitude, but also throws himself and his operatives energetically into fatal encounters. It is this nineteenth-century version of the inward-looking, tortured Renaissance Prometheus, who attempts the rape of the goddess of reason, that became a model for the enquiring scientist and writers who were critical of science and technology's role in modern times. In the time that has followed the Enlightenment, science may have replaced religious mythology as the explanation of how the world works, but narrative myths continue to offer ways of explaining the meanings that science and technology hold.

The subtitle of Mary Shelley's novel acknowledges that her tale is of a "modern Prometheus," just as Melville's use of themes and motifs rewrites the myth in ways that cannibalize older versions. Obviously, Melville's reading comes via other sources and changing worldviews, bearing no great resemblance to Hesiod or Aeschylus, or the versions of the Promethean figure in Burton, Bacon, or even Shelley. Yet Melville used these sources, as well as digests of classical sources, for direct inspiration. It is no coincidence if we recognize shared core characteristics in the figure of Ahab, or additional variations later. Prometheus did not originally create monsters, for example, but the creature made by Shelley's modern Prometheus added this variation to the myth. Melville also incorporated this figure, insofar as the white whale is a monster of Ahab's own creation, and the whale itself carries its own mythic associations with Hephaestus and Prometheus. But "Frankenstein" has become the dominant byword for creative animation, due in no small part to Shelley's emphasis on the associated dangers, which feels relevant particularly today.

Although authors use myths critically, they do so within a society whose reading of those myths changes constantly. In the nineteenth century, "Promethean" was a positive epithet, signifying a desirable drive for progress and the glory associated with the risks of progress. This may offer one reason to explain why *Moby-Dick* was forgotten and only gained popularity in the second half of the twentieth century, when attitudes toward scientific progress (nuclear technology, for example) became more ambivalent. In the nineteenth-century United States, the hope for progress and economic independence lay with the technical skill of craftsmen or artisans. For this reason, technologists of the period may have been praised and lauded for their technical skill. Antiquity, by contrast, portrays flawed, irresponsible individuals whose inventions are luxurious or dangerous, and the inventors themselves are, to some degree, social outcasts. Technologist characters rise and fall from grace as cultural heroes. In the industrial and atomic ages, Prometheus seemed to be favoured in American culture as a symbol of development and prosperity, heralding a bright future fuelled by oil, uranium, and the spirit of invention. Yet a recent book title, *American Prometheus: The Triumph and Tragedy of J. Robert Oppenheimer* (2005), reveals that the positive associations of a mythic technologist decrease when the personal and environmental costs of progress increase.

We, too, create our own creatures when we rework myths. Our creative part in the process stems simply from reading and understanding myth-based narratives from our own standpoint: "Even the earliest items of myth that are accessible to us are already products of work on myth," Blumenberg explains, "so that the process of reception has itself become a presentation of its manner of functioning" (118). In recent incarnations, then, Promethean characters carry elements of these previous identities—plasticator and pyrphoros, dubious benefactor, enlightenment hero, revolutionary idol, and model of industrial ingenuity—whether these characters are being defined by or in opposition to them, but only insofar as these elements remain familiar and historically relevant for the storyteller and the audience.

Conclusion

Ancient texts may well have seen things in a simple way: Hephaestus was ugly, Prometheus a criminal, Daedalus bad, and all deserved the constraints and deprivations they suffered. But at any moment, and certainly among the historically varied texts discussed here, such views may change: Homer, Hesiod, and Aeschylus were themselves hundreds of years apart and did not share the same attitudes, aside from being distinct from the radically changed versions of the archetypal (rebel) artisan we find handed down via Renaissance, Enlightenment, romantic, and modern reworkings of mythic material.

We have seen how the meanings of technologist myths have changed at different times and within varying literary circles—from comic to tragic, melodramatic to morally instructive (Daedalus), ridiculous to insignificant (Hephaestus), and suspect to heroic (Prometheus). When

Mary Shelley, Herman Melville, and Thomas Pynchon challenge the heroic quality of the technologist at times when, historically, the rapid progress of science and technology seemed both frightening and promising, they are not simply resurrecting the classical technologists mistrusted by their own times. If suspicion surrounds the technologists of recent literature, this is not wholly coincidental (the core myth allows for that interpretation): the mythology has evolved and has a different basis. The core myth does not imply that technologists are *essentially* dangerous or dubious characters. Literary variations have repeatedly enabled that reading to make certain points about the specific historical contexts in which these variations find expression. This is why the "Prometheus" you might meet in literature or popular culture today is not a reference to a classical figure but a mythic one. The former is a historical artifact, the latter a malleable organism, an open narrative that invites continuous reworking.

Works Cited

Aeschylus. *Prometheus Bound: The Suppliants, Seven against Thebes, The Persians.* Trans. Philip Vellacott. Harmondsworth: Penguin, 1961.

Apollodorus. *The Library (Bibliotheca).* Trans. James George Frazer. Vol. 2. London: Heinemann, 1996.

Armytage, W. H. G. *A Social History of Engineering.* 4th ed. 1961. London: Faber, 1976.

Bacon, Francis. *The Essays: The Wisdom of the Ancients and the New Atlantis.* London: Odhams, 1935.

Bird, Kai, and Martin J. Sherwin. *American Prometheus: The Triumph and Tragedy of J. Robert Oppenheimer.* New York: Knopf, 2005.

Blumenberg, Hans. *Work on Myth.* Trans. Robert M. Wallace. 1979. Cambridge, MA: MIT P, 1985.

Brunel, Pierre. *Companion to Literary Myths, Heroes, and Archetypes.* 1988. London: Routledge, 1996.

Burton, Robert. *The Anatomy of Melancholy: What It Is, with All the Kinds, Causes, Symptoms, Prognostics, and Several Cures of It.* London: Tegg, 1849.

Čapek, Josef, and Karel. *R.U.R. and the Insect Play.* Trans. Paul Selver. 1923. Oxford: Oxford UP, 1961.

Gillispie, Charles Coulston. *Dictionary of Scientific Biography.* Vol. 6. New York: Scribner, 1972.

Heiberg, I. L. *Geschichte der Mathematik und Naturwissenschaften in Altertum.* München: C. H. Beck'sche, 1925.

Hesiod. *Theogony and Works and Days*. Trans. M. L. West. Oxford: Oxford UP, 1988.

Homer. *The Iliad*. Trans. Robert Fagles. New York: Penguin, 1990.

Katz, Barry M. *Technology and Culture: A Historical Romance*. Stanford: Stanford Alumni Assn., 1990.

Melville, Herman. "The Bell-Tower." *Billy Budd, Sailor, and Other Stories*. Ed. Harold Beaver. Harmondsworth: Penguin, 1970. 195–213.

———. *Moby-Dick*. 1851. Ed. Harold Beaver. Harmondsworth: Penguin, 1972.

———. "The Paradise of Bachelors and the Tartarus of Maids." *Billy Budd, Sailor, and Other Stories*. Ed. A. Robert Lee. London: Dent, 1993, 187–207.

Morris, Sarah P. *Daidalos and the Origins of Greek Art*. Princeton: Princeton UP, 1992.

Pynchon, Thomas. *Gravity's Rainbow*. 1973. London: Picador, 1975.

Segal, Robert A. *Theorizing about Myth*. Amherst: U of Massachusetts P, 1999.

Shelley, Mary. *Frankenstein, or the Modern Prometheus*. 1818. London: J. M. Dent, 1992.

Sweeney, Gerard M. *Melville's Use of Classical Mythology*. Amsterdam: Rodopi, 1975.

U.S. News and World Report 10 Feb. 1986: 20.

Warner, Marina. *Monuments and Maidens: The Allegory of the Female Form*. 1985. London: Pan, 1987.

Wolfe, Tom. *The Right Stuff*. 1979. London: Bantam, 1980.

"Now Let Us Meet the World": Being, Appearing, and Seeing in Hawthorne's *The House of the Seven Gables*

Abigail Glogower

> All of human progress is in a circle; or, to use a more accurate and beautiful figure, in an ascending spiral curve. While we fancy ourselves going straight forward and attaining at every step, an entirely new position of affairs, we do actually return to something long ago tried and abandoned, but which we now find etherealized, refined, and perfected to its ideal. The past is but a coarse and sensual prophecy of the present and the future.
>
> —Nathaniel Hawthorne, *The House of the Seven Gables*

These lines are part of a vivid soliloquy that Nathaniel Hawthorne's character, Clifford Pyncheon, delivers against a dizzying backdrop of quickly moving scenery. The time: the late 1840s. The place: New England. The occasion: the old man's first experience aboard one of the greatest (and most disorienting) technological marvels of the age: the passenger train. This new form of travel—which covers massive distances at unprecedented speeds—so enthralls him that it would have been easy for Clifford instead to compare human progress to a straight line; after all, that is exactly how we envision trains moving. Yet, despite the overwhelming novelty of his situation, Clifford discerns some shred of familiarity in the experience. This struggle to locate continuity within radical change is not his alone. Amid the new, a collective amnesia tends to emerge, an attitude that at once exalts and laments our coordinates on the great continuum of technological progress as completely fresh and wholly uncharted. In an effort to orient ourselves, we might pause to indulge a feeling of déjà vu and wonder whether some of the problems we assume to be completely unprecedented are, in fact, different manifestations of older issues.

If we find ourselves at a loss for reference points, literature provides a good resource. Stories reveal more than just captivating plots and compelling characters; they also convey a great deal about the attitudes, issues, and anxieties of the author's place and time. The ability for an invention such as the train to convey people, objects, and information in ways that altered definitions of distance and time clearly was something that people in Hawthorne's moment thought about a great deal. But there is another new, exciting, and problematic technology that figures prominently in *House of the Seven Gables*: the camera. Here was a machine that stood to transform meaning. Just as the train altered what was possible for space and time, the camera, and the pictures it produced, shifted the possibilities for accuracy and truth in visual representation. In short, the camera would change the very way we see and are seen.

How can a book from 150 years ago speak to the chaos and excitement we experience now, in the digital landscape that is Web 2.0? Perhaps, contrary to what we might assume, contemporary society is not so different from Hawthorne's own. In 2011, the number of news articles devoted to matters of privacy settings, tagging, geocoding, and the instantaneous circulation of "private" pictures indicates that, a decade and a half after the first digital cameras hit the consumer market, even the younger consumers among us are still struggling to negotiate life as digital subjects. The world we inhabit is one populated not just by people but by images of people. Deciding which images accurately portray the original persons they represent is a skill that we have been forced to develop almost unconsciously to navigate a digital environment. A mainstay of tabloid magazine covers, for instance, are those "shocking" and "real-life" photographs of beautiful celebrities, caught off guard by the camera's trained eye and revealed to be, presumably, "real people": pimpled, pudgy, and disheveled. Usually, these candid pictures—the ones "the stars don't want you to see"—are presented alongside more legitimate photos of the same person smiling glamorously and coiffed perfectly at a celebrity event. Here the reader becomes a judge, charged with determining the portrait that more accurately depicts the subject's true essence. After years of living with photographs, we still regard them with a split consciousness. We know that pictures lie and yet we still appeal to them for truth.

Perhaps it is for this reason that Nathaniel Hawthorne's 1851 romance *The House of the Seven Gables* enjoys a kind of interdisciplinary fame. A hallmark of the American literary canon, the work is also a perennial text in the history of early photography, for it deals extensively with one of the major social and technological phenomena of Hawthorne's moment: America's fascination with a new kind of image, the daguerreotype. Named for its French inventor, Louis Jacques Mandé Daguerre, the daguerreotype was a short-lived forerunner of the film-based format that we would eventually call photography. Debuting in 1839, daguerreotypy was one of several similar mechanical and chemical processes that all aspired to create a direct, reliable, and enduring copy of the visible world, untainted by the intermediary hand of the painter or illustrator. These processes brought new kinds of images into the world—pictures that, as photography historian Alan Trachtenberg observed, "seemed reassuringly familiar and disconcertingly new, recognizable as pictures, but with a difference" (3). Distinguishing the familiar from the new is not an easy task, because we do not readily understand new things until we have, to some degree, made them familiar. Attempts to do so necessarily require sensitivity to nuance and willingness to embrace contradiction. Hawthorne's *House of the Seven Gables* is one such attempt, for it is a messy, confused, and endlessly fascinating record of people in an historical moment struggling to adopt new ways of seeing and, by extension, new ways of being.

Hawthorne understood well the importance of looking backward. The first of his four novels, *The Scarlet Letter* (1850), functions as a coda to a project upon which he embarked in the mid-1830s, returning to his birthplace of Salem, Massachusetts, to live in seclusion and explore his ancestral Puritan roots. The stories generated during this period and published in the collection *Twice-Told Tales* (1837) transport Hawthorne's readers not only to another time but also to a different moral, social, and political order. Such a journey, however, was no mere flight of fancy. As Milette Shamir has astutely noted, stories like "The Minister's Black Veil" address a "problem that belongs more to Hawthorne's New-England, middle-class, mid-nineteenth century milieu than to the Puritan village. . . . a product of the widening of the borders of the private sphere in Hawthorne's own time and the problems of intrusions into that sphere" (752). Again and again, Hawthorne can be seen probing the tensions of the past to describe the anxieties of the present.

In *The House of the Seven Gables*, Hawthorne evokes the conventions of gothic romance to combine past and present into one story. In the preface, he explains that whereas novels "aim at a very minute fidelity . . . to the probable and ordinary course of man's experience," the romance, "while, as a work of art, it must rigidly subject itself to laws, and while it sins unpardonably so far as it may swerve aside from the truth of the human heart—has fairly a right to present that truth, under circumstances, to a great extent, of the writer's own choosing or creation" (3). Hawthorne makes a powerful bid for the prerogatives of the storyteller by claiming that to tell a story that is *useful*, the reader will have to tolerate a good deal of information that is ambiguous or even untrue. What could the author hope to accomplish by this? "The attempt to connect a bygone time with the very Present that is flitting away from us" (3). To this end, Hawthorne weaves together familiar themes of greed, family drama, magic, and divine providence with urgent contemporary problems of shifting social relations amid a swell of industrial and technological progress. As if foreshadowing one of the central themes, this quote also references the language of representation, preparing the reader for a serious social and technological problem of the time: who or what is visible—and therefore knowable—and under what conditions can things be seen and known?

In a gossipy tone of local lore, Hawthorne opens *House of the Seven Gables* with the unfortunate, one hundred-and-fifty-year-old backstory that presages the current action. The saga begins in the distant past, when a wealthy and well-regarded Puritan leader, Colonel Pyncheon, erects the imposing house of the seven gables on land stolen from his neighbor, a modest craftsman named Matthew Maule. Evicted from his home and sentenced to death for the dubious charge of witchcraft, Maule curses the Colonel from the gallows, declaring ominously that he "will have blood to drink." The curse manifests itself in many forms, from the instantaneous souring of the property's well water, to a mysterious, congenital respiratory illness that claims the Colonel's life on the very day of his public housewarming. The curse persists in plaguing generations of Pyncheons to come, and from this point forward the family line spirals into decline. A pall settles over the magnificent estate, condemning future Pyncheons to poor health, weak character, and slipping social status:

> In every generation, nevertheless, there happen[s] to be some descendent of the family, gifted with a portion of the hard keen sense, and practical energy that had so remarkably distinguished the original founder. His character, indeed, might be traced all the way down, as distinctly as if the Colonel himself, a little diluted, had been gifted with a sort of immortality on earth. (16)

Having asserted this almost supernatural link between an "original" person and his proliferating representations, Hawthorne here brings readers into the present.

By this point in time, the Pyncheon clan has dwindled to a virtual terminus. The family consists of an aged sister and brother, Hepzibah and Clifford, their lovely young niece from the country, Phoebe, and their cousin, the wealthy and well-regarded Judge Jaffrey Pyncheon. Hepzibah and Clifford live entirely in the shadow of their troubled lineage. Their imprisonment in the dark, decrepit House of the Seven Gables is symptomatic of higher-order bondage. They are also oppressed by the suspicious gazes and gossip of the town, and the cruel intentions of the Judge, this generation's spitting image of the wicked original. Something much more powerful than pride prevents Hepzibah from accepting the financial support offered by her kinsman; a passionate hatred drives her to spend her entire adult life languishing in seclusion and penury. When the reader first meets "the unfortunate old maid," Hepzibah's situation has become so dire that she has resorted to opening a low-class odds-and-ends shop in the first floor of her home.

Hepzibah's self-professed "only friend" is a peculiar young man known only as Holgrave, who rents a room in the house. Though charismatic and likeable, Holgrave is regarded with suspicion both by the townspeople and by Hawthorne himself. A drifter, espouser of radical reformist politics, practitioner of the new pseudoscience mesmerism (hypnosis), and dabbler in various professions, Holgrave currently supports himself as a "daguerreotype artist," making people's "likenesses" with photographic equipment in his modest studio. Hepzibah concedes that his ways are strange, but she is comforted by the warmth of his companionship. Whereas the rest of the townsfolk whisper that her haggard face and perpetual scowl spoil the goods in her shop, Holgrave treats her with kindness.

Indeed, Holgrave seems to be a special kind of seer. As it turns out, his specular abilities cannot be divorced from his craft as a conjurer of images. He knows Clifford and Hepzibah's dark secret, that in their youth their cousin the Judge robbed Jaffrey Pyncheon the elder—their father and his uncle—and pinned the blame on Clifford. The fact that Jaffrey was found dead at the scene of the robbery gave the case another character entirely. Not wanting to implicate himself, the Judge, then a wayward youth, chose not to clear his dear cousin of the charge of murder, and this simple omission of truth sent Clifford to prison for a quarter of a century. Newly reinstalled in his home, the mentally and physically infirm Clifford is hardly a free man; the Judge continues to hound him for information about a mythical, lost family land deed. Convinced that Clifford possesses such information, the Judge threatens to have him committed to an asylum. Not only does Holgrave understand this plot well in advance of the reader, his work with pictures also brings about the revelation and ultimate resolution of the Pyncheons' suffering.

Understanding Holgrave's role as a seer requires further discussion of how daguerreotypes were made and how they were regarded in popular culture. Unlike film or digital pictures, which could be reproduced *ad infinitum*, each daguerreotype image was a one-of-a-kind object. Production consisted of fitting a chemically treated, silver-coated copper plate into a camera (essentially an empty, darkened box) and then exposing the plate to light entering through a lens in the front of the box. A reverse image of whatever sat before the lens was thereby transferred onto the plate within. To render the image visible, the plate had to be developed in a separate container, where by somewhat ghostly means steam vapors from heated mercury made the picture slowly appear. After rinsing and drying, the plates were covered with protective sheets of glass. Larger daguerreotypes—about the size of a standard sheet of notebook paper—were framed and placed on walls to inspire reverence and emulation. Cheaper and more common pocket-sized plates were installed in pretty decorative cases as intimate keepsakes.

Daguerreotypy was an immediate sensation. The precision of these "light drawings" was unmatched by the hands of the most skilled draughtsman. They captured details that until then either had gone unobserved by painters and sketchers or had been intentionally excluded in an effort to portray the subject in the most favorable manner. They seemed to possess an uncanny "surfeit of truth." Suddenly, people did not quite recognize themselves or one another. Stories abound about daguerreotypes being returned to the artist by family members who insisted that the person in the picture did not resemble—and could not possibly represent—their loved ones.[1] Not only were the details so unprecedentedly sharp, but the mirrored silver surface beneath the sheet of glass emanated a kind of flickering effect, causing the image to shift and shimmer when moved. The fineness of the lines and the magnification of the glass combined to lend the visual plane a strange optical depth not achieved in painting or drawing. Whether a portrait displayed on a wall or a miniature held in private, the daguerreotype facilitated a powerful communion between image and viewer. This almost magical object was also fairly cheap and easy to produce, especially after rapid improvements made to materials and techniques translated into affordable prices. Ordinary people who could not commission painted portraits and who had never seen themselves or others as images now began doing so.

Since no patent laws existed in 1839 to protect such a novelty sufficiently, Daguerre knew it would be difficult to profit from his invention. Therefore, he opted to surrender the process to the French government, which could then donate it freely to the world in a grand political gesture of generosity. In exchange for a lifetime pension for himself and the son of his deceased collaborator Nicéphore Niépce, Daguerre drafted the manual *An Historical and Descriptive Account of the Various Processes of the Daguerreotype and the Diorama* (1839), detailing his materials and methods. The first American to witness daguerreotypy was Samuel Morse, who interestingly enough had traveled to France in early 1839 to show Daguerre his plans for a communication invention that would revolutionize the world further: the telegraph. Proclaiming daguerreotypy "one of the most beautiful discoveries of the age," Morse foresaw the medium's boundless capabilities, further avowing that "this discovery is about to open a new field of research in the depths of the microscope . . . we are soon to see if the minute has discoverable limits" (qtd. in Rudisill 45). He quickly taught himself the process and became instrumental in promoting it in America.

In autumn, an English translation of Daguerre's pamphlet hit the United States—patent-free instructions available to any who cared to learn. With a modest equipment investment and some self-taught skill, anyone could go into the business (most often as a purveyor of portraits). Daguerreotypy was, in short, remarkably well poised to succeed in America's socioeconomic climate. Following an economic downturn two years earlier, many traditional businesses remained stalled, and lots of young men flocked to the new invention in the hope of turning a dollar. Secondary industries quickly sprang up to produce and supply the various elements that these budding entrepreneurs and artists needed for their enterprise. Within just a few years, and with the aid of rapid standardization, pocket-sized daguerreotypes were available in some places for a mere twenty-five cents. At that price, many struggling Americans could afford to indulge. Rather early, such daguerreotypists as Mathew Brady in New York, and Southworth and Hawes in Boston, built distinguished studios with elegant lobbies and portrait galleries that catered to the higher and upper-middle classes. Most others adopted a more fly-by-night approach, often moving from town to town, setting up shop for a while before drifting to the next town.

Holgrave, whose very name evokes "holy" and "graven image," is among the latter group. Here was a new type of person on the social stage, purveying a new kind of product that sparked wonder and speculation. Who they were and what exactly they were selling, however, was not completely clear to customers. Although some viewed daguerreotypy as a delightful modern invention, others dismissed the entire process as humbug. Hawthorne entertains both opinions. Though he chides Holgrave for being a callow enthusiast of novelties, Hawthorne reserves no small amount of respect for the man and his craft. As it turns out, Holgrave is more than a random, itinerant stranger lodging accidentally at the Pyncheon family's dreary, seven-gabled estate: he is a descendant of the alleged wizard Matthew Maule. Whether the daguerreotypist or his progenitor in fact possessed magical powers is left to the reader's interpretation.

It has often been suggested that the narrator's offhand critiques of Holgrave exhibit a wholesale rejection or suspicion of such novel phenomena as railroads, daguerreotypy, and mesmerism. In fact, Hawthorne's feelings were more complicated. We know he took mesmerism seriously enough to warn his fiancée Sophia Peabody, in an 1841 letter, to cease the hypnosis she underwent to treat migraines: "Do not let an earthly effluence from (the mesmerist's) corporeal system bewilder thee, and perhaps contaminate something spiritual and sacred. . . . I love thee. . . . love is the true magnetism" (307). We know also that he sat for daguerreotypes at established studios in 1841 and

1848. The new art of daguerreotypy influenced his literary consciousness as well. As he wrote in another letter to Sophia: "I wish there was something in the intellectual world analagous to the Daguerreotype (is that the name of it?) in the visible—something which should print off our deepest, and subtlest, and delicatest thoughts and feelings, as minutely as the above-mentioned instrument paints the various aspects of Nature" (Mattison). Clearly, both mesmerism and daguerreotypy had entered collective consciousness as fascinating and troubling phenomena that could not be dismissed easily.

"I make pictures out of sunshine," Holgrave says when introducing himself to Phoebe in the Pyncheon's garden. His offer to show her one of his specimens prompts the first philosophical exchange in the novel regarding photography. Phoebe is not impressed by his craft, expressing a common sentiment of her time: "I don't much like pictures of that sort—they are so hard and stern; besides dodging away from the eye, and trying to escape altogether. They are conscious of looking very unamiable, I suppose, and therefore hate to be seen" (67). As end-products, daguerreotypes prompted a unique kind of visual communion with their viewers, but this relationship was mirrored, so to speak, in the way a subject was first made to commune with the camera. "Having one's likeness taken" meant holding a pose for about twenty seconds while being coached by the daguerreotypist to focus on objects in one's field of vision or the camera lens itself. Although not a terribly long period of time, twenty seconds was just long enough to convince subjects of the artificiality of sitting before a camera.

More importantly, the subject was called upon to project himself or herself as a representation. This was not easy if you did not know how to do it. As Walter Benjamin elegantly observed:

The first people to be reproduced entered the visual space of photography with their innocence intact—or rather, without inscription . . . photography had not yet become a journalistic tool and ordinary people had yet to see their names in print. In short, the portraiture of this period owes its effect to the absence of contact between contemporary relevance and photography. (512)

Benjamin's language is difficult but worth unpacking. Being innocent and without inscription means being without precedent—that is, visible in an entirely new way. Having no point of reference for this kind of image, people raised questions: What are these pictures supposed do? Who is meant to see them? Are they supposed to give us a mere snapshot of a moment in a person's life, or are they meant as enduring signs of character? Such questions, combined with the harsh, exacting detail captured in the pictures, generated as much disdain as amazement, and many people were dissatisfied with—even repulsed by—their daguerreotype portraits. Ralph Waldo Emerson complained that his picture "looked like a pirate," and a daguerreotype portrait of President John Tyler was bemoaned in one magazine for its "unflattering fidelity" (Carlebach 17, 27).

Hawthorne's story probes the reasons behind these unseemly results. Did the eye of the camera really provide a new, superhuman way of seeing the natural world? If so, Holgrave is more than a practitioner of mere mechanical processes. As he tells Phoebe, in an effort to change her opinion of his craft:

If you would permit me . . . I should like to try whether the daguerreotype can bring out disagreeable traits on a perfectly amiable face. . . . Most of my likenesses do look unamiable; but the very sufficient reason, I fancy, is, because the originals are so. . . . While we give it credit for depicting only the merest surface, it actually brings out the secret character with a truth that no painter would ever venture upon, even could he detect it. There is, at least, no flattery in my humble line of art. (67)

A sour face does not fare well before the camera, but interestingly Holgrave seems to already have an answer to his question: under certain circumstances, handsome faces do not fare well either. He produces for Phoebe his latest unsatisfactory attempt at daguerreotyping Judge Pyncheon, who is running for public office. Holgrave muses:

> Now the remarkable point is, that the original wears, to the world's eye— and, for aught I know, his most intimate friends,—an exceedingly pleasant countenance, indicative of benevolence, openness of heart, sunny good-humor and other praiseworthy qualities of the cast. The sun, as you see, tells quite another story, and will not be coaxed out of it, after half-a-dozen patient attempts on my part. Here we have the man, sly, subtle, hard, imperious and, withal, cold as ice. Look at that eye! Would you like to be at its mercy? At that mouth! Could it ever smile? And yet, if you could only see the benign smile of the original! It is so much the more unfortunate, as he is a public character of some eminence, and the likeness was intended to be engraved. (68)

The Judge's charismatic appearance might fool everyone in town, but his true character cannot hide from the camera. This convenient "truth detector" would have indeed provided a comforting service in a time of rapid urbanization and increased travel—a world, in short, increasingly populated by unfamiliar faces, rendering unknown characters and intentions. But before accepting this device as magical, let us pause to consider the daguerreotype through the photographic reality that Holgrave is proposing. By this logic, poor ugly Hepzibah, though innocent of any crime, would not appear any better as a daguerreotype then the duplicitous Judge. The lesson seems to be that there is only one kind of successful daguerreotype portrait: a subject who not only *is* good but *looks* good. If this is the case, the camera might fail to confirm whether what we see reflects what is really there.

This dynamic becomes even more problematic if we consider two important aspects of the daguerreotype's function and reception in society. The first is the interference of the camera's truth-seeking gaze that results from efforts to better a subject's typical appearance. Daguerreotypists went to great lengths to pose their subjects in the most flattering manner, but the photographer and the "mesmeric" mechanism were but two players in the studio. The subject was the third player, and where each role began and ended is unclear. As the poet Nathaniel Parker Willis observed, in his final collection of sketches *The Convalescent* (1859):

> Some are handsome only when talking, some only when the features are in repose; some have more character in the full face, some in the profile; some do the writhings of life's agonies with their hearts and wear smooth faces; some do the same work with their nostrils. A portrait-painter usually takes all these matters into account, and, with his dozen or more long sittings, has time enough to make a careful study of how the character is worked out in the physiognomy, and to paint accordingly. But in daguerreotyping, the sitter has to employ this knowledge and exercise this judgment for himself. (qtd. in Newhall 78)

The implication here is that, while the camera may make unnatural demands of its "sitter," the subject can, with "training" through repeated exposure, become more adept at responding to those demands.[2]

The second complication concerns Holgrave's allusion to what remains an under-researched aspect of early photographic history: the daguerreotype's relationship with print culture. As a one-of-a-kind image, the daguerreotype represented a paradox of reproducibility. The only way to copy a daguerreotype was to place one in front of the camera. Obviously, this method was unsuited to mass production. Yet there were labor-intensive processes by which to reproduce daguerreotypes, processes that usually required several steps of removal from the original photograph. Daguerreotypes could be traced onto paper and transferred, through etching, onto stone, copper, or steel printing plates.[3] Original daguerreotypes could also serve as studies for artists to produce freehand renderings of the original, to be similarly etched into plates. The result of these processes was a hybrid image that possessed elements commonly considered to be opposites: the truth claims of photography and the mediating hand of the artist.

These engraved prints quickly began to appear in a variety of print media, from newspaper and magazine illustrations, promotional materials and folios, to more intimately circulated items, such as invitations, cards, and frontice pieces—often labeled with text announcing their photographic ancestry, "from (or based on) a daguerreotype." The fascination with discrete daguerreotypes was part of a generally expanding appetite and economy for images. The very processes that enabled the dissemination of the daguerreotype's truth value also acted upon that truth value, as artists inevitably softened and improved the appearances of their subjects in translation. Comparing a daguerreotype to its engraved print is an interesting exercise, for people almost always look better in the latter.[4] Holgrave wrongly assumes his unfriendly picture of the Judge would not make a suitable engraving. Arguably, the engraving was meant, in part, to accomplish this: promulgating a likeness "more-truthful" than an ordinary drawing, and yet not as harshly truthful as the original photograph. If these were the images people were apt to encounter—for they circulated more easily and more widely than their singular sources—they are also the ones they might, on some level, strive to emulate. This visual feedback loop helped to influence what took place before the camera. *Seeing* images informs the attendant mode of *being* an image.

If this consideration of photography's constraints and possibilities reminds the reader of very contemporary conversations about the visual mechanics and social politics of photo-retouching, then this essay, hopefully, has begun to come full circle, or, rather, incomplete spiral. Before winding down we must consider the other important photographic exchange between Holgrave and Phoebe, this one toward the end of the novel. Holgrave shows Phoebe a second daguerreotype of the Judge, but this time she has no trouble identifying it, nor does she resist its facticity. The reader is not offered any description of the photograph. We only experience it through Phoebe, who recoils in horror and proclaims, "This is death! . . . Judge Pyncheon is dead!" (213). Since the Judge died in the parlor of the mansion, and Clifford and Hepzibah are nowhere to be found (in fact, they were out experiencing their first train ride), the death appears highly suspicious. But, as Holgrave explains, "*if the matter can be fairly considered and candidly interpreted*," this daguerreotype would make it "evident that Judge Pyncheon could not have come unfairly to his end" (214, emphasis mine). This image-document also could exonerate Clifford from the specious old murder charges, demonstrating retroactively that Jaffrey the elder in fact had died as another victim of Maule's medical curse.

An evident reversal of attitude promptly follows. Prim, bourgeois Phoebe now has no aversion to the daguerreotype. Enlightened by her time at Seven Gables, the young woman, who once dismissed daguerreotypes with confusion and disdain, exhorts Holgrave to make the image public: "Why do we delay so? . . . This secret takes away my breath! Let us throw open the doors!" (214). Phoebe is prepared to transgress the specular dictations of polite society—both to claim a hideous image as truth and to inject it into the world. A similar urgency would soon motivate the entire enterprise of photojournalism, which at this point in history was in its infancy. Holgrave, however, pauses to relish the secret that he and Phoebe now share, reluctant to break their intimacy. Whereas to her the image is public property, to him it feels private and bonds him to her. The wandering radical now professes his love to Phoebe: "I have a presentiment that, hereafter, it will be my lot . . . in a word, to conform myself to laws, and the peaceful practice of society. Your poise will be more powerful than any oscillating tendency of mine" (214). This change of heart often is read as Hawthorne's condemnation of the hackneyed daguerreotypist and, by extension, technological progress and the pseudosciences writ large.

Yet this is too simplistic an ending. A reader would be remiss not to note that Phoebe herself has been changing throughout the story as well. Intimate and public image, objective and interpreted truth, all collapse into one another along with the young lovers.[5] Their union can be read as a compromise, an attempt to navigate a course through the complexities of the new visual landscape. Armed with their love and their evidence, Holgrave says, "Now let us meet the world! . . . We have no way but to meet it. Let us open the door at once" (215).

The House of the Seven Gables acknowledges the uneasy relationship that always has existed between being and appearing, simultaneously exploring a particularly troubled moment in this dynamic history. In returning to Hawthorne's work and time, we echo Clifford's bid to regard progress as indirect, recursive, and confused. If we pay attention, we occasionally are granted opportunities to glimpse where we have been. What we manage to glean, even at a distance, can inform, illuminate, and negotiate what is around the bend. A century and a half later, Hawthorne's story remains a valuable opportunity for readers to observe and engage with the struggle—both familiar and strange—to continually adapt our ways of seeing and being in an ever-changing world.

Notes

1. In an 1851 story in *Photographic Art Journal*, daguerreotype portraitist and editor Michael Snelling recounts how one of his photographers was having a particularly trying time with a man whose wife had sat for several portraits. Her husband was disappointed by each one, insisting they did not resemble his wife, who demonstrated "a very disagreeable stare." Snelling recounts: "Had the operator paid more attention to his subject, he would have studied her face more minutely, detected the defect, and watched his opportunity to secure the impression of the image, at the moment when a more pleasing expression crossed the features. This he might readily have produced by some pleasant remark, or delicate compliment." The problem also could have been avoided, presumably, if the woman had not made a strange face in the first place.

2. See note above on Michael Snelling.

3. In the early 1840s, scientist Hippolyte-Louis Fizeau invented a chemical means to effectively turn the daguerreotype plate into a printing plate. Although the resulting prints conveyed much of the daguerreotype's atmospheric clarity and detail, it was an expensive and unwieldy process that was not widely adopted.

4. A rare pair of images in the archives at the George Eastman House in Rochester, New York, illustrates this phenomenon well. The set consists of an etched steel engraving plate and a mid-size daguerreotype by an unknown photographer, upon which the former piece was based. The little information we can gather on the objects comes from the text engraved beneath the portrait in the steel plate. The text reads: "Complimentarily engraved and respectfully dedicated to the friends of the Rev. WP Hinds, by the Engraver H. S. Wagner," followed by an engraved handwritten script signature "Yours Truly, WP Hinds." From these images we can gather the basics: Reverend Hinds is a Caucasian man who appears to be somewhere between middle- and old-aged. Well dressed, portly and bespectacled, he maintains an air of importance and authority. One could easily recognize the man in the plate as the man in the daguerreotype, but upon close inspection they look quite different. In the daguerreotype, Hinds's wrinkled, jowly visage wears a pinched stare. In the plate, his wrinkles are fewer; his eyes are wider and slightly farther apart. In the daguerreotype, Hinds's stout head seems to protrude directly out of his dark silk cravat; in the plate, his neck is elongated and dignified. In fact, the figure's entire torso is longer and slimmer in the plate. By all appearances, the engraved Hinds appears younger and more attractive.

5. Milette Shamir examines the story in light of contemporaneous changes in the legal system regarding rights of property and privacy. The right to privacy was not established, even hazily, until Samuel D. Warren and Louis Brandeis's 1890 article in the *Harvard Law Review*, "The Right to Privacy: The Implicit Made Explicit." Shamir cites a letter Brandeis wrote to his fiancée, reflecting "that he should have published a 'companion piece' on 'The Duty of Publicity'" (775).

Works Cited

Benjamin, Walter. "Little History of Photography." *Selected Writings*. Vol. 2. Ed. Michael W. Jennings, Howard Eiland, and Gary Smith. Cambridge, MA: Harvard UP, 1999.

Carlebach, Michael L. *The Origins of Photojournalism in America*. Washington: Smithsonian, 1992.

Daguerre, Louis Jacques Mandé. *An Historical Account and Descriptive Account of the Varieties and Processes of the Daguerreotype and the Diorama*. 1839. New York: Kraus, 1969.

Hawthorne, Nathaniel. *The House of the Seven Gables*. 1851. Ed. Robert S. Levine. New York: Norton, 2006.

Mattison, Ben. "The American Reception." *The Social Construction of the American Daguerreotype Portrait*, 1995. Web. 24 June 2011.

Newhall, Beaumont. *The Daguerreotype in America*. New York: Duell, 1961.

Rev. W. P. Hinds. 1855. Daguerreotype. George Eastman House International Museum of Photography, Rochester.

Rudisill, Richard. *Mirror Image: The Influence of the Daguerreotype on American Society*. Albuquerque: U of New Mexico P, 1971.

Shamir, Milette. "Hawthorne's Romance and the Right to Privacy." *American Quarterly* 49.4 (Dec. 1997): 746–79.

Trachtenberg, Alan. *Reading American Photographs: Images as History, Mathew Brady to Walker Evans*. New York: Hill, 1989.

Wagner, H. S. *Rev. W. P. Hinds*. 1860. Steel printing plate. George Eastman House International Museum of Photography, Rochester.

Opposing Perspectives: Technology in Modernist Literature

Melissa Dinsman

First published in 1897, Bram Stoker's *Dracula* marks a shift in literature's relationship with technology. A novel centering on a band of friends and their attempt to destroy an old-world demon, the now infamous Count Dracula, this text combines the traditions of a premodern state and the technological advances of the Second Industrial Revolution. Even a quick flip through the pages of *Dracula* suggests the pervasiveness of technology within the novel; chapters include a bevy of recent technological innovations: the phonograph, telegram, and clippings from the *Pall Mall Gazette*. It is, in part, this influx of technical apparatuses that allows literary critic Jennifer Wicke to assert that *Dracula*, a novel traditionally read as Victorian, should instead "be read as the first great *modern* novel in British literature" (467).

Although technology is, indeed, ubiquitous throughout the text—typewriters, trains, stenography, phonography, Kodak cameras, newspapers, and Winchesters all find a home in the novel—the real significance of technology is not its inclusion but its use. From Dr. Seward's clinical notes on phonographic records to Mina Murray's transcription of these notes in typewritten form, and from daily newspaper reports (a product of an improved printing press) to trains that travel quickly throughout Europe, the band of friends is able to track Dracula and intersect him before he reaches his final destination. Technology, albeit in combination with old-world traditions, facilitates Dracula's defeat. As Dr. Van Helsing states, "We have on our side power of combination—a power denied to the vampire kind; we have resources of science; we are free to act and think; and the hours of the day and the night are ours equally" (243).

Yet Stoker's portrayal of technology should not be misread as one-sided, for Dracula is drawn to London: the center of the British empire, a consumer of men, and home to the Industrial Revolution and mass production. Thus, if London is the quintessential site of consumption, then Dracula is the quintessential consumer. A very complex depiction of technology, specifically technology associated with mass media, is presented in *Dracula*. On the one hand, technology helps the heroes defeat Dracula; on the other hand, there is, as Wicke suggests, a connection between Dracula as consumer and mass media as consuming. For Wicke, *Dracula* is a novel about modern consumption (or vampirism), and this consumption is mirrored in technology throughout the text: the gramophone consumes speech, the Kodak camera extracts essence, and newspapers feed off tragedies, including the newly vampiric Lucy Westenra, who is consumed by the newspapers and transformed into the "bloofer lady" (471–73). The ambivalent representation of technology in *Dracula* is indicative of a trend that would grow in literary modernism with the turn of the century.

Referred to as "the second machine age" by Richard Cork, and more poetically as "the age of mechanical reproduction" by Marxist critic Walter Benjamin, the modern era was a time of great technical innovation and political upheaval. Extending roughly from the 1880s to the 1930s, the machine age of the modern era was noted for mass production and the assembly line; improved transport (car, tram, train, and airplane); modern warfare devices (tanks, submarines, manufactured gasses); radio and phonograph technology; and the high-speed printing press, all of which contributed to social upheaval, such as increased consumerism, cultural leveling, and an enlarged working class. It was an era that saw the death of Queen Victoria, the advent of Fordism, Charles Lindbergh's flight across the Atlantic Ocean, and the devastating atrocities of World War I. With such foundation-shifting events, it is not surprising that depictions of technology were omnipresent in modern literature; however, as with Stoker's *Dracula*, technological advances were portrayed as both an aid and an evil. In the following essay, I will examine modernist ambivalence toward technology after radical transformations in the manufacturing process and the horrific outcome of World War I. Focusing on a broad overview of four late-nineteenth-century and early-twentieth-century technological categories (war, transport, manufacturing, and communications), I will contrast texts that embrace technology's power and potential with texts that reject its negative outcomes.

The relationship between technology and modern literature[1] has been a topic of debate among literary critics for decades. The traditional approach to modern literature, in particular high-modernist literature, states that high modernism was a reaction against modernity, specifically mass culture. This position, theorized most famously by the Marxist and literary critic Theodor Adorno, suggests that the complexity of high-modernist writing is a challenge to linguistic conventions and thereby modernity itself. There is, as Andreas Huyssen reminds us, a "great divide" between high art and technology. Since the 1980s, there has been a shift in perception with regard to technology's role in modern literature. Stephen Kern's *The Culture of Time and Space, 1880–1918* (1983) and Hugh Kenner's *The Mechanic Muse* (1987) suggest that the "great divide" is, in fact, not so great. Modern writers both responded to the past and reflected their present; thus, it is not surprising that omnipresent technology found itself infused in both the literary subject and style of modern writers. As Hugh Kenner states: "New ways of writing, then, for new order of experience; urban experience; Modernism is distinctively urban. . . . But like all live writing it ingests what's around it" (14). The fragmentary nature of a poem such as T. S. Eliot's *The Waste Land* (1922) has been argued to be a result of both quicker modes of transportation (trams) and communications technology (telephones).

A more recent trend in the literature has turned inward, to the human body and its mechanisms. Tim Armstrong's *Modernism, Technology, and the Body* (1998) looks at the relationship between the body and technology as found in literary modernism. Sara Danius focuses on the senses, specifically sight and sound, in connection to technological innovation as the means of high modernist aesthetic practice. In *The Senses of Modernism* (2002), Danius argues that technology is not only reflected in modern literature but that it also influenced high-modernist aesthetics: "technology is in a specific sense *constitutive* of high-modernist aesthetics" (3). Continuing in the mode of recent scholarship, this essay aims to challenge the idea of a "great divide," favoring instead a discussion of high-modernist texts as inundated with technological innovation, and considering the form and content of select literary texts from European and American authors.

War!

The shift in perception of technological advances due to World War I is perhaps nowhere better played out than among modernism's literary elite. For the futurists, an Italian avant-garde movement, the technologies of war were a windfall and a means to a progressive end; yet, for those poets who experienced the war firsthand, it was anything but. For both groups, the war largely meant the end, as the futurists lost momentum and many World War I-era poets lost their lives on the front.

The futurist movement began with the publication of F. T. Marinetti's "The Founding and the Manifesto of Futurism" in the Parisian newspaper *Le Figaro* on February 20, 1909, and spawned the creation of other avant-garde groups, including vorticism,[2] imagism, dadaism, and surrealism. Rapidly spreading throughout Europe and the United States, futurism had a broad artistic influence on literature, drama, photography, music, and the visual arts, and suggested a relationship between art and power, specifically political, industrial, and technological power. As Marinetti states, "Art, in fact, can be nothing if not violence, cruelty, and injustice" ("Founding," 6). Yet, with the outbreak of World War I in 1914, transnational interest in futurism declined, particularly in Great Britain and the United States, as the violence advocated in the manifestoes became all too real.

The futurists wanted to move away from what they saw as a decrepit past, which they emphasized by writing the manifesto as if in the moment (Marinetti describes the process of creating the futurist movement as a joyride and eventual car crash). Reveling in the destructive capability of technology, the futurist manifesto is filled with violent images, such as a "guillotine blade" and anthropomorphized automobiles described as "famished . . . roaring beneath the windows" ("Founding," 3). These striking images of glorified violence and technology are reflected in the manifesto's guidelines: technology and struggle are positioned as beautiful, and poetry must be a "violent assault"; war is glorified as "the only hygiene of the world"; and history must be annihilated to move forward. Marinetti writes, "we had crushed our ancestral lethargy" ("Founding," 4, 3).

Yet the futurists wanted to liberate artists from more than the chains of history; they wanted to liberate language. A new form of writing was invented that destroyed syntax and focused on the momentum of verbs and nouns in combination. Mathematical symbols replaced punctuation, and the first-person *I* was banished. Language was to imitate the new tumultuous life of the second machine age. "We want literature to render the life of a motor," Marinetti states, "a new instinctive animal whose guiding principle we will recognize when we have come to know the instincts of the various forces that compose it" ("Technical Manifesto," 18). Through their glorification of technological innovation, specifically technology of destructive power, the futurists spoke for an era of rupture and rebellion, an era entering World War I.

In Great Britain, there also was excitement about entering the war. It was marketed as an honorable cause, giving young men a chance to fight for "God, King, and Country." But this excitement was not unanimous among British poets, a great number of whom fought in the trenches and did not survive to see the war's end. As Candice Ward states, "Some, like Rupert Brooke and John McCrae, believed their services were part of a noble and just cause. Others—most notably Siegfried Sassoon and Wilfred Owen—entered the military through a sense of duty" (iii). The war that was supposed to be over by Christmas 1914 waged on until November 1918, resulting in disillusionment for artists and soldiers alike. Wilfred Owen's poem "Dulce et Decorum Est" ("It Is a Sweet and Fitting Thing"), a horrific and realistic depiction of war and its technologies, is a perfect representation of this disillusionment.

In "Dulce et Decorum Est," Owen presents the reader with an ironic juxtaposition. The title, referencing the good and just in war, is immediately challenged by the opening image of young soldiers "Bent double, like old beggars under sacks, / Knock-kneed, coughing like hags" (1–2). Owen openly questions Britain's patriotic depictions of a noble war and offers his readers—the British public—a dose of reality. Owen's poem, which follows the retreat of Allied forces, offers gruesome, realistic depictions of war and the new technologies that made it so devastating. The marching of soldiers without boots and the dropping of "Five-Nines" (5.9-inch artillery shells) silence the heroic sweetness of the title. Instead, these soldiers are depicted as "limp," "blood-shod," "lame," and "blind" (8, 6) in just the first stanza.

In the second and third stanzas, Owen depicts the cruelties of chemical warfare and its aftermath. A soldier, too slow with his gas mask, begins "guttering, choking, drowning" (16). Owen heightens the gruesome language in the third stanza, as the death of the gassed man is described in horrid detail:

> the blood
> Come gargling from the froth-corrupted lungs,
> Obscene as cancer, bitter as the cud
> Of vile, incurable sores on innocent tongues (21–24)

The soldier's slow, horrific death leads Owen to the climax of the poem and a lesson about the lies of war and the glorification of its technologies:

> My friend, you would not tell with such high zest
> To children ardent for some desperate glory,
> The old lie: Dulce et decorum est
> Pro patria mori. (25–28)

The final two lines, taken from Horace's *Odes* and meant to exhort Roman citizens into battle ("It is a sweet and fitting thing to die for your country"), challenge both unchecked patriotism and England's literary history.

The very form of Owen's poem poses this challenge as well. The rhyme scheme *abab*, *cdcd*, a twist on the traditional Shakespearian sonnet (*abab*, *cdcd*, *efef*, *gg*), further juxtaposes the realities of war with the idealized image of an all-powerful England. This alteration in form suggests the inability of older models of literature to accurately portray the war's tumult and devastation. By modernizing the Shakespearean sonnet, an immediately recognizable form, Owen strengthens his claim that the patriotic English message does not hold true to the realities of modern warfare. While the large divide in perceptions of war and war technology may be expected, this ambivalent relationship with modernization also affected innovations in transportation.

Planes, Trains, and Automobiles

The turn of the century also saw large developments in transportation technology: the Wright brothers' first flight on December 17, 1903, faster trains that raced through Europe, the advent of the automobile in 1885 by Germany's Karl Benz, and the introduction of the automotive assembly line by Ransom Olds (1902) and, later, Henry Ford (1914). Both public and private transportation improved, making the world a smaller and speedier place. But these developments also produced fear and new safety concerns. Authors began to include in their work the dangers of transportation as a reality of life. The opening pages of Robert Musil's epic novel *The Man Without Qualities* (1930–42) starts with an automotive collision, and Mikhail Bulgakov includes a gruesome (albeit humorous within the context) description of a tram accident in *The Master and Margarita* (1967): "Run clean over! I was a witness. Believe me—bang! and the head's gone! Crunch—there goes the right leg! Crunch—there goes the left leg! That's what these trams have brought us to" (198).

Yet not all modernists deplored these new powerful modes of transportation. As noted in the first section, the futurists used the automobile as the symbol of the modern age, showing its power to be both seductive and destructive. After the noted car collision in his manifesto, Marinetti combines his anthropomorphism and violent imagery to describe the crashed automobile as a shark: "They thought it was dead, my beautiful shark, but one caress from me was enough to revive it, and there it was again, once more alive, running on its powerful fins" ("Founding," 4). Described as a semidomesticated predator, the automobile has the power to both kill and follow the command of its master. The motor and its power were to bring in a new age of velocity, a key theme in the work of futurism, in which the faster the movement, the faster the retreat from the past. For American novelist F. Scott Fitzgerald, however, the faster one goes, the more destruction one causes, as is evident in the motif of the automobile crash in *The Great Gatsby*.

The Great Gatsby (1925) is peppered with automobile language and imagery, all foreshadowing the tragic car accident to come. Fitzgerald includes subtle references, such as "interior rules that act as *brakes* on my desires" and "*roaring* noon" (Fitzgerald 64, 73; emphasis added), and larger, more thematic images, such as the sign over George Wilson's shop, which reads "Repairs. GEORGE B. WILSON. Cars Bought and Sold" (29). The automobile is the site of numerous conversations, and the locale where the narrator, Nick Carraway, first begins to learn the truth about the mysterious Jay Gatsby. More significantly, Fitzgerald offers his readers four car collisions, the first three of which provide hints as to the fourth as they increase in danger and violence. The first collision occurs during one of Gatsby's parties, where an inebriated party guest drives one of Gatsby's cars off the road; the confusion regarding the driver and the trope of driving someone else's automobile return in the final accident. The second incident is Jordan Baker's near-fatal collision. The narrator describes Jordan's driving as so "rotten" that "she passed so close to some workmen that [the] fender flicked a button on one man's coat" (63). Much like Daisy Buchannan near the end of the novel, Jordan continues driving without once looking back. The third accident occurs on Tom and Daisy Buchannan's honeymoon and, with Tom driving, results in the broken arm of a hotel chambermaid—upping the collateral damage of the earlier two accidents from automobile damage to personal injury.

Yet not one of these incidents is as devastating as the fourth and final collision, which results in the death of Myrtle Wilson, Tom Buchannan's lover. After a tremendous fight in the city, Daisy and Gatsby leave, Daisy driving Gatsby's car. Believing it to be Tom (as Tom was driving Gatsby's car into the city), Myrtle runs out into the street and is struck and left for dead. Claiming to be the driver of the car, Gatsby sets off a chain of events that ultimately claims the lives of George Wilson and Gatsby himself. This tragic end at the hands of the automobile (Fitzgerald's "death car," 144) and the self-indulgent Daisy represents more than technology's destructive capacity. For Fitzgerald, the image of the automobile was a symbol of the decadent upper class and the tumult of the 1920s. As literary critic Lawrence MacPhee claims, "Fitzgerald employs the automobile as part of a pattern of images embodying the disorder of the Twenties and, particularly, the chaotic lives of the central characters" (207). Thus, Fitzgerald presents his readers with, at best, an ambivalent image of the automobile. Fitzgerald's cars, associated with consumption, amorality, and death, seduce readers by suggesting the romance of high society and freedom of travel.

Buying Cheap and Selling Dear

As noted in the last section, the freedom of travel would not have been possible without the mass production brought about by Fordism. Charlie Chaplin's *Modern Times* (1936), one of the most iconic films in cinematic history, offers the viewer entry into the monotony of the assembly line, where goods are rapidly produced at the expense of the individual worker. Unable to keep up with the factory's production level, Chaplin's character, the Little Tramp, gets caught inside the machine. Twisting and turning within the gears, the Little Tramp loses control of his own body, eventually moving to the rhythm of the factory. While humorous, this film speaks volumes about public opinion on mass production, for while consumerism continued to increase in the twentieth century, so did the fear that man was becoming a machine.

For American novelists Upton Sinclair and John Steinbeck, the manufacturing technologies of the modern era had a devastating impact on factory work and farming in the United States. Sinclair's eye-opening exposé of the meat-packing industry in *The Jungle* (1906) gives an alarming account of working-class conditions and, more specifically, the life-threatening factory practices that arose from the assembly line. For Sinclair, these unskilled laborers were "cog[s] in this marvelous machine" (41). Sinclair argues, as Chaplin does in *Modern Times*, that the performance of repetitive tasks dehumanizes the workforce; their lives become part of the larger machine as they live, work, and die on factory ground. Yet Sinclair does not advocate returning to a preindustrialized state, nor does he present manufacturing technology as inherently evil. What Sinclair requests, successfully so, is new regulations to match new innovation, for humanity should not be lost at the expense of the machine.

Technological modernization affected the farming community as well, and, like Sinclair, Steinbeck is critical of the "advances" being made. Following the Joad family's exodus from Oklahoma, Steinbeck's *The Grapes of Wrath* (1939) offers a critical account of big-business farming and new technologies. The main culprit is the tractor: "The tractors came over the roads and into the fields, great crawlers moving like insects, having the incredible strength of insects. They crawled over the ground, laying the track and rolling on it and picking it up" (35). Described as a plague of hungry locusts (befitting the Biblical theme of exodus), the tractors devour rather than harvest the land, destroying the "close bond between Man and Nature" (Groene 27). Steinbeck describes those who operate the tractors as robots: "gloved, goggled, rubber dust mask over nose and mouth, he was a part of the monster, a robot in the seat" (35). Although not in a factory, these drivers have become part of the machines they operate: dehumanized "cogs" working for big business to produce consumable goods.[3]

A more ambiguous account of production technologies is found in texts that outwardly have little to do with manufacturing and consumption. Virginia Woolf's *Mrs. Dalloway* (1925) and James Joyce's *Ulysses* (1922), two of the great modernist novels, make reference to this consumption as a means of female empowerment and as a connection to issues of empire. Woolf's novel begins with consumption: "Mrs. Dalloway said she would buy the flowers herself" (3). The small, independent act of purchasing flowers for an evening party introduces a concept that floats, as it does in life, in the background of the novel. Consumption drives it just as it drives the modern age. In a later passage, as Clarissa Dalloway makes her way down Bond Street in London, her eye focuses upon commodities (gloves and hats) and the royal car passing through the street. The connection of these seemingly disparate images causes Mrs. Dalloway to think of death and empire: "for in all the hat shops and tailors' shops strangers looked at each other and thought of the dead; of the flag; of Empire"; then she imagines violence breaking out between colonizer and colonized in a local pub (18). These reflections bring Mrs. Dalloway back to the thought of consumed materials, particularly ribbon on a wedding day. In these musings, Woolf is suggesting the unspoken truth that the influx of commodities in Britain is made possible on the backs of others, through empire and death.

Similar scenes occur in Joyce's *Ulysses*, in which Leopold Bloom purchases various items as he wanders around Dublin. Yet it is Gerty MacDowell's little drawer of treasures in "Nausicaa" that best illustrates the power of consumption on an unsuspecting public:

> It was there she kept her girlish treasure trove, the tortoiseshell combs, her child of Mary badge, the whiterose scent, the eyebrowleine, her alabaster

pouncetbox and the ribbons to change when her things came home from the wash and there were some beautiful thoughts written in it in violet ink that she bought in Hely's of Dame Street for she felt that she too could write poetry if she could only express herself like that poem. (298)

Each of these collected items gives Gerty a sense of self-worth and empowerment, and, as Wicke argues in "Joyce and Consumer Culture," each is an example of consumerism providing identity. But Gerty's consuming also holds a connection to empire. "Nausicaa" is largely a chapter about the fashion industry and the uneven relations between the lower-class Gerty and the items she wishes to possess. It is fashion magazines from England that tell Gerty she needs to look like a Brighton seaside girl. Living in a colonized Ireland, Gerty watches as raw materials leave her country for England, only to be transformed into mass-produced goods to be sold back to Ireland. The disparity between Gerty's reality and Gerty's imagined state is ultimately a commentary on Ireland's uneven relationship with the imperial center of England, an unevenness between those who produce and buy goods and those who sell them.

Language in the Air

Having considered manufacturing and consumption, this fourth and final section focuses on the types of technology purchased in the modern era, specifically communications technology. The increased speed of the turn of the century affected not only transportation but the very means by which people communicated. Large distances were traversed in a matter of seconds by telegrams and telephones; thoughts were recorded by typewriters and gramophones; music and news were brought to an entire nation by radio. While some of these technologies, such as the telegram and telephone, existed before the modern era, improvements to these older forms and assembly-line production meant that these technologies could be produced and sold for less, making the technology available to a much larger and now more connected population.

The omnipresence of these technologies caught the attention of modern writers, three of whom (Henry James, Virginia Woolf, and Bertolt Brecht) used the technology to an advantage in their writing.

Like Stoker's *Dracula*, James's novella *In the Cage* (1898) involves some detective work on the part of the characters and the reader, and, like *Dracula*, the reason for this is due to communications technology. Just as Mina Harker collects scraps of communication from letters, telegrams, newspapers, and phonographic records, the unnamed female telegraphist of *In the Cage* pieces together the story of two lovers via a series of telegrams. The very form of the novella reflects this mystery-inspiring medium. The plot, chapters, and sentences are fragmented, mimicking the nature of the telegraphed message: "the prose imitates the curt, implicit syntax of telegrams . . . by making the sentence 'click' with repetition, disjointment, and an irregular number of pauses" (Pollard 82). Yet James's novella is more than just a story that explores and mimics a new technology. For James, the telegram marks a general shift in power in the new communications age: stenographers, telephone operators, and telegraphers all stood as observers rather than practitioners. Thus, the telegraph, a medium that enables new interconnections, also marks a class division, a division mirrored by the very space one enters to send a telegram. From behind the glass partition that separates her space from the grocery store, the female telegraphist observes rather than acts in life: "It had occurred to her early that in her position—that of a young person spending, in framed and wired confinement, the life of a guinea-pig or a magpie—she should know a great many persons without their recognizing the acquaintance" (2). According to Richard Menke, *In the Cage* is a study of the psychological and sociological impact of telegraphy. Without championing or condemning the telegraph, James's novella presents the realities of a world both brought together and divided by new technology.

In her last novel, *Between the Acts* (1941), Woolf attempts to show the psychological and sociological impact of communications technology on a listening public. Set in 1939, before the outbreak of World

War II, and following the lives of a small English village and Miss La Trobe's attempt to put on a pageant-play celebrating English history, the novel represents a last grasp at an "authentic" English community before it is dispersed and disintegrated by war. Relying heavily upon the gramophone, Miss La Trobe's play unites this diverse village with patriotic songs and childhood nursery rhymes. Speaking throughout the novel, even when the pageant-play is in intermission, the gramophone marks the remaining time before the devastation of another world war: "Tick, tick, tick, the machine continued. Time was passing. The audience was wandering, dispersing. Only the tick, tick of the gramophone held them together" (154). This unification, albeit a fleeting unification, challenges Adorno's reading of the gramophone as "the pregnant stillness of individuals" ("Curves of the Needle," 605). As the novel and play reach their climax, the gramophone voice gains command of the narrative. Dispersing at the end of the play, the audience and the reader know that war and irrevocable change are on the horizon for this small community. The gramophone, the unifier of the novel, suggests that unification is fleeting and inauthentic, just like the "Englishness" captured by the play: "*Dispersed are we*, the gramophone triumphed, yet lamented, *Dispersed are we*" (198). The gramophone, like the play, is unable to bring perpetual unity to a divided community, a community that still longs, at the end of the novel, for a center. The coming war will provide a brief resurgence of unity, but, as the gramophone foreshadows, this unity will end as well: "The gramophone gurgled *Unity—Dispersity*. It gurgled *Un.. dis...* And ceased" (201).

Of all modern writers, the German playwright Brecht was perhaps the most invested in technological innovation. A true media writer, Brecht wrote not only for the stage, but also for radio, cinema, and the opera. Radio, as a listener and a writer, was a particular passion for Brecht, who believed that radio had the potential to be democratic, educational, and communicative ("Suggestions"). This fascination with radio turns into dependence as Brecht is forced to flee Nazi Germany. In the poem "To a Portable Radio" (1938), Brecht discusses his need for this technological lifeline.[4] The short poem begins with Brecht's flight from Nazi Germany, radio in hand, as he travels into exile. The second and final stanzas describe his dependence on the radio as a link to the outside world. In exile, the radio was a necessity. Brecht was able to carry the portable device with him as he left Germany "from house to train, from train to ship" (3) before the outbreak of World War II. This radio became Brecht's means of hearing news of his enemies ("Feinde") in that "hated jargon" from Nazi Germany (4). The right-wing propaganda and swift advancement across Europe struck fear into the listener. Strikingly, this "fear" serves two purposes, for Brecht fears not only Nazi "victories" but also the death of his radio, his access to the outside world (7–8). Similar to Woolf's gramophone and James's telegraph, listening to the radio connects Brecht to a larger community of radio listeners, particularly Germans in exile. Yet there is a more ominous element at work in Brecht's poem. As the realities of the coming war are broadcast daily, the isolation and fear of the listener grow, so much so that this poem is written in dedication to an object, rather than a person, or even the community of radio listeners.

Whether as a lifeline or a danger, a windfall or a mere fact of modern life, technology of the second mechanical age powered its way into modern literature. An ambivalent relationship between writers and the technological age was to be expected, as new hazards arose alongside increased speed and efficiency. This division can be located in such areas of technological advancement as war, transport, manufacturing, and communication. Some writers, such as the futurists, Owen, and Steinbeck, present a relatively one-sided opinion of technology, while others, such as Stoker, Fitzgerald, and James, offer more ambiguity. Then there are writers, such as Woolf and Joyce, who include technology merely as a fact of life but also provide larger sociological implications and commentaries. No matter the depiction, albeit celebration or censure, the modern writer was far from rejecting modernity. Technology's ubiquitous presence in modern literature challenges the notion that there was a "great divide." Even the fragmented form, as in James's *In the Cage* and Joyce's *Ulysses*, is influenced in part by the speed of the technological age.

The demonization of the machine—iconically captured in the form of "Moloch"[5] in Fritz Lang's *Metropolis* (1927)—offers a lasting image of the relationship between modern man and technology. But in actuality technology was and remains neither godsend nor evil. Technology is a reality of a rapidly changing world, a world that modern writers wanted to capture in their art. The ambiguity that arises is a result of the newness of those technologies, for any world-changing innovation will cause rupture and unease until it is accepted as a societal norm. Still, a warning can be gleaned from modern writing: in the pursuit of technological advancement, we should not forsake our humanity. We must strive, as Sinclair tells us, to keep from becoming "cogs" in a machine. Perhaps more fittingly for the digital age is this warning: we must keep from becoming a mere node in the network.

Notes

1. Traditionally, modern literature is considered to have taken place between 1890 and 1940. In "The New Modernist Studies," modernist critics Douglas Mao and Rebecca Walkowitz argue that literary modernism might become more inclusive in terms of historical time and place (modernist authors are no longer strictly American and European), and "low" and "high" modernism. Mao and Walkowitz refer to these inclusive shifts as temporal, horizontal, and vertical expansions.

2. Although not a focus of this chapter, the vorticists, a short-lived English avant-garde group, also focused on machinery, stating in their literary magazine *Blast*: "Machinery is the greatest Earth-medium: incidentally it seeps away the doctrines of a narrow and pedantic Realism at one stroke" (Lewis 205).

3. Although largely critical of new farming practices, Steinbeck does praise the new irrigation systems in California (Groene 29). In *Grapes of Wrath*, praise for technology is in minimal.

4. Brecht's original poem is titled "Auf den kleinen Radioapparat."

5. Fritz Lang uses "Moloch" (traditionally, the name of an ancient god associated with sacrifice) to describe the sacrifices humanity, specifically workers, have to make to industrialization. As the hero of the film travels into the workers' city, he watches as his fellow men are consumed by, and made slave to, their work, which is symbolized by the transformation of the giant machine into a man-devouring demon ("Moloch").

Works Cited

Adorno, Theodor. *The Culture Industry.* Ed. J. M. Bernstein. London: Routledge, 1991.

_____. "The Curves of the Needle." *The Weimar Republic Sourcebook.* Eds. Anton Kaes, Martin Jay, and Edward Dimendberg. Berkeley: U of California P, 1994. 605–607.

Armstrong, Tim. *Modernism, Technology, and the Body.* Cambridge, England: Cambridge UP, 1998.

Brecht, Bertolt. "Auf den kleinen Radioapparat." *Gedichte 4.* Frankfurt: Suhrkamp, 1961.

_____. "Suggestions for the Director of Radio Broadcasting." *Brecht on Film and Radio.* Ed. and trans. Marc Silberman. London: Methuen, 2000.

_____. "To a Portable Radio." *Bertolt Brecht: Poems 1913–1956.* Eds. John Willett and Ralph Manheim. London: Methuen, 1976.

Bulgakov, Mikhail. *The Master and Margarita.* Trans. Richard Pevear and Larissa Volokhonsky. New York: Penguin, 1997.

Danius, Sara. *The Senses of Modernism: Technology, Perception, and Aesthetics.* Ithaca: Cornell UP, 2002.

Fitzgerald, F. Scott. *The Great Gatsby.* 1925. New York: Simon, 1995.

Groene, Horst. "Agrarianism and Technology in Steinbeck's *The Grapes of Wrath.*" *Southern Review* 9.1 (1976): 27–31.

Huyssen, Andreas. *After the Great Divide: Modernism, Mass Culture, Postmodernism.* Bloomington: Indiana UP, 1986.

James, Henry. *In the Cage.* 1898. New York: Quill Pen, 2008.

Joyce, James. *Ulysses.* 1922. Ed. Hans Walter Gabler. New York: Vintage, 1986.

Kenner, Hugh. *The Mechanic Muse.* New York: Oxford UP, 1987.

Kern, Stephen. *The Culture of Time and Space, 1880–1918.* Cambridge, MA: Harvard UP, 1983.

Lewis, Wyndham. "Manifesto." *Modernism: An Anthology.* Ed. Lawrence Rainey. Malden: Blackwell, 2005. 201–206.

MacPhee, Laurence E. "The Great Gatsby's 'Romance Motoring': Nick Carraway and Jordan Baker." *Modern Fiction Studies* 18.2 (1972): 207–12.

Mao, Douglas, and Rebecca L. Walkowitz. "The New Modernist Studies." *PMLA* 123.3 (2008): 737–48.

Marinetti, F. T. "The Founding and the Manifesto of Futurism." *Modernism: An Anthology.* Ed. Lawrence Rainey. Malden: Blackwell, 2005. 3–6.

_____. "Technical Manifesto of Futurist Literature." *Modernism: An Anthology.* Ed. Lawrence Rainey. Malden: Blackwell, 2005. 15–19.

Menke, Richard. "Telegraphic Realism: Henry James's *In the Cage.*" *PMLA* 115.5 (2000): 975–90.

Metropolis. Dir. Fritz Lang. Perf. Brigitte Helm and Alfred Abel. Paramount, 1927. DVD.

Modern Times. Dir. Charles Chaplin. Perf. Charles Chaplin and Paulette Goddard. Warner, 1936. DVD.

Owen, Wilfred. "Dulce et Decorum Est." *World War One British Poets*. Ed. Candice Ward. Mineola: Dover, 1997. 21–22.

Pollard, Tomas. "Telegraphing the Sentence and the Story: Iconicity in *In the Cage* by Henry James." *European Journal of English Studies* 5.1 (2001): 81–96.

Sinclair, Upton. *The Jungle*. 1906. New York: Penguin, 1986.

Steinbeck, John. *The Grapes of Wrath*. 1939. New York: Penguin, 2006.

Stoker, Bram. *Dracula*. 1897. Ed. John Paul Riquelme. New York: Bedford, 2002.

Ward, Candice, ed. *World War One British Poets*. Mineola: Dover, 1997.

Wicke, Jennifer. "Joyce and Consumer Culture." *Cambridge Companion to James Joyce*. Ed. Derek Attridge. 2nd ed. Cambridge, England: Cambridge UP, 2004. 234–53.

_____. "Vampiric Typewriting: *Dracula* and Its Media." *ELH* 59.2 (1992): 467–93.

Woolf, Virginia. *Between the Acts*. New York: Harcourt, 1970.

_____. *Mrs. Dalloway*. New York: Harcourt, 1981.

Inventions in Literature: Time Travel in the Works of H. G. Wells, Mark Twain, and Douglas Adams _____

Claire Menck

In 1819, Washington Irving published a short story about an old man named Rip Van Winkle who falls asleep and is mysteriously transported forward in time. In the Western canon, this is perhaps the earliest work of fiction to mention the idea of traveling through time. Literature about time travel has since evolved to address complex social, philosophical, and technological issues. Travel through multiple dimensions, including the fourth dimension (time), and potential fifth dimensions (possible or parallel worlds), assumes that we can transport our consciousness into other realms. Time travel prompts the question: what happens when we transfer our forward, linear-moving consciousness backward or forward in time? Authors have used this core dilemma of time travel to introduce interesting and provocative elements into their narratives.

Time travelers are confronted with a series of complex paradoxes as they move forward and backward in time, including parallel worlds, causal loops, and multiple consciousness. The incorporation of time travel transforms linear narratives (that is, stories that start at point A and move logically to points B, C, and beyond) into nonlinear narratives, in which characters move back and forth on their own timelines and interact with others at multiple points in their life journeys. The popular British science-fiction character Doctor Who aptly sums up this alteration to the conventional narrative arc when he explains that time does not just move forward but instead is sort of "wibbly-wobbly, timey-wimey stuff" ("Blink"), looping backward and forward in a series of paradoxical but interconnected loops.

Literature that addresses the problems and potential of time travel has several consistent themes and characteristics. Some of the most popular representations of the genre include Mark Twain's *A Connecticut Yankee in King Arthur's Court* (1889) and H. G. Wells's *The Time Machine* (1895), as well as more modern interpretations, such as

Douglas Adams's *The Hitchhiker's Guide to the Galaxy* (1979), *Doctor Who* (1963–89; 2005–), C. S. Lewis's *Narnia Chronicles* (1950–56), Madeleine L'Engle's *Wrinkle in Time* series (1962–86), and the BBC series *Life on Mars* (2006–2007). The authors of these texts employ the technology of time travel to influence character choices within the narrative structure of the story. They also illustrate the critical difference between time travelers who actively chose to travel through time and those who are thrust into time travel unwillingly. The distinction between choice and happenstance defines the science fiction genre as distinct from fantasy, and integrates the topics of science and technology as important components of the narrative construction. Indeed, as we will see, the time-travel machine (or ship) becomes a character within the narrative itself.

As the idea of time travel evolves, contemporary issues arise, including the evolution of noncyclical narratives addressing wormholes to other versions of our world, in which unlimited outcomes of a single event are played out simultaneously. In this way, authors imply the potential of multiple consciousnesses across parallel and possible worlds. Characters are introduced into earlier periods in their own lives and the lives of others who will impact their own destiny. One of many philosophical issues raised by time travel in literature is the following question (also known as the "grandfather paradox"): to what extent can people change their destiny? This plot device acts as a "machine for producing possible worlds" (Eco 246), in which authors can radically alter the narrative timeline and introduce conflicts based on the paradox of multiple temporal and spatial realities. By shifting a character's location in space and time, an author develops the narrative arc of a story.

The History and Themes of Time Travel in Literature

The concept of time travel in Western literature first shows up in eighteenth-century fantastic fictions that focused on the idea of people being transported into the future, such as Samuel Madden's *Memoirs of the Twentieth Century* (1733). In these tales, magical forces take travelers away from their present time and move them into the future.

In the nineteenth century, time travel became a more popular topic for authors. A notable example is Charles Dickens's *A Christmas Carol* (1843), one of the first works of fiction to deal with the concept of altered narrative time. Dickens's story relies on time travel as a plot device, allowing characters to move back and forth on their own timeline in order to alter their future. Ebenezer Scrooge is confronted with his past, present, and future selves so that he can make changes in his present that will alter his future.

Time travel is a plot mechanism that allows the author to introduce the potential of altered outcomes through technology, albeit magical technology. Mark Twain uses a similar approach in *A Connecticut Yankee in King Arthur's Court*. The main character, Hank Morgan, is transported to the distant past after he is struck on the head. It is not until H. G. Wells introduces us to *The Time Machine* that we first encounter intentional time travel enabled through the application of science and technology.

The concept of traveling forward and backward in time presents several philosophical and scientific dilemmas. D. H. Mellor reminds us that to be present in any time means "you must be able to affect, as well as be affected by, whatever else is there. In other words, you must be able to *interact* with it" (51). In this worldview, simply reading about or imagining another time, no matter how detailed, does not place you in that time. The core conflict with the concept of time travel is that we do not have a technological way to transport ourselves to another physical reality. H. G. Wells makes the first attempt to address this problem by introducing a machine that allows the user to physically transport himself or herself to another place in time.

Aside from the issue of technical transport to another place in time, there are multiple philosophical paradoxes associated with time travel that emerge throughout nineteenth-century and twentieth-century literature. The concept of travel in a fourth dimension is first noted in

Jean d'Alembert's "Dimensions" (1754), in which he introduced the idea of "space-time," merging space and time into a single mathematical formula. Throughout the nineteenth and early twentieth centuries, philosophers and mathematicians took up the idea of a fourth dimension—most notably Charles Howard Hilton, Bertrand Russell, and writer H. P. Lovecraft.[1]

In the nineteenth century, the study of physics and quantum theory advanced the conversation about the potential for and problems with time travel. Albert Einstein's theory of relativity allowed for a theoretical model that engaged with time travel's possibility. This potential opened up deeper questions about some of the inherent paradoxes of traveling in time, including, for example, the grandfather paradox. Alasdair Richmond sums up the paradox's basic premise:

> The standard objection to time travel runs: if time travel were possible, backward time travelers would be able to create contradictory states of affairs, for instance by killing their own grandfathers before those grandfathers have become parents and thereby making their own existence impossible. (299)

This dilemma draws on a concept of causal loops, or events that rely on each other and directly impact one another. If one were to kill one's grandfather, for instance, one would not exist, rendering the event impossible. If one of those events were to be changed, it would change all subsequent events.

From a literary standpoint, a causal loop introduces a dramatic shift in narrative time and structure. Traditional linear time allows characters to move forward and references to events in the past as flashbacks. In science fiction, characters can exist in multiple times simultaneously. One such example occurs in an episode of the popular British television show *Doctor Who*, "Blink." The tenth iteration of the Doctor directs characters' actions through a series of DVD recordings made from a transcript that he received from a future self.[2] Over the course of the story, Larry transcribes as the future Doctor reads to him on a series of DVDs. The transcript is being both read and written at the same time. Past events are dependent on future events; they are a paired event, forming a causal loop that moves in on itself. The plot relies on the paradox of the paired event to move the narrative forward. The technology of time travel is not only a narrative strategy that raises the question of how characters influence future events but also a central topic of the story. The causal loop of the two Doctors existing at the same time is the central dilemma of the narrative. The characters must work through how time is moving to escape and survive.

Causal loops also raise a question of multiple consciousnesses. If two versions of the Doctor rely on each other for their existence, which Doctor is the real one? Which consciousness is valid? Arguably, the answer is both. Narrative structures that include two temporal spaces at the same time open up the potential for characters with multiple consciousnesses—that is, characters that exist in two places at the same time. How we know and understand the world—our epistemological worldview in general—is suddenly expanded if the narrative structure of a story allows each character to exist and influence events in such a way.

Characters are confronted with a series of disorienting dilemmas brought about by shifts in time. Time travel causes a "kind of back and forth movement [that] is culturally disorienting, since it involves a constant shifting of perspectives and hence a questioning of traditional assumptions" (Cantor and Hufnagel 49). These changes in time require that characters engage with events, either by chance or by circumstance. Time travel becomes the central motivating aspect of the narrative, as characters must work through the question of how time affects and is affected by their actions. In this way, authors engage the possibility of multiple outcomes and altered states. The distinction between intentional and forced time travel is also important because it introduces the use of technology as a tool for facilitating time travel, regardless of its philosophical and mathematical dilemmas. Characters that choose to travel in time invite the possibilities of altered states, for they are willing and, often, eager to understand the past or influence the future.

Choice

In H. G. Wells's *The Time Machine*, the unnamed main character builds a time machine that allows him to travel far into the future, and eventually back to his own time. Wells's narrative represents time travel as intentional, and it uses technology to engage and explain movement in time. Wells begins his story with a detailed description of how time travel is possible, finishing with an eloquent description of the time machine itself:

> I remember vividly the flickering light, his queer, broad head in silhouette, the dance of the shadows, how we all followed him, puzzled but incredulous, and how there in the laboratory we beheld a larger edition of the little mechanism we had seen vanish from before our eyes. Parts were of nickel, parts of ivory, parts had certainly been filed or sawn out of rock crystal. The thing was generally complete, but the twisted crystalline bars lay unfinished upon the bench (10).

The time machine ultimately becomes a character in the story when it is stolen by the underworld race of creatures called Morlocks. Wells's main character spends the majority of the narrative trapped in a future time because he is separated from the machine and cannot return home. This separation introduces a deep internal conflict when the protagonist realizes that he is separated from his own world and everything in it. The radical change in the world over the centuries he has traveled virtually renders it a new place, although geographically it is the same as the one he has left in the past.

Many themes in *The Time Machine* are consistent with other literature of the period. The main character is essentially engaged in a voyage of discovery not unlike Conrad's *Heart of Darkness* (1902). Cantor and Hufnagel remind us that this contemporary influence on

Wells impacted his narrative tale: "It is therefore understandable that when he was trying to imagine a journey into the future, he ended up modeling it on something more familiar, a journey to the imperial frontier" (36). The storytelling is clearly linear; we hear about the journey as the main character tells it to friends over dinner. The story deals with another world, in which two rival races coexist in apparent harmony, but as the story unfolds we realize that one race clearly dominates the other. The main character is an explorer from another world entering into a new and exotic time. The only clear difference between this narrative form and other colonial adventure stories is the introduction of time-travel technology in the time machine itself.

Similarly, the television show *Doctor Who* relies heavily on the ship the Doctor uses to travel through time and space, the TARDIS (an acronym for Time and Relative Dimension in Space). The Doctor is a Time Lord, one of a race of historian-scholars with the ability to travel through time. The series' basic premise is based on his theft of the TARDIS to escape his home planet and travel on his own. Even in its earliest iterations in the early 1960s, the TARDIS was shown to have its own distinct personality, often sending its occupants off course or trying to communicate through a series of mechanical messages. When the series was introduced a second time in 2005, the TARDIS was personified as a living being.[3] In the episode "The Doctor's Wife," the TARDIS is brought into human form and expresses her deep love and devotion to the Doctor. The personification of the ship advances Wells's idea of technology merely as a tool for exploration, imagining the Doctor as having a relationship with her. At a critical point in the episode, the Doctor and the personified TARDIS (named Idris) are trapped in another dimension. Idris is rapidly dying and must be returned to the physical space of the TARDIS, so her consciousness can reenter its true form. The Doctor builds a temporary time machine but cannot get it to work. When he gives up hope and tells Idris he has nothing left, she leans into him and says: "My silly fool, you have what you've always had—you have me," and breathes her own essence into the machine, causing it to hum into life.

In this narrative, the technology of time travel is personified in the physical being of Idris—she literally breathes the force required to engage the machine. In this way, time travel evolves into a form of consciousness itself. Writer Neil Gaiman appropriately titled the episode "The Doctor's Wife" to imply that a time traveler is married to his ship. The time traveler of *The Time Machine* and the Doctor both struggle to control their time machines, which careen them through time and take them on adventures they do not necessarily anticipate but have engaged in willingly. Technology is a critical part of the narratives, and a key earmark of the science-fiction genre. Technology is the aspect of the genre that sets it in stark contrast to the unintentional time travel of fantasy fiction, in which characters are removed from the linear time stream and placed in another time against their will or without their consent.

Happenstance

Mark Twain's *A Connecticut Yankee in King Arthur's Court* tells the story of a man who is hit on the head and transported through time and space to medieval England. The story places Hank Morgan in prison, sentenced to die on June 22, 528—coincidentally the date of a full solar eclipse. Having been transported to the past, Hank is aware of the event and prophesizes it to the court, eventually winning favor and saving his life. Later, a magic spell transports Hank 1,300 years into the future.

In this case, time travel is the result of an accident and magical spells. Twain uses time travel as a mechanism to make a commentary on chivalry and the monarchy. Hank states: "men write many fine and plausible arguments in support of monarchy, but the fact remains that where every man in a State has a vote, brutal laws are impossible" (169). Twain also juxtaposes the magical belief system of medieval

England with Hank's own nineteenth-century logic, founded in the rationality of the scientific method.

In the chapter "A Competitive Examination," Hank shows off his modern knowledge of reading, arithmetic, and science to cross-examine a potential army officer and influence the competition for the post. He uses knowledge of the future to impact events in the past with no concern for the effect they might have on later events. Twain is not interested in the grandfather paradox, in which future knowledge is introduced into a prior age; instead, he uses time travel as a plot device to advance his underlying focus: the division between science and magic, and their roles in the function of the nation state. In light of this primary focus, the mechanism of time travel in Twain's novel is less significant. Time travel allows Twain to compare two different social and belief systems, as he uses Hank to elaborate on his own judgments. The technology of time travel is secondary to the central project of contrasting of the belief systems of the past and the present.

Similarly, the contemporary BBC series *Life on Mars* tells the story of Sam Tyler, who is hit by a car and transported from the early 2000s to 1973. It is never stated clearly if Sam has really traveled back in time or if he is in a coma and dreaming, but eventually he comes to prefer his new time, fighting to go back to the 1970s after he has been returned to the future. In the first episode, we find Sam, a police detective, struggling to solve a murder in 1973 that bears an eerie resemblance to a murder he had been investigating in 2006, before his accident. As the story unfolds, we discover that the murderer was sent to a mental institution in 1973 and released thirty years later, only to commit the same crimes again. At the end of the episode, Sam finds a piece of evidence showing that the man accused of the crime is mentally insane. Sam's boss, Gene Hunt, tells him that if he reveals the evidence in court the murderer will be released. Years before computers and expert witnesses, Sam confronts the choice of destroying the evidence that will prevent further murders in the future. He applies his knowledge to change future events. This ethical dilemma establishes

Sam's character within the context of the narrative. As in Twain's novel, this use of time travel is a simple plot device, not an investigation of the technological, scientific, or philosophical paradoxes of time travel.

These narratives, and others like them, use time travel as an incidental tool to introduce conflict into the plot. They explore time travel as fantasy, not as an extension of science and technology. In contrast, Wells and *Doctor Who* employ time travel as an essential element within the plot. Wells goes to great lengths in the first chapter of *The Time Machine* to explain how the machine works, and the TARDIS in *Doctor Who* is arguably the only consistent character throughout the new and classic series (even the character of the Doctor changes every time he regenerates). Science fiction engages the technology and science of time travel, whereas works of fantasy and social commentary use time travel primarily as a plot device. In the latter category, the randomness of time travel stands in contrast to the intentional and technological investigation of time travel in the former. This difference is visible in the role that time travel plays in terms of plot. In science fiction, time travel becomes a character (as illustrated by Idris, the Doctor's time machine), and engages in the plot as an actor. Conversely, fantasy incorporates time travel as a plot device for introducing more salient topics. As the technology of space travel has advanced, however, so has the philosophical and epistemological function of time travel within narrative constructions. These technologies open up new possibilities for authors to radically alter the narrative timelines of their works.

The Future Is Over There

In contemporary literature, time travel has evolved to confront several complex issues that bend the lines between fantasy and science fiction. In contrast to the idea of a fourth dimension, a second school of thought arose in the late twentieth century concerning the possibility of parallel or possible worlds. Possible world theory purports that reality is "the sum of the imaginable rather than . . . the sum of what exists" (Ryan 644). Based in large part on David Lewis's *On the Plurality of*

Worlds (1986), which suggests that multiple worlds exist and that each world is a distinct and real entity, this theory does not draw a distinction between lived and imagined experience. In a parallel world, the same individuals inhabit the same space, but they live out different potential outcomes. This theory is based on the idea that with every choice we leave aside other choices. In a parallel world, those other choices are lived out, leading to new outcomes and possibilities. Similarly, in a possible world, events are based on a complete modal system, which is a world of its own reality. The literary scholar and critic Marie-Laure Ryan explains:

> When we read a text of narrative fiction, we take some statements as establishing hard facts for the story world and others as describing what is merely possible or what exists only in the minds of the characters. In other words, a fiction is not just a nonactual possible world; it is a complete modal system centered around its own actual world (Ryan 646).

The narrative structure created by the author is a total world structure; it exists when the reader engages it. Possible worlds allow authors to use multiple interpretations of a world to illustrate how a character's specific choices influence outcomes.

Madeleine L'Engle's *A Wrinkle in Time* and J. K. Rowling's *Harry Potter* series also represent time travel in possible worlds. In *Harry Potter*, students must enter the world of Hogwarts School by running at a train platform that is invisible to all but those chosen. The story also uses magical tools: "portkeys" allow characters to travel between places and times. "Floo powder" and the "Floo network" allow characters to travel through time and space, and to see other realities and potential outcomes. Authors use these magical technologies to show characters and readers critical events from the past. Harry Potter learns about his parents and his teachers by glimpsing episodes of their distant past.

In *A Wrinkle in Time*, L'Engle uses a similar device, called "tessering," to allow characters to move into a fifth dimension within a fold of time and space. In both series, these travels are planned and orchestrated. Characters do not engage a specific form of machinery to travel, yet they interact with technology that allows skilled users to travel intentionally through time and space into parallel and possible worlds. Albus Dumbledore demonstrates this skill when, in need of a quick escape from Hogwarts, he produces a portkey (Rowling). Madeleine L'Engle employs a similar event when the character Mrs. Whatsit transports the primary characters, Meg and Charles Wallace and Meg's schoolmate Calvin, to a variety of worlds and times, so that they may understand what is happening in their present time (L'Engle). These examples illustrate authors' use of time travel as a way to show past events and their influence on the present. They are also employed intentionally to influence character choices and, subsequently, future events.

C. S. Lewis and Douglas Adams employ a third example of this kind of travel through time and space in the series *The Chronicles of Narnia* and *The Hitchhiker's Guide to the Galaxy*. In Lewis's series, characters travel to the possible world of Narnia through a clothes wardrobe. The physical travel device is the wardrobe (an intentional entrance to Narnia), which allows the four main characters to travel back and forth between this world and the other. In *Life, the Universe, and Everything* (1982), Adams uses the "anachronistic sofa" as an intentional device for traveling through the continuum of time and space. Both stories employ technological tools (the wardrobe and the sofa) in a manner similar to Wells' time machine and the Doctor's TARDIS, but neither employs traditional machines; rather the wardrobe and the sofa are wormholes into other parts of the space-time continuum and alternate worlds. As defined by philosophers Craig Callender and Ralph Edney, "a wormhole is a tunnel, made out of spacetime, between two different points of spacetime" (Callender and Edney 115).

In all of these stories, technology allows characters to travel through the dimensions of space and time to parallel worlds, or possible realities.

These technologies enable fantastical and unexplained abilities that play on the use of time travel in fantasy literature. Authors, however, clearly define these as acquired and valid skill sets. While such skills may be magical in our own reality, Albus Dumbledore is clearly in control of the knowledge and skills that produce a portkey at his command. This draws on the intentionality of travel through time and space in the more traditional science-fiction realm. There is an implied acceptance of the possibility of travel through space and multiple dimensions. This acceptance marks an evolution from earlier uses of time travel, in which it appeared as an accidental event to move along a plot line; contemporary literature uses the technology of time travel as a critical component of the skills and knowledge that characters need to survive. Authors empower their characters with the skill to move through time and space as a way to engage the plot and move the narrative forward. Making time travel inextricable from character raises a critical question: how do we come to know our world and our place in it?

How Do We Know What We Know?

Philosophers such as Edward Husserl, Maurice Merleau-Ponty, and Jean-Paul Sartre have asked the question, how do we know what we know about our own experience? Epistemology is the examination and study of how we experience and know our world, and focusing in particular on the interface between consciousness and reality. The examples given thus far engage time and dimensional travel as a way to move a traditional plot forward in a linear manner: characters start at point A and travel through a series of events that eventually resolve the plot. Even though characters might move back and forth in time, their own personal journey is linear in nature.

Contemporary literature that deals with time and dimensional travel has begun to question the linearity of characters' consciousness. Authors like Milorad Pavić develop stories that require the reader to jump throughout the text to build a coherent storyline. Different characters travel in different directions throughout the text, intersecting one another at various points in their timelines, and sometimes crossing over in the future and the past. Perhaps the most contemporary example of this kind of ergodic literature is the series of *Doctor Who* episodes written primarily by Steven Moffatt. The character River Song is introduced in series four of the new series.[4] She returns in series five and six as a primary character. As we progress through the story, we become aware that River's narrative progression moves counterclockwise to the Doctor's—every time he experiences something with her for the first time (for example, a kiss), she experiences it for the last time. Their narrative consciousnesses move in counter directions.

The shift in how characters experience their own consciousness marks a fundamental shift in how authors use time to tell a story. In traditional science fiction, the technology and basic philosophical questions of time travel are investigated and play a critical role in the telling of the story, as is the case in Wells's *Time Machine*. Fantasy literature relies on time and dimensional travel to advance traditionally linear plots, as is the case in Twain's *Connecticut Yankee*. Contemporary literature advances the concept of time travel by questioning the construction of linear consciousness. Subsequently, the plot moves forward and backward through the same events simultaneously. A character's story is told by moving along nonlinear points in their timeline, and even backward (as is the case with River Song).

The ubiquitousness of time travel in modern narratives means audiences are more alert to its occurrences and more astute about its use in defining character, setting, and plot. The ability of characters to manipulate the sequence of time marks a fundamental shift in how authors construct narrative timelines, and how readers (or viewers) interact with those characters. Readers (and viewers) no longer simply witness the development of linear events, we are asked now to engage with the characters, discovering multiple narratives as they do. For example, the Doctor ages as his companion, River Song, grows younger. The same story is told from two different perspectives with shared events. This narrative strategy indicates an evolution from the philosophical potential of early interpretations of time travel. If time can move backward and forward, why can it not do so at the same time? Indeed, as the good Doctor reminds us, this new narratology is "wibbly-wobbly, timey-wimey stuff."

In *Hamlet on the Holodeck* (1997), Janet Murray suggests that new technologies, like time travel, pose disorienting dilemmas for tech-savvy readers used to interacting with digital media through computers, mobile media, and gaming devices. Murray points out that the computer

> is first and foremost a representational medium, a means for modeling the world that adds its own potent properties to the traditional media it has assimilated so quickly. As the most powerful representational medium yet invented, it should be put to the highest tasks of society. (284)

Authors must create narratives that draw readers into the progress of the story because readers demand interaction with the characters in new ways. In the case of *Doctor Who*, it is not uncommon to see lively debate about River Song's identity and origins on Internet social media sites like Tumblr. In this way, readers interact with the stories themselves, even generating their own fictional versions of the stories in "fanfics" (fan fictions), websites such as A Teaspoon and an Open Mind, or through "cosplay" (costume play) at science-fiction conventions like Comic-Con. The technology of time travel offers a unique and disorienting way to simulate interactive storytelling between authors and readers, expanding their narrative universe throughout time and space.

Notes

1. For a more complete description of this lineage, please see Halperin and Labrosse, 2009.
2. The character of the Doctor is a Time Lord, a species from the planet Gallifrey, who can regenerate twelve times. By 2011, there were eleven iterations of the character.

3. The original *Doctor Who* series (often referred to as *Classic Who*) aired on the BBC from 1963 to 1989. It was brought back briefly in a film version in 1996. The new series (often referred to as *New Who*) was brought back in 2005.
4. The original *Doctor Who* series ran for twenty-three seasons between 1963 and 1989. The new series has had six seasons between 2005 and 2011.

Works Cited

Adams, Douglas. *Life, the Universe, and Everything.* New York: Harmony, 1982.

"Blink." *Doctor Who.* Dir. Hettie MacDonald. BBC. 9 June 2007.

Callender, Craig, and Ralph Edney. *Introducing Time.* Cambridge, England: Totem, 2001.

Cantor, Paul A., and Peter Hufnagel. "The Empire of the Future: Imperialism and Modernism in H. G. Wells." *Studies in the Novel* 38.1 (2006): 36–56.

Dickens, Charles. *A Christmas Carol.* Illus. John Leech. Baltimore: Ottenheimer, 1989.

"The Doctor's Wife." *Doctor Who.* Dir. Richard Clark. BBC. 14 May 2011.

Eco, Umberto. *Semiotics and the Philosophy of Language.* Bloomington: Indiana UP, 1984.

Halpern, Paul, and Michael C. LaBossiere. "Mind Out of Time: Identity, Perception, and the Fourth Dimension in H. P. Lovecraft's 'The Shadow Out of Time' and 'The Dreams in the Witch House." *Extrapolation* 50.3 (2009): 512–33.

L'Engle, Madeleine. *A Wrinkle in Time.* New York: Farrar, 1962.

Lewis, C. S. *The Lion, the Witch, and the Wardrobe.* 1950. Vol. 2. New York: Harper, 2005.

Lewis, David. *On the Plurality of Worlds.* New York: Blackwell, 1986.

_____. "The Paradoxes of Time Travel." *American Philosophical Quarterly* (1976): 145–52.

Life on Mars. By Matthew Graham, Tory Jordan, and Ashley Pharoah. BBC, 9 Jan. 2006.

Mellor, D. H. "Time Travel." *Time.* Ed. Katinka Ridderbos. New York: Cambridge UP, 2002.

Murray, Janet H. *Hamlet on the Holodeck: The Future of Narrative in Cyberspace.* New York: Free Press, 1997.

Richmond, Alasdair. "Recent Work on Time Travel." *Philosophical Books* 44.4 (2003): 297–309.

Rowling, J. K. *Harry Potter and the Order of the Phoenix.* New York: Scholastic, 2007.

Ryan, Marie-Laure. "From Parallel Universes to Possible Worlds: Ontological Pluralism in Physics, Narratology, and Narrative." *Poetics Today* 27.4 (2006): 633–74.

Twain, Mark. *A Connecticut Yankee in King Arthur's Court.* New York: Harper, 1889.

Wells, H. G. *The Time Machine, an Invention.* New York: Holt, 1895.

Literary Models of Technological Mediation: Jean-Paul Sartre's *Nausea* and Julio Cortázar's "The Treasure of Youth"

Luis O. Arata

Literature has the capacity to create models for human behavior, including those affecting use of technology. Argentine writer Julio Cortázar offers a comic vision of how human desires shape technology, while French existentialist writer and philosopher Jean-Paul Sartre depicts how technology helps to solidify a sense of human identity. Both Cortázar's short story "El Tesoro de la Juventud" (1969) and Sartre's novel *Nausea* (1938) describe our relation to technology in ways that enhance our sense of being human.

Technology to Live By

Argentine writer Julio Cortázar included in his collection *Último round* (1969) a brief history of technology entitled "El Tesoro de la Juventud" ("The Treasure of Youth"). This hilarious reverse history begins with a reminder to young students that they should be grateful for the efforts that went into developing the marvels of technology that they enjoy. The narrator proposes to use examples of transportation technology to illustrate the brilliant story of human ingenuity. Surprisingly, his starting point is the jet plane. Young ones should understand that in spite of the convenience of jet planes, they had many disadvantages. It took great skill to invent the propeller plane that brought about the advantages of flying at lower altitude, greater appreciation of the landscape, and increased safety due to slower speed. Further breakthroughs pushed transportation technology beyond the dangers of flying. The railroad allowed for travel at ground level and was quickly followed by the bicycle. The steamship was created for seafaring, and the sailboat soon surpassed it. The narrator concludes that presently it seems unimaginable to think how technology might possibly take us beyond the latest advances, which finally have given us the ability to walk and swim.

Cortázar's playful history of technology hinges on an imagined relentless human appetite for safer, simpler, and more intimate forms of transportation. In a comic way, his ingeniously absurd chronology offers a model of how technological progress follows human wishes rather than the other way around. This story was published in 1969, before global warming became a pressing issue and before there was widespread interest in green technologies. In this respect, the story was ahead of its time, depicting what looks like technological regression as the desired way forward—advancement along the lines of less is more. In a time of increasing interest in smaller, more economical cars, wind technology, and the development of walkways and bicycle lanes, among other apparent regressions, Cortázar's view seems prescient (as well as comical).

Personally, my transportation technology for commuting to work evolved from the climate-controlled comfort of a car to a sturdy pair of shoes and appropriate weather gear. I walk to work and derive great pleasure from watching the changing scenery in a more relaxed and intimate way. Instead of dealing with car expenses, contributing to the rise in greenhouse gases, and negotiating the tense uncertainties of traffic, I get a large portion of my daily dose of exercise by going to work. At home, we are outgrowing the sophisticated technology of central heating and relying increasingly on a fireplace insert in our chimney, a technological gem that gives us a most pleasing source of warmth. I traded the wrist-action of adjusting thermostats for the upper-body action of splitting wood and the weight-lifting exercise of bringing wood to the fireplace, all of which supplement quite well the respiratory and leg training of walking. At night, the family gathers by the soothing glow of flames dancing behind a glass door that keeps smoke away and improves burning efficiency.

The Dalai Lama tells us that technological development and the science that drives it should be shaped above all by ethical considerations. The Dalai Lama, the spiritual leader of Tibet, notes in *The Universe in a Single Atom* (2005) that science, at its best, springs from our desire to reduce suffering and enhance qualities that lead to happier lives. Our quest for understanding can translate to greater wisdom when we temper scientific development with ethics and compassion. But this view is at odds with a commonly held sense that science and technology are driven by their own directions, with one discovery inevitably leading to another, like a chain reaction that cannot be stopped. The Dalai Lama, however, believes that we are more in command of such progress than we think, and therefore we should be more mindful of what we opt to do. His view resonates well with current directions in green technologies and conservation. He notes that progress hinges to a significant extent on choices we make rather than technology's blind evolution. To enhance quality of life those choices should be ones that promote human and natural well-being.

Literary models of the mediation between humans and technology, such as Cortázar's story, are one way to influence, however modestly, technological development. After all, we are the users. We drive the markets and, consequently, the products. In this respect, Cortázar underscores with sustained humor the pivotal role of education in shaping the hearts and minds that propel technological change. His story is narrated as a history lesson for young students about the motivations influencing technological evolution. Students are asked to admire the creative ingenuity that came from a shared desire for safer technologies that bring users in closer contact with nature. The history concludes with what the narrator asserts is irrefutable evidence: people are flocking to beaches in growing numbers, proving without a doubt how much they enjoy engaging at once in the two crowning achievements of human technology—to walk and to swim.

Technology's Evolutionary Direction

Technology becomes what we desire and need it to be, subject to the constraints of nature, and it evolves according to our interests. Cortázar's history gives an eccentric yet resounding thumbs-up to this view of technological development.

Former Stanford University economist and complexity studies pioneer W. Brian Arthur gives an affirmative though scholarly answer to such a view in *The Nature of Technology: What It Is and How It Evolves* (2009). Arthur reflects on technology, drawing on his background as an undergraduate electrical engineering student. He defines technology as nature organized for our purposes, a view that Cortázar's story shares. Like the Dalai Lama, Arthur does not endorse a dehumanized view of technology as evolving independently of our wishes or driven by an internal causality that pulls ahead from discovery to discovery, beyond our control. For Arthur, technological innovation is an "adaptive stretch." Innovation is not pure novelty. The new tends to be the old reconfigured and improved in novel ways, as if stretched. The stretch is adaptive in the sense that technologies evolve in step with human needs and desires as they break new ground; otherwise, they will be ignored, overlooked, misunderstood, and left behind, lacking markets capable of driving their production.

Cortázar captured this view in the way that transportation technologies develop as novel extensions of themselves, harmonizing with human desires rather than moving by unexpected leaps and bounds. From the jet we went to the propeller plane mostly through a change in engine type. Such developments then reconfigure a previous technology. The evolution from one flying machine to another maintained the basic airplane design but gave it a new twist.

Technological innovation as adaptive stretch is a concept that applies to innovation in general. In *Investigations* (2000), biologist Stuart Kauffman argued that innovation tends to happen by nudging a system into an "adjacent possible" space. For instance, propeller and jet planes are in adjacent technological spaces, as slight variations of a similar conception of a flying machine. Moving from one to the other is far easier than going from a jet plane to a rocket-propelled spaceship because their technological spaces are less linked.

Another way to look at this concept of adaptive stretch is through what Russian psychologist Lev Vygotsky called the "zone of proximal development." Vygotsky was interested in how innovation emerges through education, but his view applies to technology as well. Zones of proximal development are personally preferred regions where students can play and learn beyond structured education. To facilitate innovation, an educator tutors students to play creatively in areas in which they have special talents, motivations, and personal preferences that go beyond what is normally covered in the classroom. A tutor helps students toy with their own ideas, potentially facilitating innovations stemming from ideas they already have. This process is an adaptive stretch: the student stretches conceptually into adjacent areas of interest, and the tutor instructs the student on how to adapt constructively to the move into a zone of proximal development. Personal initiative and creativity mix with tutorial guidance to enhance the potential for innovation.

Arthur argues that human needs drive technological developments, but an internal factor drives its evolution as well. When technology is stretched in new directions, the resulting innovations inspire new desires that in turn affect our needs, as if technology seduced us to follow its way. In a similar vein, Pablo Picasso observed that, in the end, painting wins. Picasso stressed that painting cannot go beyond the constraints of the paints used and the surface being painted, no matter what the artist wishes to do. The artist has to adjust to the guiding constraints of the chosen medium and be creative within those constraints. More metaphorically, painting cannot go beyond the evolving techniques of expression, because otherwise the artwork would not resonate with the artist and, more importantly, with the human appreciation that drives the art world. Picasso would not have been a successful artist a century or two earlier. Van Gogh, slightly ahead of his time in expressing his perception of nature, was ignored during his lifetime. Arthur gives the example of painter Paul Klee, who noted that the artist adapts to the medium used. These artists illustrate how innovations come from purposeful human interactions with the limitations of the media employed. Such interactions of human and nonhuman factors inspire recombinant stretches, stimulate development, and adapt them for human use. Innovations do not come as surprises. The genius of innovators comes from how they push slightly ahead to solve pressing problems or develop new techniques within the boundaries of current desires. Genetic manipulations, for instance, do not go beyond what we are willing to accept; otherwise, there will be no funding or support, which is necessary to further that line of research.

This combination of inner and outer drives that shape technology makes its evolution uncertain. Cortázar humorously shares this view as well, noting at the end of his story that progress is unpredictable; we cannot tell what surprises may await us beyond the technological achievements of walking and swimming. Cortázar would have rejoiced at the unexpected development of the World Wide Web, for example, had he lived long enough to see it happen. The Internet enabled closer communications at a time when technology seemed to be dividing us. He would have coveted Wikipedia, as it took the encyclopedia from the heights of expert, exclusive knowledge and enabled everyone to become a potential contributor; this looks like a regressive move but, paradoxically, is a remarkable step forward. Technological innovation has enabled social connectivity to a level that we once enjoyed in small groups, lost after the Industrial Revolution, and now regained at a much higher level than anyone could have suspected three decades ago.

Arthur's view of technology rests in part on the earlier insights of Herbert Simon, recipient of a Nobel Prize in Economics. He received the award for contributing to decision-making theory with his view of bounded rationality. Simon coined the term "satisficing" to name the boundary of rational thought that seeks perfection. Ultimately, economic decisions cannot be perfect, but they should be satisfactory and sufficient for their purposes. In a similar way, Arthur stresses that technology cannot be optimized. To put it succinctly, messy vitality, not the ideal of perfection, is closer to technology's nature. Technology's messy vitality emerges from interactions in a sort of play space, in which human desires and existing tools form new combinations.

In this playful zone of proximal development, imaginative adaptive stretches shape new technologies out of existing ones.

In *The Sciences of the Artificial* (1996), Simon noted in a similar fashion that human preferences drive technological design. Beyond preferences and desires, the other factors that influence designs are the medium in which they function and the history of previous technologies. Arthur's *The Nature of Technology* presents a model of what technology might be all about, a question that remains open. The book underscores that because human purpose drives technology, its evolution is more unpredictable than a drive for greater comfort and convenience. Arthur argues that technology can either alienate us from what makes us human or affirm our humanity; it is up to us. As Cortázar's story illustrates, technology depends on what we wish for. This keeps us in the loop of technological evolution.

Stories affect our development as well, influencing choices and desires. This means that art and culture play a significant role in shaping future technologies. The narratives we cultivate help us to steer technologies in the direction of what we wish to become. With so much diversity in our midst, whose direction will it be? Looping back onto itself, technology may help to weave a shared destiny, one that emerges from our differences without homogenizing the idiosyncrasies that enrich our lives. In this circle of creation, we go hand in hand with technology.

Technology's Puzzle

French existentialist philosopher Jean-Paul Sartre considered his best work to be the novel *Nausea*, which he started writing when he was twenty-six. Originally called *Melancholia*, the novel was rejected by its prospective publisher. Resubmitted a year later with strong recommendations, it was accepted but renamed. Famously, its new title prevailed, and the novel went on to gain great success.

Nausea is written as the diary of its protagonist, Antoine Roquentin, who is carrying out historical research when he suddenly experiences something startling, yet unexplainable and hardly noticeable. The diary entries are like meticulous lab notes, as he sets off to explore the cause of what he can only vaguely describe as a sort of mental nausea.

Gradually, he begins to realize that his puzzling sense of revulsion comes from an intuitive grasp of a condition that is at the heart of existential philosophy. Roquentin senses that the meaningful activities of his life are illusions, that at its core life itself has no sense. There is only existence. Our existence is intrinsically no different than that of any other living entity in the world. Every entity that exists comes into life without reason, manages to survive as long as possible, and in the end dies by pure chance. Life is intrinsically senseless. Human existence is absurd in itself because it lacks intrinsic sense.

Roquentin is stunned when he comes to the realization that his life is meaningless, and that it amounts to nothing beyond his physical presence as a life-form. He could just as well be a crab or a tree root. Existing without reason, he feels superfluous. Whatever sense there is in life does not come from life itself but is made up, fabricated by people, and therefore entirely arbitrary, contingent, uncertain, and accidental. Roquentin's existential angst does not come from the erasing finality of death negating a lifetime's achievements. His nausea is more immediate and based in the present. His life seems to crumble into nothingness under this realization. He puts an end to his historical research because he sees it as just another story, the story of a story of someone who imagined, falsely, that his life made sense.

What eventually cures Roquentin is actually a form of technology: a record playing jazz. He is captivated by the singer's voice. His sense of nausea recedes when he hears the singer and her song repeats. It is not the woman singing that fascinates him but the enduring recording of her voice—solid, unchanging, beautiful, and ethereal.

Why would a recording make such difference in his crumbling life? What does such technology embody to cure his existential nausea?

For Roquentin, this difference does not come from a facile sense of fame. He is under no illusion that a recording confers immortality.

The artist whose voice is preserved in the record has no special human privilege. What appeases his nausea comes from something else, something that will continue even if the record is smashed. Roquentin struggles to pinpoint this paradoxical something. It is always beyond the immediate—beyond the instruments, the voices, the recording, beyond all material entities, which are existents devoid of sense. All existents come about by accident. They come into existence and pass away without making any difference to life itself, which goes on undisturbed. Existents and entities such as him have no inherent reason to be. What captivates him does not stem from natural existence. What Roquentin feels in the music is a solid *sense* of being. The sense is beyond existence, untouched by life, and unscathed by the indifference of contingencies. Breaking the record would not do away with the music. What the recording embodies is a tribute to an act of creation that happened elsewhere. This act did not save the artist as a human being. It was a model of existence to which even the artist would aspire, and the artist was able to express it as a lasting creative act. It is technology that makes possible this paradoxical act of creative defiance against life's lack of sense.

Technology's Humanity

Roquentin writes in his notebook about the night view from his hotel window. He contemplates people interacting with various types of technologies, which should facilitate their lives but fail to uplift their spirits, instead composing a somewhat dreary scene. There is the pub "Railwaymen's Rendezvous," with its lifeless red and white lights. The Paris train has just arrived and people spill out into the street. Like clockwork, tramway number seven arrives and picks up families loaded with suitcases and sleeping children. The tramway heads out into the night toward factories in the east.

The drab view of city life from the hotel window is oddly soothing. He thinks it cured him from the nausea. Yet later encounters with nature trigger the sense of nausea all over again. The nausea seems to emanate from nature itself. He begins to understand the reason for this stark contrast: the world of the city, with its own logic, is not the world of natural existence. Human creations, such as geometry and railroad systems, have solid foundations and clockwork behaviors, but they do not exist in the way a tree exists. Roquentin can understand city life but he feels incapable of understanding natural life.

Roquentin begins to sense that there is an existential difference between such human constructions as logic or geometry, and that of such natural entities as a muddy stone and a chestnut tree, which seems to dig into the undifferentiated existence of the soil and grow for no reason at all. Constructions such as a record of music are subject to reasons and explanations that are foreign to things like stones or trees. Through the reflexivity his journal entries, Roquentin comes to realize that his malaise comes from a feeling of disconnect between nature and what people do with nature. One exists beyond any logic, out of an indifferent inner drive, and the other does not. Natural entities simply exist, but systems that people build exist in a new way, beyond nature's indifference, even if they are rooted in that indifference.

Life has no logic, no meaning. The cure for this despairing realization lies at the heart of its absurdity: people have the capacity to build meaning and superpose sense on that which lacks meaning. Roquentin's malaise comes from thinking, mistakenly, that meaning is rooted in nature itself. People concoct meanings to make life at least bearable on a human scale.

Following Roquentin's reflections, technology stands above and beyond human existence. In *Nausea*, technology remains intimately linked to humanity as an extension rather than a separate entity. As an example from popular culture, the *Terminator* film series gives a quick, dystopian model of what this view might be about. Cyborgs stand above and beyond natural existence, but they also adopt a hostile attitude toward a humanity that tries to control it. *The Matrix* series takes this dystopian perspective a step further into virtual reality. These series illustrate the common trend of technology taking on a life of its own, beyond the control of human creators. Such simplistic outcomes of technological development follow the tradition of Mary Shelley's novel, *Frankenstein* (1818). Sartre, however, gives us a humanizing view of technology as the solution that pulls us out of the absurdity of life—by our own bootstraps, so to speak—and offers us the possibility of constructing meaning. This fragile, ephemeral human meaning is precariously but defiantly perched above existence. How is this possible?

Technological Concoction

On a Tuesday, Roquentin's notebook entry is just two words: "Nothing. Existed" (103). This sums up his indifferent, quiet despair. He recalls a former lover named Anny, who used to treasure what she called "perfect moments." She wanted things to happen in certain ways and would criticize Roquentin for not playing along. He found her behavior increasingly eccentric until they parted ways. Toward the end of the novel, Roquentin begins to understand that what Anny was doing instinctively was introducing meaning into life where there was none. More than just existing, she wanted to feel herself *being*. Now he longs to find a way to bring that sense of accomplishment into his own broken life.

Roquentin's way out appears first in the form of the recorded song he hears at the "Railwaymen's Rendezvous." His train for Paris leaves in forty-five minutes. The gramophone begins to play the jazz song he likes. Roquentin starts imagining a scene in New York from which the music emerges. He asks the waitress to play the record again. Suddenly, he feels that those involved in the song hover in a special realm of life. They are a bit like the heroes of a novel—suspended beyond human existence, models of what we imagine but cannot be.

It is not that the recording immortalizes the artists in any physical sense. What he imagines has little relation to how that song came about. The physicality is gone. Only the recorded music remains imperfectly reproduced through a gramophone. Nevertheless, Roquentin feels a sort of joy. Such acts of creation can justify existence, at least a little, he thinks. He resolves to engage in such acts of creation to overcome the nausea, but he would have to use a different medium and instead create a book or a novel. Behind the words of the novel, the reader would envision something as solid as steel, in the shape of adventures—something that did not exist but went shamelessly beyond. In a rather circular way, Sartre's novel *Nausea* ends as the protagonist decides to write a novel to try to justify his existence: the novel is itself a model of its proposed solution.

To extend Roquentin's solution to other creative media, from the arts to the sciences, we can see how technology mediates such interventions as well. Technology is what enables the creation of beautiful, enduring concoctions that endure, or seem to, beyond existence. Like Leonardo da Vinci's *Mona Lisa*, these works smile back at us mysteriously from a different, unreachable realm that transcends into a form of being that eases Roquentin's feeling that existence is absurd. These technologically mediated creations humanize existence. They infuse meaning where there is none to be found. They enchant nature, illuminating its indifference like a spotlight that shines on a stage of our making, where we prepare to perform. This performance is existence shaped through technologies into human adventures that otherwise would not be. Roquentin notes that such a solution to the problem of existence is an illusion as well; nevertheless, it is a marvelous one.

Modeling Technologies

For Arthur, our relation to technology ultimately hinges on trust and fear. Can we trust technology as much as we trust nature, the place where we made our home? Can we fear it on similar terms? We seem to trust nature more than technology. We tend to accept natural disasters, for instance, as an act of fate. Yet we fear the possibility of technological catastrophes. Arthur thinks this is unreasonable. We can only play along with nature, but we should be able to guide the development of technology, for it is our own creation. Fear of technology emerges when it escapes our control and affects our lives. Arthur emphasizes that people tend to fear technology if we sense that it might take away our freedom, enslaving us in its implacable machinations. Such a reaction is understandable, Arthur acknowledges, but as we develop technologies we must learn to use them properly to enhance rather than downgrade human life.

Writer Robert Pirsig makes a similar point in *Zen and the Art of Motorcycle Maintenance* (1975). He recalls that for the ancient Greeks, *techne*, the root of the word technology, meant "art." Pirsig argues that art and the perceived quality of art constitute an integral part of technology. We have the choice to manufacture nice or ugly technological objects. It is crucial not to lose sight of the fact that we are the makers of technology. Pirsig stresses that we should not feel separated from the technologies we produce. Only when in touch with technology will we be able to shape it according to our human desires in ways that enhance life. From a humanistic perspective, it is imperative that we make decisions that enhance the beauty and worthiness of our creations. The Dalai Lama stressed that technology must support the good of humanity. It is irresponsible to do otherwise. The consequences of such lack of insight are becoming increasingly costly. Maintaining a human perspective on our creative processes will help us to steer away from dystopian disasters, but we have to remain engaged in the loop of technological development, wherever our preferences might place us.

Our fear of technology will increasingly turn to trust as we become more adept at handling our creations responsibly, and steer them effectively in the direction of our dreams, as Cortázar shows with great humor. Technology has become part of what we are. It is woven into the fabric of what makes us human and what allows us to improve our existence, as Sartre portrays in *Nausea*.

We instinctively distinguish between technology that enslaves us and that which extends our nature. Arthur stresses that it is our choice to accept or reject technology that might harm us, deprive us of meaning, deaden our senses, weaken our challenges, weaken our purpose, or separate us from nature. This realization should guide our hand in modeling technologies that help us to extend what we are. Literary models of technological mediation contribute to shaping our own creations. We need to remain aware that we are in the driver's seat. We are in charge of the journey. It is our adventure and we have to keep it that way.

Cortázar and Sartre give two different examples of how technology enhances our being in the world. The ethical way to work with technology is to maintain a human perspective at every step, either with self-motivation or through regulation. We are in control of technological development and can steer in the direction of possibilities and desires, as makers and users of technologies. Ultimately, technology is about us. It extends our capacities to learn, understand, and shape our desires. This, in turn, will entice the development of new technologies, through every means at our disposal, including literary models, which illustrate the function of the human spirit interacting with technology.

Works Cited

Arthur, W. Brian. *The Nature of Technology: What It Is and How It Evolves*. New York: Free Press, 2009.

Bstan-'dzin-rgya-mtsho (Dalai Lama XIV). *The Universe in a Single Atom: The Convergence of Science and Spirituality*. New York: Morgan, 2005.

Cortázar, Julio. "El Tesoro de la Juventud." *Último Round*. Mexico: Siglo XXI, 1969, 23–28.

Kauffman, Stuart. *Investigations*. Oxford: Oxford UP, 2000.

Pirsig, Robert M. *Zen and the Art of Motorcycle Maintenance: An Inquiry into Values*. New York: Bantam, 1975.

Sartre, Jean-Paul. *Nausea*. New York: New Directions, 2007.

Simon, Herbert A. *The Sciences of the Artificial*. 3rd ed. Cambridge, MA: MIT P, 1996.

Vygotsky, L. S. *Mind in Society: The Development of Higher Psychological Processes*. Cambridge, MA: Harvard UP, 1978.

"Art as Technique": Technology, the Avant-Gardes, and the Birth of the Cinema

Annie van den Oever

> But from the perspective of the uncanny, the arrival of celluloid moving pictures constitutes a decisive moment.
>
> —Laura Mulvey, *Death 24x a Second*

An Uncanny Viewing Experience of New Technology

Eminent novelist and poet Vladimir Nabokov, born in Saint Petersburg, Russia, in April 1899, opens his memoir *Speak, Memory* (1951) with a description of the "abyssal," "disturbing," and deeply uncanny experience of watching a "homemade" movie made prior to his birth. Ironically referring to himself as a young "chronophobiac," Nabokov describes how the family movie placed him in a distinctly defamiliarizing relationship to his mother and environment at the age of four. The movie unpleasantly confronted him with the empty baby stroller on the porch, awaiting his arrival, and with his cheerful mother waving at the camera with an "unfamiliar" gesture. All of this, he noticed, took place without a trace of mourning for his absence. *Speak, Memory* opens with the experience:

> The cradle rocks above an abyss, and common sense tells us that our existence is but a brief crack of light between two eternities of darkness. Although the two are identical twins, man, as a rule, views the prenatal abyss with more calm than the one he is heading for. . . . I know, however, of a young chronophobiac who experienced something like panic when looking for the first time at homemade movies that had been taken a few weeks before his birth. He saw a world that was practically unchanged— the same house, the same people—and then realized that he did not exist there at all and that nobody mourned his absence. He caught a glimpse of his mother waving from an upstairs window, and that unfamiliar gesture

disturbed him, as if it were some mysterious farewell. But what particularly frightened him was the sight of a brand-new baby carriage standing there on the porch, with the smug, encroaching air of a coffin; even that was empty, as if, in the reverse course of events, his very bones had disintegrated. (17)

For many reasons, Nabokov's description is highly interesting for early cinema scholars and so-called media archaeologists (scholars who, among other things, excavate the impact of new techniques when they were still considered new). First of all, this short but dense description gives a clear impression of the impact a confrontation with the new medium, cinema, had on a sensitive "chronophobiac" around 1903. In fact, Nabokov only described and analyzed the experience to underline its pivotal impact on his authorship and imagination, which he sees as "the supreme delight of the immortal and the immature" (17). Typically, important sources in the study of Nabokov did not take note of this.[1] In retrospect, it is difficult to understand the disruptive impact of these now old cinematic techniques. Nevertheless, the impact of the still "young" cinema on literature at the beginning of the twentieth century should not be underestimated.

The fact that attention for the medium is missing in so many literary sources also seems, in part, to be a typical institutional misrepresentation of history, suggesting that the field of literature had no real interest in the field of (early) cinema. Generally speaking, one has always taken the assumption for granted that it was the well-established and respected literature and theater traditions that had an impact on the young medium, and not the other way round. This supposition has been thoroughly undermined by the study of early cinema (by Tom Gunning, André Gaudreault, Ian Christie, Richard Taylor, Miriam Hansen, Laura Mulvey, Yuri Tsivian, Frank Kessler, Wanda Strauven, and many others). At last, early cinema studies have been able to make clear that the cinema, especially in its early days in what has now become known as the "medium-specific period," had an enormous impact on audience members who viewed it as a new technology, one that carried intense and estranging impressions for a great many people. As Nabokov writes, the dancing patches of light on the film screen might have had an impact on the imagination of the "immortal and the immature" in those early years of cinema (17). Again, cinema's impact in the other art forms is not necessarily due to masterful craftsmanship. Rather, the impact stemmed from the uncanny "strangeness" of the new medium—that is, cinema's ability to make everything it displayed simultaneously real and strange. The cinema opened up and touched upon regressive and nightmarish material: visions viewers would not necessarily have wanted to be confronted with. Nabokov immediately and ironically thinks of Sigmund Freud in this respect, as he is wont to do:

> I have ransacked my oldest dreams for keys and clues—and let me say at once that I reject completely the vulgar, shabby, fundamentally medieval world of Freud, with its crankish quest for sexual symbols . . . and its bitter little embryos, spying, from their natural nooks, upon the love life of their parents. (18)

Cinema created a wholly new perceptual experience of the world. How deeply the experience of the new technique went becomes clear from the following:

> I felt myself plunged abruptly into a radiant and mobile medium that was none other than the pure element of time. One shared it—just as exited bathers share shining seawater—with creatures that were not oneself but that were joined to one by time's common flow, an environment quite different from the spatial world, which not only man but apes and butterflies can perceive. (19)

As with so many poets, novelists, and artists of the day, the new "cinema machine" (Mulvey) suddenly facilitated the imagining of existential metaphors regarding life, death, and time, as well as a deeply felt and prolonged sense of the present. The experience of the "new" also would trigger slightly utopian and futuristic views of the twentieth century.

The Early Cinema Experience and New Optical Techniques

Seeing a movie in those early days was a deeply alienating experience for most people. It is important to understand that in this very context Nabokov's fellow townsman, the young art scholar Victor Shklovsky, wrote his reflection on "ostranenie," or the way techniques *defamiliarize*. Russian writer Maxim Gorky phrased it famously in his often cited critique of 1896 (and it is constructive to cite him, to evoke the experience of stupor and excitement at seeing the first moving images)—that aspect of strangeness that a twenty-first-century audience has lost:

> If you only knew how *strange* it felt. There were no sounds and no colours. Everything—earth, trees, people, water, air—was portrayed in a grey monotone: in a grey sky there were grey rays of sunlight; in grey faces—grey eyes. . . . Silently the ash-grey foliage of the trees swayed in the wind and the grey silhouettes of the people glided silently along the grey ground, as if condemned to eternal silence and cruelly punished by being deprived of all life's colours. (qtd. in Tsivian 2)

After more than a century of film, the medium has stabilized into a mimetic tradition. In retrospect, it is very hard, almost impossible, to understand such experiences and exclamations when viewed from our current perspective, because both film and viewing practices have changed radically since 1896. Film scholar Tom Gunning described the *stupefying* effect of early cinema on its early spectators in several pieces. Judging from the responses of those early moviegoers, it seems that for them seeing movies was an "astonishing" experience.[2] For this reason, it should come as no surprise to twenty-first-century readers that the cinema triggered an immense outpouring of reactions in response to the distorting power of the new optical technology. Such responses as Maxim Gorky's are in many ways indicative of "the period of the discovery of the cinema" (Gunning, *Early Cinema* xxi) as a "medium-specific period in film history," with a "medium-sensitive film viewer" (Tsivian 217). This viewer "went to see a film show in order to experience the new medium more than to see a specific film" (Gunning, *Early Cinema* xxi). Gunning described and analyzed other confrontations with new technologies (such as electricity) in similar terms: one was utterly thrilled and surprised by the spectacle that the new technology made possible. In response to the Philadelphia Centennial Exposition—one of many such world-famous events during the turn of the century—one spectator sent home a postcard that read only "Oh Oh oooooooo!"[3]

Not all experiences of new technologies were as impressive as those that attended the optical technologies that changed the face of the twentieth century. Optical technologies may have made a deep impression on individuals and culture for several reasons. First, sight and sound tend to define our relation to the world. For this very reason, even the slightest change in the technologies that allow us to see and hear the world may affect and change our imagination and vision of the world. Regarding the "birth" of the cinema, it is important to realize that the "birth" of the photographic image had made quite an impression half a century earlier. Cinema, however, seemed to move even closer to the "real." Going from still to moving images confronted viewers with a moving world, one that suddenly seemed alive and animated. Unlike photography, the cinema created a wholly new viewing culture: a "shared" viewing experience that transformed the viewing of images from an individual to a cultural event. This development may have contributed to cinema's impact on culture at large.

In its early days, film triggered a true cascade of descriptions and reflections by poets and novelists. In 1912, Virginia Woolf famously remarked that film was deeply and utterly "barbaric" (Marcus 102). From Woolf's notebooks we can gather that early audiences responded initially with silence, only to expatiate their excitement an instant later, by means of vivid chatter. Loud chatter, however, does not necessarily indicate that they had found the right words to "frame" the extraordinary viewing experience. Woolf was not the only one who noticed that the experience of an initial confrontation with the "new" could not be verbalized properly at first. Interestingly, Victor Shklovsky made a similar observation, stating that the initial impact of new techniques would not normally be visible in the first instance but only after some time.

How can we explain that new technologies tend to create such a stir both in individuals and in the arts and culture, as historical discourses have testified? And why is the impact of new technologies on art, culture, and the humanities not only overwhelming but also enduring? These questions are very relevant today, for we too are part of a medium-specific interval in history, one that is comparable in many ways to the early decades of the last century. The birth of the avant-garde in Russia, considered in relation to the birth of cinema, illustrates the impact of technology on historical avant-garde movements. In this context and era, the relation between art and technique was radically redefined.

The Early Cinema Experience, the Symbolist Poets, and the Historical Avant-Garde in Russia

Symbolist Poets

For a good understanding of the specific historical context in Russia, it is wise to single out parties and individuals who made their voices heard in the debate of the time: the symbolist poets, the futurist poets, and the so-called Russian formalists, a group of young academics from the fields of language and literature studies, Victor Shklovsky their intellectual leader.[4] It is essential to see that the symbolist poets were more senior than the futurist poets and already established when the younger avant-gardists entered the literary scene. The symbolists simply dominated the debate on the arts in Russia at the time. As such, they also played a crucial role in the cultural reception of the cinema in Russia. Like all other movie-goers, symbolist poets, Andrei Bely among them, were medium-sensitive viewers. The hushing sound of the projector; the scratches on the reel; the unusual ("deadly") silence surrounding the moving and animated figures on the screen; the grayish ("ghostly") tones of the on-screen world; the changing scale of figures and things moving toward the camera, abnormally enlarged at some moments; the seeing of oneself on the screen; or a reversed projection, presenting a reversed course of events—all that was new and unusual to these "inexperienced" viewers was linked to a thing or theme they were familiar with (Tsivian 12). In retrospect, it is obvious that the symbolists "thematized" the technical fallacies and specialties of early cinema in their discourses on the new medium: the theme of "death" was used to refer to moving images when they looked less animated, "doubles" and "double identity" when one saw a familiar face presented in an unfamiliar way, and so on. Thus, the shock effects of the new were channeled and smoothed along old and familiar thematic lines and motives that the symbolist authors knew all too well.

The Futurists: "A Slap in the Face of Public Taste"

Whereas the symbolists were intrigued by the themes they saw displayed on the screen, the futurists' attention was drawn by the very techniques that had such a strong and sudden impact on the imagination. In contrast to the symbolists, the futurists shared and cherished the disruptive and evocative aspects of the early cinema experience. Technologies (optical, visual, and audio) and the ways in which they affect perception became their real focus. In fact, futurist poets immediately made use of what the cinema had to offer in their poetry. They had noted that the new optical technology had an evocative and disruptive perceptual impact on viewers (or more generally, on "percipients"), and they mimicked the fallacies and specialties of the new optical techniques in their verses to produce similarly evocative effects. The futurist poets, Velimir Khlebnikov and Vladimir Mayakovsky among them, played an essential role in the very early avant-garde movements in Europe. As such they had a strong impact not only on audiences and other artists but also on the later avant-garde movements of the 1920s in their own country and the rest of the continent. In December 1912, the futurists presented the provocative manifesto *A Slap in the Face of Public Taste*, which would make its way into history. They entered the public scene as "a bunch of half-wits" in 1913, the very year Russia's "general craze for cinema" peaked (Tsivian 12). They consciously and purposefully chose to disturb and even bully "public taste" with their verses, which were not calmly published but recited offensively and loudly. To catch the attention of the audience, a poet would rage "on raw meat like a vandal," as Mayakovsky wrote in "A Cloud in Trousers," one of his most famous poems. Provoking a disturbance was an essential part of their poetics and performances from the start. For instance, Mayakovsky traveled the country to perform for enormous audiences, dressed in a black suit, six and a half feet tall, reciting and raging with a radish in his buttonhole. It should come as no surprise that cinema and futurist poetry were often compared with each other, and that both were associated with something that was similarly "incoherent, spasmodic, senseless": that icon of modernity, "the increasingly feverish pulse of the big city" (Tsivian 10–13). In short, the futurists had taken note of a simple and obvious fact: accidental techniques, like those attending the new "cinema machine," were able to work suddenly and strongly on the viewer's imagination. This recognition made them rethink and reframe technology, (verse) technique, and the "new" in art altogether. Thus, futurists experimented with the evocative impact of "dumb" and senseless techniques, and with new forms for addressing the viewer, listener, or reader that would awaken the "static," "stupid voyeur" of traditional art forms (Marinetti 127).[5]

However provocative and effective the futurist poets may have been in terms of their performances, they were not very strong theoretically. In fact, one may argue that their poetical reflections were not half as competent as the well-known works by the symbolists, who, for good reason, had dominated the debate. This changed rapidly when Victor Shklovsky entered the scene in that famous year 1913. The young academic theorized on the "strangeness" of the perceptual experiences offered by both early cinema and futurist poets. As a "brilliant" but "brash" young scholar (Erlich 159), Shklovksy, still a freshman at the University of Petersburg, presented a lecture to his futurist friends in the Stray Dog Café called "The Place of Futurism in the History of Language." Richard Sheldon notes that Shklovsky

> maintained that futurist poetry emancipated words from their traditional significance and *restored them to perceptibility* by calling attention to their sounds. The function of art in general, he concluded, should be *to force such new perceptions of the word and the world.* (x, emphasis mine)

In retrospect, the young Victor Shklovsky indeed may have provided the theoretical framework for explaining the impact of new technologies (cinema) and artistic techniques (poetry) from the revolutionary new perspective of perception. In general, it may be said that "the tradition of the avant-garde . . . most coherently addresses the question of technology from the view point of the uncanny and de-familiarization" (Gunning, "Re-Newing Old Technologies" 18). Whereas Mayakovsky and his futurist friends created a revolutionary art practice, Shklovsky and his formalist friends provided a truly new conceptual space for explaining the impact of disruptive techniques, doing so in the form of a brilliant art theory that the futurists were unable to formulate.

Art as Technique

Victor Shklovsky was the first art theorist to understand that any new technique that breaks the automatic routines of perception by "making [the seen] strange" notably slows down, complicates, and deepens the perceptual process, and creates an "art experience." As Shklovsky explained in "Art as Technique," an "art experience" was a prolonged experience of things "as they are perceived and not as they are known" (12). The work was published in 1917 and soon became the manifesto of the so-called Russian formalists. His key word was "ostranenie," or "making strange." Making the world visible once again by making the world "strange" also became the central statement in art and film criticism in the 1920s.[5] In effect, Shklovsky helped shape and frame the experience of the "new" conceptually. Regardless of the genealogy of the idea, and whether or not it can be traced back from film criticism in the 1920s to Shklovsky's reflections on "techniques" in the 1910s, it may be argued that he was the avant-garde theorist of that decade. By theorizing on the relation between technique and art in a radically new way, he envisioned novel ways of making and studying art. In the wake of the new, modernist poetics, Shklovsky conceived a new theory of art. Within this era and context, "Art as Technique," with its emphasis on the "strange" quality of the seen and its impact on perception, stood out as extremely adequate in relation to the early cinema experience, since "making strange" was basically what the new medium did for most of its early spectators. Shklovsky envisioned truly revolutionary implications for art studies, implications that continue to apply in the twenty-first century. He presented a radical approach to art in which technique (technology) and art are studied within the same conceptual framework. His approach remains surprisingly relevant for art, film, and media studies today, as it creates a conceptual space for analyzing the responses to and the cultural impact of new techniques from one and the same perspective—namely, that of perception. Viewing experiences effectively can be conceptualized and analyzed in terms of "(de) automatization," regardless of whether effects are triggered intentionally by an artist or accidentally by a new technology. Conceptually speaking, "Art as Technique" opens new ways of reconsidering the destabilizing impact of new media in culture. If ever there was a field that might profit from the replacement of the "clumsy"[6] dichotomy of "form/content" by the concept of "technique" (or technology), it must be the humanities, and more particularly art, film, and media studies;

this conceptual framework helps us to analyze the effects of both hardware and software, technology and artistic techniques. To see the relevance and productivity of such research, one needs only to recognize that "Art as Technique" brings to light that the genealogies of art and technique are inherently connected.[7]

Technology and the Humanities

Within the broader context of the humanities it is important to understand the implications of Shklovsky's theory. First of all, it should be noted that breaking perceptual routines (a process referred to as "deautomatization") sensitizes viewers to the techniques involved in the process. Second, sensitivity to new techniques and media comes and goes through the processes of automatization and deautomatization. Being desensitized to a technique or medium means that mechanisms of habituation have overcome one's sensitivity to a technique's strangeness. As Shklovsky explained in "Art as Technique:"

> If we start to examine the general laws of perception, we see that as perception becomes habitual, it becomes automatic. Thus, for example, all of our habits retreat into the area of the unconsciously automatic. . . . The process of "algebraization," the over-automatization of an object, permits the greatest economy of perceptive effort. Either objects are assigned only one proper feature—a number, for example—or else they function as though by formula and do not even appear in cognition. (11–12)

The process of deautomatization thus leads to a sensitivity to, and awareness of, technologies and techniques. In contrast, the process of automatization inevitably leads to a decrease of sensitivity regarding the distorting powers of these once new techniques, ultimately making percipients lose sensitivity. Automatization inevitably leads to a point where the presence of techniques in the perceptual process is not noted anymore: a swift shift from medium to mediated may become not only habitual but natural. Being perceived as natural indicates that, once the mechanisms of automatization enhance a smooth shift in the perceptual process from perceptual input to cognition—fully automatic processes unnoticed by the percipients—they may stop taking note of the ontological difference between a tree or cockroach in nature and one on a canvas, photo, TV, laptop, or IMAX screen. It is for this very reason that the special ontological status of the mediated image may be automatically overlooked and go unquestioned. This lack of awareness regarding media is, in itself, an interesting symptom of percipients being desensitized to a medium (e.g., television): it easily leads to an identification of real and mediated. In other words, overlooking the medium is a predictable and almost inevitable consequence of the process of automatization. Once techniques become second nature, we lose sight of them.

What does this automatization imply for the humanities? Not only are the relations between technology, individuals, and cultures dynamic and complex, but the humanities, the field of research that teaches and studies their relationship, is seriously affected by the same processes that make us overlook the presence, history, and impact of technologies in the first place.

Everyday percipients may argue that for everyday life the cognitive mechanism of automatization is adequate and even desirable, as it enhances action that is needed to function properly and economically in everyday life. For example, if a phone rings, we need someone to pick it up right away, without having him or her experience a moment of stupor that prevents immediate action.

Researchers, however, may argue that research is affected by the mechanism of automatization in undesirable ways as well, as research and reflection generally do not benefit from quick shifts between input, cognition, and action. Research in the humanities, more specifically, does not benefit from being desensitized to technology and media, the technologies of representation and communication included. In this light, one must conclude that overlooking technology and media does occur and can be considered a structural problem. In research, automatization is the mechanism underlying the phenomenon.

Nabokov's "Nonnon"

In one of his remarkable novels, Nabokov describes a technical device that deforms and distorts the seen, but since no one knows how the device works, the problem is how to understand and interpret its projections and distortions. This paradox, which makes us realize that knowledge and meanings are unstable things, could easily drive a sensitive person, such as an artist, insane. In Nabokov's *Invitation to a Beheading* (1959), this theme bears on the problem of technology, art, and the humanities, for it adequately sums up the problematic presence of technology in the humanities. Nabokov notes that anything put in front of the device is a "nonnon." With its double negative—non! non!—this neologism acknowledges that, as long as we do not understand the media of our everyday lives, we do not really know anything about the world:

> There are, you know, all sorts of marvelous gimmicks. I remember, for instance when I was a child, there were objects called "*nonnons*" that were popular, and not only among children, but among adults too, and, you see, a special mirror came with them, not just crooked, but completely distorted. You couldn't make out anything of it, it was all gaps and jumble, and made no sense to the eye—yet the crookedness was no ordinary one, but calculated in just such a way as to . . . Or rather, to match its crookedness they had made . . . No, wait a minute, I am explaining badly. Well, you would have a crazy mirror like that and a whole collection of different "*nonnons*," absolutely absurd objects, shapeless, mottled, pockmarked, knobbly things, like some kind of fossils—but the mirror, which completely distorted ordinary objects, now, you see, got real food, that is, when you placed one of these incomprehensible, monstrous objects so that it was reflected in the incomprehensible, monstrous mirror, a marvelous thing happened; minus by minus equaled plus, everything was restored,

everything was fine, and the shapeless speckledness became in the mirror a wonderful, sensible image; flowers, a ship, a person, a landscape. You could have your own portrait custom made, that is, you received some nightmarish jumble, and this thing was you, only the key to you was held by the mirror. Oh, I remember what fun it was, and how it was a little frightening—what if suddenly nothing should come out?—to pick up a new, incomprehensible "*nonnon*" and bring it near the mirror, and see your hand get all scrambled, and at the same time see the meaningless "*nonnon*" turn into a charming picture, so very, very clear. (135)

Notes

1. Surprisingly, Boyd, Nabokov's biographer and an authority on Nabokov in many respects, does not really take note of Nabokov's reflections on film or his relation to early cinema. Scholars who did take note of the relation, in particular Alfred Appel Jr. and Richard Corliss, fully acknowledged the importance of the cinema (rather than individual films) for Nabokov and explored some elements of the relation. But as they prepared their books in the early 1970s and late 1980s, their work could not profit from the new perspectives developed in the early cinema studies of the early 1990s. In this respect, research on Nabokov and the impact of early cinema on his childhood and beyond remains underdeveloped. A rare and interesting exploration of the topic, however, comes from Galya Diment, who has shown an interest in Nabokov's relation to "pre-revolutionary Russian cinema, and, in particular, Evgenii Bauer (1865–1917), the most popular and prolific director of Nabokov's youth."

2. The Russian symbolists of the turn of the century, like the French symbolists they admired, were perfectly skilled in verse technique and often labeled as "in-geneers poetry"—poetry in which "form" and "content" were made to cohere in a sublime way. Opposing the symbolists, the futurists in the 1910s wrote evocative nonsense poetry in which they provocatively mimicked and inserted the type of fallacies created by the new so-called cinema machine. They were a younger and less established generation of poets, and an important part of the early avant-garde movement in Russia. The so-called Russian formalists were their closest friends, and in many ways they knew the avant-garde's techniques and aspirations from early on. Being linguists and philologists with an academic training in these fields, they started to theorize and conceptualize the differences between symbolist and futurist poetics, successfully creating a true revolution in approaches to literature and art. Victor Shklovsky is the recognized initiator and intellectual leader of this movement, and his essay "Art as Technique" is considered the manifesto of Russian formalism.

3. See the interview with Laura Mulvey in Oever's *Ostrannenie: On "Strangeness" and the Moving Image: The History, Reception, and Relevance of a Concept* (2010).

4. See Tom Gunning's "Re-Newing Old Technologies: Astonishment, Second Nature, and the Uncanny in Technology from the Previous Turn-of-the-Century," in *Rethinking Media Change: The Aesthetics of Transition* (2003). See also Gunning's "The Cinema of Attractions: Early Film, Its Spectator, and the Avant-Garde," in *Early Cinema: Space, Frame, Narrative* (1990). See, in particular, Gunning's analysis of the first "astonishment," which touches on the uncanny and the sublime: "An Aesthetic of Astonishment: Early Film and the (In)credulous Spectator," in *Viewing Positions: Ways of Seeing Film* (1994).

5. See Francesco Casetti's *Eye of the Century: Film, Experience, Modernity* (2008).

6. See the discussion of form and technique in Boris Eichenbaum's "The Theory of the 'Formal Method,'" in *Russian Formalist Criticism* (1965).

7. "The history of art is, at least in part, a history of the tools and materials with which art is made" (Straw). For more information, see the Daniel Langlois Foundation (Canada) and its online DOCAM research initiative, which explains the relationship between technological invention and artistic creation "from the beginning." See http://www.docam.ca/en/technological-timeline.html.

Works Cited

Appel, Alfred, Jr. *Nabokov's Dark Cinema*. New York: Oxford UP, 1974.

Boyd, Brian. *Vladimir Nabokov: The Russian Years*. Princeton: Princeton UP, 1993.

Casetti, Francesco. *Eye of the Century: Film, Experience, Modernity*. Trans. Erin Larkin and Jennifer Pranolo. New York: Columbia UP, 2008.

Clancy, Laurie. *The Novels of Vladimir Nabokov*. London: Macmillan, 1984.

Corliss, Richard. *Lolita*. London: BFI, 1994.

Diment, Galya. "From Bauer's Li to Nabokov's Lo: *Lolita* and Early Russian Film." *Cycnos* 24.1. Web. 21 May 2012.

Eichenbaum, Boris. "The Theory of the 'Formal Method.'" *Russian Formalist Criticism*. Ed. Lee T. Lemon and Marion J. Reis. Lincoln: U of Nebraska P, 1965.

Erlich, Victor. "Russian Formalism." *Journal of the History of Ideas* 34.4 (October–December 1973): 627–38.

Gunning, Tom. "An Aesthetic of Astonishment: Early Film and the (In)credulous Spectator." *Viewing Positions: Ways of Seeing Film*. Ed. Linda Williams. New Brunswick: Rutgers UP, 1994. 114–33.

_____. "The Cinema of Attractions. Early Film, Its Spectator and the Avant-Garde." *Early Cinema: Space, Frame, Narrative*. Ed. Thomas Elsaesser. London: BFI, 1990.

_____. "Re-Newing Old Technologies: Astonishment, Second Nature, and the Uncanny in Technology from the Previous Turn-of-the-Century." *Rethinking Media Change: The Aesthetics of Transition*. Ed. David Thorburn and Henry Jenkins. Cambridge, MA: MIT P, 2003. 39–60.

Hyde, G. M. *Vladimir Nabokov: America's Russian Novelist*. London: Marion Boyars, 1977.

Marcus, Laura. *The Tenth Muse: Writing about Cinema in the Modernist Period*. Oxford: Oxford UP, 2007.

Marinetti, Filippo Tommaso. "The Variety Theater 1913." *Futurist Manifestos*. Ed. Umbro Apollonio. New York: Viking, 1973.

Mulvey, Laura. *Death 24x a Second: Stillness and the Moving Image*. London: Reaktion, 2006.

Mulvey, Laura, and Annie van den Oever. "Conversation." *Ostrannenie: On "Strangeness" and the Moving Image: The History, Reception, and Relevance of a Concept*. Ed. Annie van den Oever. Amsterdam: Amsterdam UP, 2010, 185–203.

Nabokov, Vladimir. *Invitation to a Beheading*. Trans. Dimitri Nabokov. New York: Putnam, 1959.

_____. *Speak, Memory: An Autobiography Revisited*. 1947. New York: Penguin, 1982.

Oever, Annie van den. "The Medium-Sensitive Experience and the Paradigmatic Experience of the Grotesque, 'Unnatural' or 'Monstrous.'" N.d. TS.

_____. *Ostrannenie. On "Strangeness" and the Moving Image: The History, Reception, and Relevance of a Concept*. Amsterdam: Amsterdam UP, 2010.

_____. *Sensitizing the Viewer: The Impact of New Techniques and the Art Experience*. Amsterdam: U of Groningen, 2011.

Sheldon, Richard. Introduction. *A Sentimental Journey: Memoirs, 1917–1922*. By Victor Shklovsky. Trans. Richard Sheldon. Champaign: Dalkey Archive, 2004.

Shklovsky, Victor. "Art as Technique." *Russian Formalist Criticism*. Ed. Lee T. Lemon and Marion J. Reis. Lincoln: U of Nebraska P, 1965.

Straw, Will. "Introduction to the Technological Timeline." *Documentation and Conservation of the Media Arts Heritage*. DOCAM Research Alliance, n.d. Web. 25 May 2012.

Tsivian, Yuri. *Early Cinema in Russia and Its Cultural Reception*. Trans. A. Bodger. Ed. Richard Taylor. New York: Routledge, 1994.

Humanity and Technology at War_____

Robert Blaskiewicz

> Modern war. You couldn't even *pretend* it was human.
> —James Jones, *The Thin Red Line*

In conflicts where the dead are counted in the millions, the relative importance of the individual, both combatant and noncombatant, seems greatly diminished, and a number of writers who served in the military during wartime have detected this change in the status of humanity, especially in one's capacity to control and shape his or her own destiny. Many authors drew on the metaphor of the machine to describe what it meant for a human to be subject to immense, impersonal forces, and explored what it meant to be both a part and a product of that war machine. In three important America novels that emerged from the experience of the Second World War—Kurt Vonnegut's *Slaughterhouse-Five* (1968), James Jones's *The Thin Red Line* (1962), and Joseph Heller's *Catch-22* (1955)—the authors explore the process of losing one's autonomy and free will in the vast machinations of war, each author arriving at different conclusions about the capacity of man to reclaim his humanity.

While the phrase "war machine" is now widely used to describe the deployment of national power and resources to prepare for and wage war, the metaphor only came into popular use in the twentieth century. It is often difficult to determine precisely when a word or phrase first entered the language, but the use of "war machine" seems to have become widespread only at the beginning of the First World War, when it was used to describe the German national war effort. The Great War saw the first deployment of massive conscripted armies in Europe against weapons of mass effect, such as coordinated high-explosive artillery, gas, and machine guns. The lethality of these weapons was enhanced by the tactics employed by generals on all sides, which involved massed movements of soldiers, collectively large and easy targets. The devastation wrought by the machine gun and barbed wire brought about further innovations, such as tanks, which were invulnerable to the withering spray of bullets. For these reasons, most historians consider the First World War to be the first modern mechanized war.

The Second World War brought additional refinements of weaponry and tactics. Technologies and tactics that had been in their infancy during the Great War were produced and deployed on vast scales. For instance, the zeppelin raids over Britain and the dogfights between fighter pilots who had brought their side arms with them in the First World War led to converging fleets of Flying Fortresses, loaded with tons of high explosive and incendiary ordinance and protected by clouds of agile fighters in the Second World War. Long-range air flight enabled armies to drop entire divisions of light infantry to attack enemies from behind. On the ground, the tanks that appeared in the First World War now carried large artillery cannons and transformed the battlefield into a rapidly changing venue.

Technological development expanded not only the range at which military might could be projected, but also the definition of what was considered a legitimate military target. Military infrastructures that previously could be reached only by saboteurs and indirect disruption were now within the reach of military weaponry, and that infrastructure included the civilian workforce. Though war had never been kind to civilians, for the first time in global total war civilian populations (and their morale) became the targets and direct objects of military attacks. Nowhere was this more apparent than in the Blitz, the fire bombings of Dresden and Japan, and the destruction of Hiroshima and Nagasaki. The debate over whether the Allied bombings of Dresden, Nagasaki, and Hiroshima were primarily attacks against civilians or military targets is robust; however, from the point of view of attacking infrastructure and morale, and with the hindsight of history, it seems that the answer is "yes." These attacks were aimed at crippling the enemy "war machine."

Many American authors who participated in this war, such as Vonnegut, Heller, and Jones, explored the implications of the loss of autonomy in the face of immense social forces, using the language and imagery of technology as a common trope. In Vonnegut's *Slaughterhouse-Five* and Heller's *Catch-22*, the loss of autonomy results in a tragicomic view of the world, rife with gallows humor and absurdity. In *The Thin Red Line*, Jones is more interested in exploring the many possible responses to the loss of autonomy, from acceptance to ambivalence to rebellion.

During the Second World War, America's citizen-soldiers often had difficulty adjusting to the peculiarities of military life. A prerequisite for a functioning military, and fundamental to the command and control of men and materiel, is that individuals suspend a number of rights that civilians take for granted. These include privacy, free speech, and individualistic pursuits, including even the biological imperative of self-preservation. The stripping of individual identity is perhaps most clearly seen in the symbolic act of head shaving during induction, the issuing of identical uniforms, and endless hours of military parades. This standardization coincides with a psychological program designed to immerse the new soldier in the world of communal action to refine obedience. Literary scholar Edmond L. Volpe tells an anecdote of his own experience of army life during the Second World War. A college graduate, he resented the fact that, during the second week of infantry training, he was reduced to KP duty at Fort Wheeler, Georgia. Through the window, he watched platoons marching and had a disturbing revelation:

> Under identical helmets, not one man was distinguishable from another. Each uniformed figure was a stamped-out cog in a gigantic marching machine. At twenty, I had never doubted my significance and future importance to the universe. But I knew suddenly I had metamorphosed into number 31337580. That day I enjoyed KP. At least for a few hours, I had escaped that inexorable maw that chewed up unsuspecting individuals and turned them into identical links in a never-ending human sausage for the delectation of the war gods. (106)

Volpe employs a number of metaphors that are useful when thinking about the process of dehumanization that the individual undergoes as he becomes a part of the military machine. Philosopher and Second World War-veteran J. Glenn Gray finds that even civilian draftees come to see themselves in this way:

> Even the civilian soldier who finds the military way quite alien and strange can learn to hold fast to the few simple rules, to be a proper cog in the vast machine, and to suspend thoughts that might unfit him for his appointed mission. He learns to expect orders from above and to pass them along to those under his control. Thinking tends to become not only painful but more and more unnecessary. (103)

Like Volpe and Gray, Jones imagines soldiers to be mere cogs in a vast war machine. The term "cogs" is used to describe men throughout *The Thin Red Line.* Such descriptions are more frequent late in the book, when the men have been to combat and realize the nature of their relationship to the army: mechanistic, functional, and basically interchangeable. Staff Sergeant Culn reacts angrily when questioned about his feelings in combat: "He felt his rights were being infringed upon by Payne. He had plenty of feelings, but he didn't have to talk about them. He was not a cog in a machine, whatever Payne thought" (400). It is a strong response to a natural question, but it makes sense in light of what follows—that Culn's unspoken feeling, *"Whatever They say, I'm not a cog in a machine"* (408), is tacitly shared by the men: "it said for everybody what they all felt fiercely and needed to believe. They took it to themselves, and applied it to their own particular situations, and they believed it. They were not cogs in a machine, whatever *anybody* said" (408). The men of the company are holding onto their individuality, which is under the threat of the dehumanization of combat.

Jones explores what can happen to the individual when he is faced with the frightening possibility of becoming fully integrated into the military machine. He does this by contrasting the development of two characters, Private Bell and Private Witt. At the beginning of the novel, both characters are fierce individualists. Bell is a former officer who left the military for reasons that he explains to Private Fife: "It's undignified for a married man my age to be separated from his wife" (28). When he resigned, he was told that he would be drafted back into the infantry and would never receive another commission. By resigning his commission, Bell asserts his autonomy and fundamental human dignity.

Under the pressures of combat, however, Bell recognizes a change in himself and the rest of his company. As he leads a patrol to assault a strongpoint in the Japanese defenses, he realizes that if the Japanese have moved troops up to cover his intended route, he, the point man, will be "the first big fat target" (275). He curses himself: "Now here he was . . . unable to back out without looking cowardly, schmucky. Pride! Pride! What stupid foolish things it forced us to do in its goddamn fucking name!" (275). In the next instant, however, he realizes he has undergone a remarkable change: "Irritably he glanced back to motion to the others to come on and in doing so discovered something strange. He no longer cared very much. He no longer cared at all" (275). In fact, the rigors and emotions of combat "had all taken their toll of him until somewhere within the last few minutes—Bell did not know exactly when—he had ceased to feel human . . . And instead of impairing his ability to function, it enhanced it, this sense of no longer feeling human" (275). At this moment, Bell is no longer fiercely individualistic, but is becoming something else, a soldier ready to "function as he ought to function, under fire" (43).

On the heels of this realization, Bell knows that his individuality, and that of his squad, has been reduced so that he no longer decides his own actions, and he whistles to himself "*I Am An Automaton* to the tune of *God Bless America*" (275). This alteration of the patriotic standard signals a growing awareness of his squad's loss of free will:

> They thought they were men. They all thought they were real people. They really did. How funny. They thought that they made decisions and ran

their own lives, and proudly called themselves free individual human beings. The truth was that they were here, and they were going to stay here, until the state through some other automaton told them to go someplace else, and then they'd go. But they'd go freely, of their own free choice and will, because they were free individual human beings. Well, well. (275)

Bell's new cynicism extends to other social organizations. Just as Bell's group is about to begin its assault on the strongpoint, an "elderly, morose, Calvinistic-looking 2d Lieutenant from B-for-Baker" (277), stands up and is instantly machine-gunned. The squad crawls past Gray, the mortally wounded man, and as Bell crawls by he hears the officer "droning feebly on, repeating some other kind of prayer now which Bell had never heard and didn't know. Automatons. Religious automatons, irreligious automatons. The Business and Professional Automatons Club, Chaplain Gray will give the benediction. Yes, siree" (279). By conflating religion and business with his newly acquired awareness of automatic behavior, Bell begins to understand that the implication of his discovery extends well beyond the army; it applies to many institutions of American culture. Private Fife recognizes this very early on, as he watches Japanese bombers defend themselves against American fighters and detects something cold and business-like behind the scene:

> The defending fighters . . . strove to keep the price [in bombers] as high as possible. . . . And that there were men in these expensive machines which were contending with each other, was unimportant—except for the fact that they were needed to manipulate the machines. The very idea itself, and what it implied, struck a cold blade of terror into Fife's essentially defenseless vitals, a terror both of unimportance, his unimportance, and of powerlessness: his powerlessness. . . . It was terrifying. He did not mind dying in a war, a real war,—at least, he didn't think he did—but he did not want to die in a regulated business venture. (41)

Jones's detection of similarities between war and business puts into question both the free will and the value of the individual subject to those systems.

During the final assault on the Japanese strongpoint, the Americans are described in completely clinical terms, emphasizing the mechanical functions of the body that make it possible to act without emotion:

> No longer did they have to fret and stew, or worry about being brave or being cowardly. Their systems pumped full of adrenaline to constrict the peripheral blood vessels, elevate the blood pressure, make the heart beat more rapidly, and aid coagulation, they were about as near to automatons without courage or cowardice as flesh and blood can get. Numbly, they did the necessary. (305–6)

The men are performing a mere mechanical function in the larger scheme of things, and Bell simply cannot accept that they are more than interchangeable parts of the larger effort: "'Sure, sure,' he said automatically, 'of course.' Not cogs in a machine? Not cogs in a machine? What did they think they were then?" (412).

Bell comes out of the Guadalcanal campaign a fully assimilated soldier. The last human tie that distinguishes him from the rest of the men—his intense sexual relationship with his wife—ends when she writes him asking for a divorce. Once this last emotional link to civilian life is severed, Bell is "as a professional soldier, quite ready to die" (505), and the army rewards Bell for his acceptance of this role. Even though he was told that he would never receive another commission, when he asks Captain Bosche to draft him a letter granting the divorce, Bosche informs him that he has been given a field commission as first lieutenant of infantry. Having demonstrated his usefulness in battle and relieved himself of emotional encumbrances that might hamper his work, Bell has found that he has a place within the military machine.

Jones contrasts Bell's increasing skepticism of individualism with Private Witt, who happens to be in Bell's squad during the first assault on the Japanese strongpoint, and who "did think he was a man, and did believe he was a real person" (276). Witt is the most self-certain individual of the novel, never doubting that his life has worth or meaning. Having been transferred out of C-for-Charlie company to a support unit consisting of malcontents and homosexuals, he asserts his will and rejoins the company without orders or permission, because he believes that his presence might make a difference in the outcome of the fight, which is to say that he does not consider himself interchangeable with any other soldier. When Bell and Witt are the only survivors of a disastrous roadblock mission, Witt storms back to confront Lieutenant Band, who ordered the unnecessary patrol, and declares, "I love this compny better'n anything, but I wouldn't serve in no outfit commanded by a son of a bitch like you! If they ever kill you or get rid of you, I might come back" (460). By leaving the company, Witt demonstrates that he never becomes fully assimilated into the machine, though he seems unaware that his presence did not make a difference in the fate of the patrol.

While Jones provides scenarios in which characters either accept or reject their incorporation into the military machine, Heller presents a protagonist who flatly rejects the absurd demands of war in *Catch-22*. Captain Yossarian, who used to be brave, finds that as his superior officers demand more and more missions of their crews, the chances that he will survive the war shrink to zero. While Jones's characters realize and accept that eventually the law of averages will catch up with them, most of the survivors of the Guadalcanal campaign remain with the unit. Yossarian, however, rejects that notion. Heller explores the illogic and madness that keeps people within the military, business, and political organizations that ultimately destroy them. Unlike Jones, he is not interested in a realistic study of individual psychology. Heller instead focuses on the methods of coercion inherent to large social structures. The tyrannical law of Catch-22, which governs the lives of the fliers in the novel, establishes a system that, as described by one commentator, has the effect of "alienating people from their own interests and estranging them from their instincts" (Kirn).

Catch-22 is itself described as a mechanism. As applied to Orr, Yossarian's tentmate, Catch-22 stipulates: "Orr would be crazy to fly more missions and sane if he didn't, but if he was sane, he had to fly them. If he flew them, he was crazy and didn't have to; but if he didn't want to he was sane and had to" (55). Yossarian's response is to see it as an elegant machine: "Yossarian saw it clearly in all its spinning reasonableness. There was an elliptical precision about its perfect pairs of parts that was graceful and shocking" (55). As it functions in the novel, Catch-22 is invoked as a mechanism that allows the powerful to control the powerless.

Even though Orr seems to be a comparatively minor character in the book, he is important because, as his name suggests, he shows Yossarian an option, a way out of the vicious machine that designs his death. When the reader first encounters Orr, he is tinkering with a machine, a faucet that feeds gas to the stove in his tent:

> He worked without pause, taking the faucet apart, spreading all the tiny pieces out carefully, counting and then studying each one interminably as though he had never seen anything remotely similar before, and then reassembling the whole small apparatus, over and over and over and over again, with no loss of patience or interest, no sign of fatigue, no indication of ever concluding. (31–32)

Orr, who has crashed every plane he has taken up, is cryptic and full of secrets, chuckling every time he advises that Yossarian should fly with him.

When Orr disappears on a mission and does not return, he is written off as dead, but when Yossarian learns that his tentmate escaped to Sweden, he realizes that Orr had been planning his escape the entire time: "Don't you understand," Yossarian exclaims, "he planned it that way from the beginning. He even practiced getting shot down. He rehearsed for it on every mission he flew. And I wouldn't go with him! . . . Danby, bring me buck teeth too, and a valve to fix and a look of stupid innocence that nobody would ever suspect of any cleverness. I'll need them all" (460). It is clear that Orr has been examining the machinery of Catch-22 throughout the novel, and has devised a way to escape it. Yossarian follows Orr's example and lights out for Sweden.

In *Catch-22*, the military and the social forces it represents act upon the individual like a cold, indifferent, and badly flawed machine. There are, in fact, a number of machines in the novel that do to individuals literally what the military does metaphorically—act on individuals without reflection or attention to consequences. Take, for instance, the "bald and pedantic cetologist from the zoology department at Harvard who had been shanghaied ruthlessly into the Medical Corps by a faulty anode in an I.B.M. machine" (23). The same product of "International Business Machines" also destroys the life of the character Major Major Major Major. Having already been cursed with a likeness to the actor Henry Fonda, the boy who thought that his name was Caleb Major learns that his father signed his birth certificate Major Major Major. When he enters the army, Major Major Major finds himself "promoted by an I.B.M. machine with a sense of humor almost as keen as his father's" (96) to the rank of Major, alienating him from his comrades and making him a pariah in an institution where he might have thrived.

Throughout the novels of Second World War veterans, authors invariably describe a soldier as someone who, in a sense, no longer belongs to himself. When Yossarian rises from his bed in the hospital, Nurse Cramer orders him back to bed and remarks:

> "I suppose you just don't care if you kill yourself, do you?"
> "It's my self," he reminded her.
> "I suppose you just don't care if you lose your leg, do you?"
> "It's my leg."
> "It certainly is not your leg!" Nurse Cramer retorted. "That leg belongs to the U.S. government. It's no different than a gear or a bedpan. The Army has invested a lot of money to make you an airplane pilot, and you've no right to disobey the doctor's orders." (301–2)

Similarly, General Peckem sees the addition of a colonel to his staff as an exercise in acquiring materiel:

> An additional colonel on his staff meant that he could now begin agitating for two additional majors, four additional captains, sixteen additional lieutenants and untold quantities of additional enlisted men, typewriters, desks, filing cabinets, automobiles and other substantial equipment and supplies that would contribute to the prestige of his position and increase his striking power in the war he had declared against General Dreedle. (328)

In the same way that Jones opens *The Thin Red Line* with the evaluation of the men onboard the troop transport—"All their lives they had been cargo; never supercargo" (1)—the conflation of people and property, to use Gray's term, diminishes the significance of the individual to "so much material potentiality" (146). With more bitterness than irony, Jones equates the wounded soldier and broken field equipment: "in a way, a wounded soldier who stays up on the line might very well be accused of damaging government property (himself) needlessly" (Jones, "Phony" 66). Even the common term for an American soldier, a "G.I.," suggests that the soldier is "Government Issue," like any other piece of battlefield equipment.

In Vonnegut's work, the relationship between technology and humanity is complicated. Despite Vonnegut's protestations to the contrary, it is difficult to imagine that his experiences during the Second World War did not deeply color his understanding of technology and its uses in the hands of humanity, whose ethical and moral development has not kept pace with technological developments. After all, Vonnegut survived one of the greatest engineered disasters in human history, the burning of Dresden, and later wrote about the experience in *Slaughterhouse-Five*. Not surprisingly, Vonnegut's writing presents numerous apocalypses that result from the misuse of technology. In his first novel, *Player Piano* (1951), Vonnegut's protagonist, engineer Paul Proteus, wages all-out war against what seems to be inexorable technological progress (he is defeated). In *Cat's Cradle* (1963), the world is destroyed by a type of water crystal, Ice-Nine, that rearranges the molecules of liquid water into a solid that is stable at room temperature.[1] Vonnegut's apocalypse in *Slaughterhouse-Five*, however, makes his other versions of the end of the world seem puny. Even though science fiction has primed the protagonist Billy Pilgrim to imagine that somehow "the Earthling combination of ferocity and spectacular weaponry might eventually destroy part or maybe all of the innocent universe" (147–48), humanity does not participate in the destruction of the universe. Billy's Tralfamadorian zookeeper explains: "We blow it up, experimenting with new fuels for our flying saucers. A Tralfamadorian test pilot presses a starter button, and the whole Universe disappears" (149).

In the face of such catastrophic forces, the individual is rendered almost completely powerless. Indeed, Billy Pilgrim is the embodiment of a powerless victim. From the beginning of his life, Billy is almost completely passive, never an active agent in his life, merely pushed around through space and time. Like Heller and Jones, Vonnegut plays with the idea of people as a kind of military cargo, describing Billy Pilgrim's mother as "standard-issue" (130), for instance, or describing the attitude of German guards opening the boxcars at the prisoner of war camp: "They had never dealt with Americans before, but they surely understood this general sort of freight. They knew that it was essentially a liquid which could be induced to flow slowly toward cooing and light" (102). Vonnegut's primary concern, however, is the similarity between the operation of machines, without volition or reflection, and the behavior of people.

The most striking instance comes when Billy meets Kilgore Trout. The narrator injects a dark amusing aside about Kilgore's career as a science-fiction writer, particularly about a book called *The Gutless Wonder*:

It was about a robot who had bad breath, who became popular after his halitosis was cured. But what made the story remarkable, since it was written in 1932, was that it predicted the widespread use of burning jellied gasoline on human beings.

It was dropped on them from airplanes. Robots did the dropping. They had no conscience, and no circuits which would allow them to imagine what was happening to the people on the ground.

Trout's leading robot looked like a human being, and could talk and dance and so on, and go out with girls. And nobody held it against him that he dropped jellied gasoline on people. But they found his halitosis unforgivable. But then he cleared that up, and he was welcomed to the human race. (213–14)

Vonnegut's narrator paints an odd picture of what it takes to qualify as "human;" it does not depend on one's capacity to behave ethically or express empathy for other humans but is a matter of aesthetics. It is not by accident that Vonnegut talks about jellied gasoline dropped from airplanes, as the aerial deployment of napalm was often used against enemies in Vietnam, which was ongoing at the time Vonnegut wrote *Slaughterhouse-Five* and lingers in the background of the novel.[2]

Two details relevant to the prosecution of wars stand out in the last passage. First, of course, is the similarity of the fire bombings of the gutless wonders to the attack on Dresden that Vonnegut survived. The second is Vonnegut's comparison of U.S. airmen, both in Vietnam and the Second World War, to robots. Because of technological developments, the act of bombing physically separates the actions of bombardiers from the experiences of people on the ground; even if American fliers have the conscience and imagination to understand their actions' results, the technology of war so removes the suffering that they might as well lack those empathic qualities. In this sense, the gutless wonders are indistinguishable from the typical flier who carries out his duties. As such, Vonnegut likely would have agreed with other writers of the war, including the philosopher Gray, who was astonished by "how much of the business of warfare can still be carried on by men who act as automatons, behaving almost as mechanically as the machines they operate" (102).

Vonnegut goes out of his way to blur the lines between humanity and robots. In the Tralfamadorian reality, which Billy comes to accept, man *is* a machine. One might look to the conception of Billy's son as an instance of the cold construction of a fighting machine, much in the same way that, at the beginning of the book, Mary O'Hare considers a romantic view of war: "Valencia questioned her funny-looking husband about war. It was a simply minded thing for a female Earthling to do, to associate sex and glamor with war" (154). While she imagines this romanticized version of war, deep inside her body, Valencia is "assembling the materials for a Green Beret" (155), as if her body were some sort of soldier factory. Valencia's father is also described in mechanical terms: "Lionel Merble was a machine. Tralfamadorians, of course, say that every creature and plant in the Universe is a machine. It amuses them that so many Earthlings are offended by the idea of being machines" (196).

To associate humans with machines is to limit the range of decisions and actions that an individual can make. Machines cannot choose not to do what they were designed to do, and this is exactly the reality that the Tralfamadorians perceive for themselves and for Earthlings. Take, for instance, their explanation for why the universe has to be destroyed by their test pilot: "He has *always* pressed it, and he always *will*. We always let him and we always *will* let him. The moment is *structured* that way" (149). Placing the Tralfamadorian pilot within a larger, structured history, in which he has no ability to deviate from his preordained role in the destruction of the universe, reduces his agency to that of a mechanism, and seems to relieve the Tralfamadorians of responsibility for the universal disaster. They do not seem to betray any concern, guilt, or anxiety about the end of the universe they bring about; they could not prevent it. The notion that one could have made other decisions is literally alien to the Tralfamadorians: "Only on Earth is there any talk of free will" (109). The ambiguous lesson that Billy takes away is that "the idea of preventing war on Earth is stupid" (149). It is a sobering, tragic view of life that Billy adopts.

Yet Vonnegut allows a glimpse into a world where war can be undone, when Billy becomes "slightly unstuck in time" (93). On his daughter's wedding night, Billy watches a movie about war production that ultimately leads to a bombing raid on Germany, which he watches in reverse. By running the clock of the war backwards—damaged planes taking off backward from England, getting repaired in the skies over Germany, gathering the explosions on the ground into bombs that leap into the bellies of the bombers, and depositing the bomb material back into the earth, where it can never hurt people again (93–95)—it is as if Vonnegut, through imagination, takes apart the war machine in the same way that Orr disassembles the gas valve in Yossarian's tent, allowing us to imagine a version of the war in which the machine never needs to be reassembled.

Notes

1. Peter G. Jones has identified and discussed Vonnegut's attitude about technology in *War and the Novelist* (1976).
2. Christina Jarvis discusses the relationship between these two conflicts in "The Vietnamization of World War II in *Slaughterhouse-Five* and *Gravity's Rainbow*," in *War, Literature and the Arts* 15.1–2. (2003).

Works Cited

Gray, J. Glenn. *The Warriors: Reflections on Men in Battle*. 1959. New York: Harper, 1970.

Heller, Joseph. *Catch-22*. 1955. New York: Simon, 1996.

Jarvis, Christina. "The Vietnamization of World War II in *Slaughterhouse-Five* and *Gravity's Rainbow*." *War, Literature and the Arts* 15.1–2 (2003): 95–117.

Jones, James. "Phony War Films." *Saturday Evening Post* (30 Mar. 1963): 64–67.

_____. *The Thin Red Line*. 1962. New York: Dell, 1998.

_____. *WWII: A Chronicle of Soldiering*. New York: Ballantine, 1975.

Jones, Peter G. *War and the Novelist*. Columbia: U of Missouri P, 1976.

Kirn, Walter. "War Is Heller." *Slate*. Slate Group, 2 Aug. 2011. Web. 25 May 2012.

Volpe, Edmond L. "James Jones–Norman Mailer." *Contemporary American Novelists*. Ed. Harry T. Moore. Carbondale: Southern Illinois UP, 1968. 106–19.

Vonnegut, Kurt. *Slaughterhouse-Five*. 1968. New York: Laurel, 1991.

Android Dreams and Human Imaginings _____

Aaron Barlow

What is not human? Does the fact of biological humanity divide "us" from everything else? What about something that acts with all of the intelligence, compassion, and sense of shared mission of the best human beings? What if these qualities were constructed, not born? Is such a being not human? What about someone who has withdrawn from knowledge, feelings, and any sort of interaction with others? Is that person no longer human? While these are good questions, they are not the only ones that science-fiction writers address when examining human relations with their creations; they are merely starting points. Such examinations lead back to a fundamental question: "What are we?"

Science-fiction writers, such as Alfred Bester, Philip K. Dick, Stanisław Lem, and William Gibson, use robots, androids, and artificial worlds not to explore what is "out there" in fictional universes but to seek what is "in here," in each of us. As Patricia Warrick writes, "Finding an answer to the question of what is truly human and what only masquerades as human is, for Dick, the most important difficulty facing us" (189). The same could be said of the other writers as well. Dick has written that nonhuman "creatures are among us, although morphologically they do not differ from us; we must not posit a difference of essence, but a difference of behavior. . . . A human being without the proper empathy or feeling is the same as an android built so as to lack it" ("Man, Android and Machine," 202). As Joseph Francavilla puts it, "not only will the contrasts and oppositions between the human and the android become blurred, but . . . also the contrasting characteristics of each life form will switch sides. The human will become more inanimate; the nonhuman, more animate" (9). Understanding the implications and veracity of such a notion became these writers' core endeavor.

Early on, science fiction in literature and film tended to interpret the relationship between humans and their creations in a paradigm of threat and opposition (such a paradigm stemming from golem tales and, in part, Mary Shelley's 1818 novel *Frankenstein, or The Modern Prometheus*). Later, within a controlled framework of creation and mastery, the genre viewed human creations as something more "scientific" but still maintained an underlying dichotomy, difference, and subservient position within a hierarchy of control. Toward the beginning of the 1956 film *Forbidden Planet*, a crew, newly arrived on a distant planet, encounters a robot whose owner explains:

> DR. MORBIUS. Don't attribute feeling to him, gentlemen. Robby is simply a
> tool. Tremendously strong, of course. He could quite easily topple this
> house off its foundation.
> DOC OSTROW. In the wrong hands, mightn't such a tool become a deadly
> weapon?
> DR. MORBIUS. No, Doctor, not even though I were the mad scientist of
> the tape thrillers because, you see, there happens to be a built-in safety
> factor. Commander, may I borrow that formidable-looking sidearm of
> yours? Thank you. Robby, point this thing at that *Althaea frutex* out
> there on the terrace. Fire. You understand the mechanism?
> ROBBY. Yes, Morbius. A simple blaster.
> DR. MORBIUS. All right. Now turn around here. Point it at the commander.
> Aim right between the eyes. Fire. You see, he's helpless, locked in a
> sub-electronic dilemma between my direct orders and his basic inhibi-
> tions against harming rational beings. Canceled. If I were to allow that
> to continue he would blow every circuit in his body.

Here, the creation (though not one made by humans, it turns out) is a mere extension of human will, its vast power completely in human hands. The dangerous creation has been brought under control, or, rather, the illusion of control.

The bringing to life of the inanimate has been a prominent theme for eons, the sculptor of antiquity Pygmalion being perhaps the most well-known classical example; the potential dangers, however, are more recently recognized. Not surprisingly, the most influential nineteenth-century discussion of the risks of such creation is Shelley's *Franken-stein*. A little over a century later, Karel Čapek's play *R.U.R.* (1920)—the initials standing for "Rossum's Universal Robots"—introduced the word "robot" and provided another examination of the creation's possible dangers to its human engineers. Such tales, as literary scholar Istvan Csicsery-Ronay Jr. argues in a discussion of Ridley Scott's 1982 film *Blade Runner*,

> show the slave either attaining equality with the Handy Man, refusing to consent to his domination, or revealing the illusory nature of the master-slave relationship. This shift entails the alien or subject creature assert-ing its equality via technological power. . . . All these deformations are condensed in *Blade Runner*'s Nexus 6. These Replicants were originally constructed to serve human purposes. As programmed beings, they had al-most no free will; nonetheless, some were required to improve their func-tions as soldiers and sex slaves. They have sufficient freedom to become aware of their predicament. (253)

The difference is that the Replicants are no longer the enemy, except when humans make them so, and they have increased their free will, becoming as human as many humans.

In 1939, a tale called "I, Robot"—attributed to Eando Binder, the pen name of the brothers Earl and Otto Binder—appeared in *Amazing Stories* magazine. The story focuses on a self-aware robot called Adam Link, and attempts to balance earlier conceptions of the hazards of human creation by presenting a case in which a robot is wrongly per-ceived as evil. Unjustly accused of killing its creator, the robot even-tually decides that it is not worth trying to clear itself and prepares to deactivate. Soon after this story appeared, science-fiction writer Isaac Asimov began a robot-themed series for *Astonishing Stories*, *Super Science Stories*, and, most importantly, *Astounding Science Fiction*. Asimov believed that any "real" robots would need to be designed so that they could not threaten humans.

In these stories, Asimov develops what came to be known as "the three laws of robotics," which appeared for the first time in his 1942 story "Runaround" in *Astounding Science Fiction*. Two characters discuss these rules:

> "Now, look, let's start with the three fundamental Rules of Robotics—the three rules that are built most deeply into a robot's positronic brain." In the darkness, his gloved fingers ticked off each point.
> "We have: One, a robot may not injure a human being, or, through inaction, allow a human being to come to harm."
> "Right!"
> "Two," continued Powell, "a robot must obey the orders given it by human beings except where such orders would conflict with the First Law."
> "Right!"
> "And three, a robot must protect its own existence as long as such protection does not conflict with the First or Second Laws."
> "Right! Now where are we?" (36–37)

We have been asking that same question in relation to robots, androids, and other creations (real and imagined) ever since. Though Robby of *Forbidden Planet*—whose name is taken from one of Asimov's stories—follows the three laws, we have realized since his appearance that the laws are based on a simplistic hierarchy of human and machine that is unlikely ever to exist, a relationship that Csicsery-Ronay Jr. sees as that of "the Willing Slave." He writes, "The selfhood of the Willing Slave is, of course, a subset of his Master's, and will not extend beyond that the boundaries that the [master] inscribes. But he is independently conscious to the degree that he can learn higher rationality, and willingly choose his subaltern position" (*Seven Beauties of Fiction*, 229). As robots, the Willing Slaves "are aware that it is possible to act against the interests of human beings. Yet they cannot" (252).

French writer and filmmaker Emmanuel Carrère claims:

From the earliest science fiction on, the robot—like the golem and Frankenstein's monster before it—had been cast in the role of villain, its human creator's most cunning adversary. . . . Isaac Asimov had tried to impose a code of good conduct on robots and their writer-creators, to reduce the theme of robot rebellion to the scientific absurdity and cheap literary convention it was, but he did not succeed. (131)

Just as Asimov, the Binders, and other early science-fiction writers found faults in the traditions of *Frankenstein*, other writers soon began to chaff under the simplicity of the three laws and worry about the conundrum of androids or robots being both able and unable to act against humans.

Francavilla sees androids as "constructions of organic artificial life resembling humans" (as in the Replicants of *Blade Runner*) and robots as "inorganic artificial life resembling humans which is fundamentally a machine or mechanical being" (7). In either case, the resemblance of robots to humans raises another question, one not just of physical resemblance but of mind. This question was brought to the attention of science-fiction writers through mathematician Alan Turing's 1950 essay "Computing Machinery and Intelligence." Turing begins: "I propose to consider the question, 'Can machines think?'" (433). This question piqued the interest of the science-fiction community, especially. Carrère writes:

Turing takes up the range of objections that had been raised against the possibility of artificial intelligence—that what computers do is too specialized to be called thinking, that they lack spontaneity, moral sense, desire, and taste, and so forth. Turning dispatches these arguments one by one, and proposes instead a single criterion by which to answer the question of whether a machine can think. That criterion is whether the machine is capable of making a human being *believe* that it thinks as he does. (132)

Not only did Turing provide new legitimacy to an area that science-fiction writers were exploring, but his work also led to the so-called Turing test, in which a human is presented with two responses to one question. If that person cannot tell which response comes from a machine and which comes from another human, the machine has passed the test.

In response to Turing, science-fiction writers began to wonder about not just how to control androids and robots, who were sure to eventually "think," but also how to understand the community that humans and their creations were sure to become one day. Among these writers was Alfred Bester, whose "Fondly Fahrenheit" appeared in *The Magazine of Fantasy and of Science Fiction* in 1954. In the story, the relationship between human and machine becomes much more complex than anything found in Asimov. The last lines are particularly instructive:

> Vandaleur didn't die. I got away. They missed him while they watched the android caper and die. But I don't know which of us he is these days. Projection, Wanda warned me. Projection, Nan Webb told him. If you live with a crazy machine long enough, I become crazy too. Reet!
>
> But we know the truth. We know that they were wrong. The new robot and Vandaleur know that because the new robot's started twitching too. Reet! Here on cold Pollux, the robot is twitching and singing. No heat, but my fingers writhe. No heat, but it's taken the little Talley girl off for a solitary walk. A cheap labor robot. A servo-mechanism . . . all I could afford . . . but it's twitching and humming and walking alone with the child somewhere and I can't find them. Christ! Vandaleur can't find me before it's too late. Cool and discreet, honey, in the dancing frost while the thermometer registers 10° fondly Fahrenheit. (489)

With its structure—the narrator moving from human to robot to both, seemingly at random—Bester's story questions the possibility of an absolute distinction between owner and the property owned, between humanity and those it has created to "serve." Such ideas set the stage for the next two decades and the complex explorations of such writers as Dick, Lem, and Gibson. The distinctions and lack thereof between humanity and machinery have had significant impacts on science-fiction film, including works as divergent as Stanley Kubrick's *2001: A Space Odyssey* (1968), Ridley Scott's *Blade Runner*, Steven Lisberger's *Tron* (1982) and Joseph Kosinski's *Tron: Legacy* (2010), Mamoru Oshii's *Ghost in the Shell* (1995), and Andy and Larry Wachowski's *Matrix* trilogy (1999; 2003; 2003).

Perhaps the most influential science-fiction writer in terms of attitudes toward human and machine relations, Dick still had ambivalent feelings with regard to the relations between people and their creations. This ambivalence is evident in his earliest stories, including "The Defenders," which appeared in *Galaxy* magazine in January 1953 and was later incorporated into Dick's novel *The Penultimate Truth* (1964). A war has driven both Americans and Russians underground, leaving the conduct of the war to "leadies," robots able to survive the highly radiated surface. One of them speaks to a group of humans it is trying to block from returning to the surface: "I am sorry," the leader said, "but it is for your own protection. We are watching over you, literally. You must stay below and let us conduct the war. In a sense, it has come to be *our* war. We must fight it as we see fit" (78). The humans manage to turn the tables on the leadies and get to the surface, which they find is not radioactive but has been restored as a pristine human environment:

"But why?" Taylor asked, dazed. He stared down at the vast valley below. "Why?"

"You created us," the leady said, "to pursue the war for you, while you human beings went below the ground in order to survive. But before we could continue the war, it was necessary to analyze it to determine what its purpose was. We did this, and we found that it had no purpose, except, perhaps, in terms of human needs. Even this was questionable." (80)

Created with one vision and purpose, created with a specific desire built-in, the leadies reimagined that desire—even including human desire alongside their own—for the sake of the humans.

In "The Defenders," Dick puts his finger directly on the great weakness of Asimov's three laws: robot "desires" are not necessarily the same as those of their creators. No matter the restrictions placed on them, robots will work to fulfill their own desires. But how, one may ask, can a robot desire? It lacks the self-awareness of humans, and therefore lacks feelings. To Turing, however, this question may be irrelevant. If a robot seems to desire, it desires. Furthermore, desires are not simply feelings or caught up with volition and will—capacities that we associate with human beings and not with machines. Other entities certainly desire, as plants desire the sun, turning their flowers to catch its rays. Desire encompasses much more than human yearning and, as with the leadies, can be built into machines: a streetcar desires to run along its tracks. If it does not, it is no longer a streetcar.

In another of his early stories, "The Short Happy Life of the Brown Oxford," Dick approaches this issue from another angle. Instead of portraying desire as crucial to life or the power of decision, he imagines desire as an irritation. The character Doc Labyrinth explains:

> "The Principle came to me this way. One day I was sitting on a rock at the beach. The sun was shining and it was very hot. I was perspiring and quite uncomfortable. All at once a pebble next to me got up and crawled off. The heat of the sun had annoyed it."
>
> "Really? A pebble?"
>
> "At once the realization of the Principle of Sufficient Irritation came to me. Here was the origin of life. Eons ago, in the remote past, a bit of inanimate matter had become so irritated by something that it crawled away, moved by indignation. Here was my life work: to discover the perfect irritant, annoying enough to bring inanimate matter to life." (250)

Humor aside, the anthropomorphism that Dick lampoons (and that Turing sidesteps) can be a real problem in coming to an understanding of human and machine relations—but that does not mean that such human traits as desire do not have machine analogues.

The leadies of "The Defenders" desire to do the best for the humans they are programmed to serve, even if that means fooling the humans into circumventing their warlike nature to establish peace. Whatever the ontology of their desires, the leadies ended up as independent actors, making their own decisions and following plans of their own design. They act as though they have will of their own. Indeed, they would pass any Turing test that attempted to differentiate their responses from human ones.

Turing's logic and Dick's stories lead one to believe that robots, androids, and other creations in fact could become independent actors with individual volition. Would nothing make them different from human beings? Would they have individual consciousness behind that will? Would they desire in the ways that humans desire, or would their desires remain a mere metaphor of ours? To Turing, such questions probably would have no relevance; to science-fiction writers like Dick and Lem, they are fascinating.

With the exception of "The Short Happy Life of the Brown Oxford," Lem generally has more fun with human and machine relations than Dick. Part of Lem's intent is to lampoon the clichés of the science-fiction genre and beyond (similarly to how English writer Douglas Adams would create his own satire one generation later in his *Hitchhiker's Guide* series), but he also points to the serious consequences of ill-conceived human and machine interactions. His characters are often powerful, whereas Dick's characters generally are people oppressed in some way. The "constructors" of Lem's *Cyberiad* (1974), Trurl and Klapaucius, succeed; Dick's characters reach but rarely manage to grasp.

A focus on the nuances of human and machine relations is quite clear in Lem's stories featuring Pirx, a spaceship pilot; these stories are collected as *Tales of Pirx the Pilot* (1979) and *More Tales of Pirx the Pilot* (1982). As literary historian Jerzy Jarzębski submits:

> in the person of Pirx Lem intended to test mankind. He set out to find a place, in the world of triumphant technology, where human weakness and human imperfection are no longer defects. It is simple to say: "Machines cannot think, machines have no consciousness!" From where do we derive this certainty? . . . Whence come the criteria that allow us to define "thought" in an apodictic way—and what if not thinking shall we call machine operations that have analogous results for their "output"? Lem's robots are not primitive machines; they represent a serious challenge to man. (120)

Ultimately, for both Dick and Lem, the questions should be turned around, away from the robots and back to human beings. What makes us human? What makes us fundamentally different from self-aware machines? Over the course of the half-century since Bester's story, the attempts to answer such questions have provided some of the most intriguing work of the science-fiction genre.

For Dick, Lem, and Gibson, the questions become even more complex, for the very natures of humans and machines are dependent on environment. How can one be truly human in an inhuman environment? How can one be real in an unreal world? In *I Hope I Shall Arrive Soon* (1985), Dick writes:

> I consider that the matter of defining what is real—that is a serious topic, even a vital topic. And in there somewhere is the other topic, the definition of the authentic human. Because the bombardment of pseudo-realities begins to produce inauthentic humans very quickly, spurious humans—as fake as the data pressing at them from all sides. My two topics are really one topic; they unite at this point. Fake realities will create fake humans.

Or fake humans will generate fake realities and then sell them to other humans, turning them, eventually, into forgeries of themselves. So we wind up with fake humans inventing fake realities and then peddling them to other fake humans. (6)

If a human can become a fake human, why cannot a fake human, an android, become a real human? Where, in other words, does humanity lie? This is something Turing does not bother to answer. Is it simply something physical, or is there also a necessary spiritual aspect?

Perhaps these questions miss the point. Toward the end of *Do Androids Dream of Electric Sheep?* (1968), Rick Deckard remarks, "The electric things have their lives, too. Paltry as those lives are" (241). With this statement, Deckard erases the distinction between human and machine, and with it the notion that humanity constitutes an exclusive and discrete set of qualities. Yet Dick cannot let the question go and continues to explore it throughout his career—even though he clearly knows that, on some level, Turing and Deckard are right.

In the 1980s, Gibson took a different approach, exploring the interface of humanity and machines in *Neuromancer* (1984), *Count Zero* (1987), and *Mona Lisa Overdrive* (1988), novels in which the two meld in a "cyberspace" that is separate from "normal" reality—something of a sensorial Internet accessed through computer portals. For Gibson, the intersection of machine life and human life allows both to bleed into each other. Robert Longo's 1995 film *Johnny Mnemonic* reflects this blurred relationship, as information stored in the title character's brain threatens his memories and his life.

Of course, Gibson's most important contribution to discussions of humanity and machines comes from his concept of cyberspace, also known as virtual reality. In his article "The Sentimental Futurist: Cybernetics and Art in William Gibson's *Neuromancer*," Istvan Csicsery-Ronay Jr. sees cyberspace primarily in terms of science fiction. He claims that by developing the concept

Gibson restored the heroic spatial expanse that SF had lost in outer space and laid the groundwork for developing a system of symbols for cybernetic implosion. Cyberspace, after all, is a purely human system, a "consensual hallucination," with no objective status. . . . It cannot be conquered for humanity because it is an aspect of humanity at the outset. The best that can be hoped for is its conquest for unalienated, enlightened human beings from the powers of avarice, fetishization, and global reification that control the cyberspace field. (223–24)

Though humanity has yet to conquer cyberspace, things have changed since Csicsery-Ronay Jr.'s article. The Internet has achieved a position of objective status. The "consensual hallucination" has become a human reality, but it is one that we still do not completely understand. Through its social networks and its tendency to isolate individuals behind screens, the impact of this reality on our sense of humanity remains to be seen. Whatever the case may be, the Internet is certainly changing ideas of our relations to machines, as we become more and more dependent on the mechanical aspect of our lives, which already anticipates the efficiency of Dick's leadies.

There may be another Turing test yet to be developed, one that does not test human intelligence but rather human empathy—a test that addresses Dick's concern for humans drifting away from humanity, not machines' movement toward it. In one of his last novels, *The Divine Invasion* (1981), Dick writes of the "Beside-Helper," who offers to assist the newly dead with the test of judgment to come:

He offered to present his own bill of particulars to the retribution mechanism in place of the bill of particulars of the person. If the person were innocent this would make no difference but, for the guilty, it would yield up a sentence of exculpation rather than guilt. . . .

"What does the Beside-Helper's bill of particulars list?" he asked.

"It is blank." . . .

"The retributive machinery could not process that." . . .

"It would process it. It would imagine that it had received a compilation of a totally spotless person." (127–28)

Everybody believes, however, that they are more good than bad, so the balance is already in their favor.

The way in which Dick sets up this situation—with "retributive machinery" making the decision and not a human—turns the Turing test on its head, much like CAPTCHA (Completely Automated Public Turing test to tell Computers and Humans Apart) tests, and proves that online responses are supplied by humans, not machines. In *Blade Runner*, Scott conveys an understanding of this turnaround, and incorporates it into the film's ending, when Deckard (a human who may be a Replicant) and Rachel (a Replicant who has been led to believe she is human) exit together. Literary scholar Judith Kerman writes:

> I do not hear the closing elevator doors that end the Director's Cut of *Blade Runner* as the clap of doom for Deckard and Rachel. . . . They have been expelled even from the dubious Eden of protection by the forces of Tyrell and his police apparatus, and now they must earn their bread in a hard world by the sweat of their brows. As in our own society and our own lives, we do not know the end of *Blade Runner*, but we can anticipate that the hard road of . . . reality lies ahead. (39)

Yet Deckard and Rachel seem to be among the few who have taken on the assistance of the Beside-Helper: They are going into their future with a clean slate, the distinctions of human and machine erased.

This is a far cry from the end of Shelley's *Frankenstein*, which includes the last words of Victor Frankenstein's abandoned creation:

> "Farewell, Frankenstein! If thou wert yet alive and yet cherished a desire of revenge against me, it would be better satiated in my life than in my destruction. But it was not so; thou didst seek my extinction, that I might not cause greater wretchedness. . . . Blasted as thou wert, my agony was still

superior to thine; for the bitter sting of remorse will not cease to rankle in my wounds until death shall close them for ever.

"But soon," he cried, with sad and solemn enthusiasm, "I shall die, and what I now feel be no longer felt. Soon these burning miseries will be extinct. . . . My spirit will sleep in peace; or if it thinks, it will not surely think thus. Farewell."

He sprung from the cabin-window, as he said this, upon the ice-raft which lay close to the vessel. He was soon borne away by the waves, and lost in darkness and distance. (225)

Blade Runner's parallel comes earlier, in the death of the android Roy Baty, the inheritor of the mantle of *Frankenstein* monster's. Similarly aware of his own being and the circumstances of his creation, Baty is torn between the strength of his being and the weakness of his origin. In *Blade Runner*, however, the road does not end at the point of the creation's death but continues. While Deckard defeats his own "monster," something different from any past relationship between human and machine is portended as he and Rachel exit.

As it winds into unknown territory, Deckard and Rachel's path also winds back to ancient human mythology. Ovid's *Metamorphoses*, written over two thousand years ago, contains the tale of Pygmalion, who weds an ivory statue of his own creation after it comes to life. Perhaps, in our contemporary vision of human and machine relationships, the same good life might meet Deckard and Rachel, and the audience as well.

Works Cited

Asimov, Isaac. "Runaround." *I, Robot*. New York: Bantam, 2004. 25–45.
Bester, Alfred. "Fondly Fahrenheit." Ed. Robert Silverberg. *The Science Fiction Hall of Fame: Volume One, 1929–1964*. New York: Tor, 2003. 472–89.
Binder, Eando. "I, Robot." *Isaac Asimov Presents: Great Science Fiction Stories of 1939*. Ed. Isaac Asimov and Martin H. Greenberg. New York: Dorset, 2001.
Blade Runner: Final Cut. Dir. Ridley Scott. Warner Home Video. 2007. DVD.

Carrère, Emmanuel. *I Am Alive and You Are Dead: A Journey into the Mind of Philip K. Dick.* Trans. Timothy Bent. New York: Metropolitan, 2004.

Csicsery-Ronay Jr., Istvan. "The Sentimental Futurist: Cybernetics and Art in William Gibson's *Neuromancer*." *Critique* 33.3 (Spring 1992): 221–40.

_____. *The Seven Beauties of Science Fiction.* Middletown: Wesleyan UP, 2008.

Dick, Philip K. "The Defenders." *The Collected Stories of Philip K. Dick: Volume 1.* New York: Citadel, 1987. 67–85.

_____. *The Divine Invasion.* 1981. New York: Vintage, 1991.

_____. *Do Androids Dream of Electric Sheep?* 1968. New York: Ballantine, 1996.

_____. *I Hope I Shall Arrive Soon.* Garden City: Doubleday, 1985.

_____. "Man, Android and Machine." *Science Fiction at Large: A Collection of Essays, by Various Hands, About the Interface Between Science Fiction and Reality.* Ed. Peter Nicholls. London: Gollancz, 1976. 202–24.

_____. "The Short Happy Life of the Brown Oxford. *Paycheck and Other Classic Stories.* New York: Kensington, 1990. 249–57.

Forbidden Planet. Dir. Fred M. Wilcox. Warner Home Video. 2006. DVD.

Francavilla, Joseph. "The Android as *Doppelgänger*." *Retrofitting* Blade Runner. Ed. Judith Kerman. Bowling Green: Bowling Green UP, 1991. 4–15.

Gibson, William. *Count Zero.* New York: Ace, 1987.

_____. *Mona Lisa Overdrive.* Toronto: Bantam, 1988.

_____. *Neuromancer.* New York: Ace, 1984.

Greenberg, Martin H, and Joseph D. Olander. *Philip K. Dick.* New York: Taplinger, 1983.

Jarzębski, Jerzy. "Stanislaw Lem, Rationalist and Visionary." Trans. Franz Rottensteiner. *Science Fiction Studies* 4.2 (July 1977): 110–26.

Kerman, Judith. "Post-Millennium *Blade Runner*." *The* Blade Runner *Experience: The Legacy of a Science Fiction Classic.* Ed. Will Brooker. London: Wallflower, 2005. 31–39.

Lem, Stanisław. *The Cyberiad: Fables for the Cybernetic Age.* Trans. Michael Kandel. San Diego: Harcourt, 2002.

_____. *More Tales of Pirx the Pilot.* Trans. Louis Iribarne. San Diego: Harcourt, 1982.

_____. *Tales of Pirx the Pilot.* Trans. Louis Iribarne. New York: Harcourt, 1979.

Shelley, Mary. *Frankenstein, or The Modern Prometheus.* 1818. London: Penguin: 2003.

Silverberg, Robert. *The Science Fiction Hall of Fame: Volume One, 1929-1964.* New York: Tor, 2003.

Turing, Alan M. "Computing Machinery and Intelligence." *Mind* 59 (October 1950): 433–60.

Warrick, Patricia. "The Labyrinthian Process of the Artificial: Philip K. Dick's Androids and Mechanical Constructs." *Philip K. Dick.* Ed. Martin H. Greenberg and Joseph D. Olander. New York: Taplinger, 1983. 189–214.

Death of the Digital Messiah: Increased Complexity in Virtual Narratives _____

Mike Griffith

> A hero ventures forth from the world of common day into a region of supernatural wonder; fabulous forces are there encountered and a decisive victory is won; the hero comes back from this mysterious adventure with the power to bestow boons on his fellow man.
>
> —Joseph Campbell

In his seminal work, *The Hero with a Thousand Faces* (1949), Joseph Campbell identifies aspects of what he refers to as the monomyth, a schema by which archetypal stories progress (through any combination of seventeen possible steps) from the hero's "call to adventure" to the "freedom to live"—the moment when mastery of the world of the story frees the hero from the fear of death and pushes him or her into a existence of pure being (221). The meaning of the story will vary depending on which steps a character takes and how his or her world is presented to the audience. The steps impact not only the development of the character but also the way the character is understood by the audience. These models often are applied to genres such as science fiction. Many films and texts identify and explore the shifting relationship between characters and the immersive digital technologies that make up their cultural space. As the media landscape becomes more complex and impossible to quantify accurately, the narratives that imagine future digital milieus shift the types of agency available to the protagonists. When Campbell's theories are applied to the heroes of William Gibson's novel *Neuromancer* (1984) and Stephen Lisberger's film *Tron* (1982), the relationship between society and technology is revealed in the development of their characters.

Sprawling Spaces

In the early 1980s, two landmark works of science fiction moved the genre in entirely new directions visually and spatially. *Tron* pushed computer animation into the mainstream under the powerful stamp of the Walt Disney animation studio. Two years later, Gibson's novel *Neuromancer* established cyberpunk as a unique genre within postmodern literature. Together, these texts represent a moment of fantastic speculation on the future of the relationship between humankind and machines. Both the film and the novel are focused on characters who enter an electronic world and possess the unique skills necessary to manipulate that world. In each, the hero—Flynn in *Tron* and Case in *Neuromancer*—follows a pattern that conforms to Campbell's monomyth: they are ambivalent about undertaking their journey, receive some manner of supernatural (technological) help, and ultimately become a master of both worlds (digital and physical). The hero's journey grants both characters what Campbell calls a "freedom to live."

At the start of *Neuromancer*, Case is separated from the digital environment where he feels most at home. Some of his clients, in retaliation for his embezzling, have destroyed his nervous system, and in response Case takes on physically and socially destructive habits to account for his lack of digital agency. When Molly and Armitage approach Case about a new job, they confront him directly with these destructive tendencies: "Our profile says you're trying to con the street into killing you when you're not looking. . . . You're suicidal, Case." (28–29). Case identifies himself as a "cowboy," a ruler of the untamed, digital frontier. The destruction of his nervous system isolates him from that identity, for he is actively (if unconsciously) trying to kill himself. When offered a deal to restore his hacking ability, Case only asks about the terms of the agreement; he cares nothing for the job itself or the implications inherent in its completion. As Campbell says, "the individual is drawn into a relationship with forces that are not rightly understood" (46). For Case, the restoration of his digital abilities also means the restoration of his identity. He is so wedded to the idea of this recovery that he does not want to examine the conditions that may be attached.

Armitage, Case's superior and benefactor, is under the control of an artificial intelligence named Wintermute. The AI has assembled the team in order to merge with another AI, Neuromancer. The two AIs were constructed together but later separated, in accordance with the Turing laws (a reference to English mathematician and computer scientists Alan Turing) of Gibson's future society. Throughout the text, the merging is represented as a return to completion for the AIs. For Case, the freedom from "meatspace" and the ability to reinhabit the digital world is worth any cost. Fortunately for him, the united AI is relatively benevolent, or at least unconcerned about the future affairs of humanity. Case is far enough down the chain of command that he can act on purely selfish motivations. In accordance with Campbell, Case becomes more aware of the repercussions of his actions as his power develops.

To achieve personal growth, Case has the help of a native guide, who provides what Campbell refers to as "supernatural aid": "For those who have not refused the call, the first encounter of the hero-journey is with a protective figure (often a little old crone or old man) who provides the adventurer with amulets against the dragon forces he is about to pass" (63).

An important aspect of these characters is their illumination, for both the hero and the audience, of the difference between agency in the supernatural (technological) realm and the real (physical) realm. Case's guide comes in the form of Dix, who is also called the Dixie Flatline. A flatline construct is a read-only hard drive that contains an individual's entire consciousness. Gibson uses Dix to express ambivalence about the increasing control of digital technologies over everyday life. Since Dix is read-only, he cannot create new memories unless he is connected to an external memory source. The flatline construct represents a permanent kind of digital memory, as his personality is frozen in time. When he was still alive, Dix was Case's first cyber-crime mentor, and his presence is a constant reminder to Case of his dual existence. In life, Dix was a successful hacker, his timing governed by a digital device. Dix was known for having died multiple times while plugged into cyberspace, making his existence that much more supernatural. Dix's disappointment with his constrained life as a construct and his demand to be erased remind Case that he cannot exist solely within the digital realm. Although his understanding of digital space is complete, Dix cannot, in his present form, execute commands without Case's agency: " 'Here,' said the voice, 'I'll do it for you.' The Flatline began to chant a series of digits, Case keying them on his deck, trying to catch the pauses the construct used to indicate timing. It took three tries" (82).

This scene reveals much about the relationship between Case and Dix, as well as the understanding of technology in the space created by the novel. Dix easily can read the code that Case needs but cannot act on the knowledge. Case has to act as a conduit between Dix and cyberspace, which involves his physical being negotiating the language of technology on both ends of the exchange. On one side, he has to account for the digital nature of the messages that he receives from Dix. Even though Dix speaks conversationally, his personality is mediated by the construct he inhabits. Interacting with Case, Dix jokes as though he is human, but the computer accessing his memory calculates his decisions; Case cannot be sure that the real Dix would have responded in the same ways that the flatline construct responds.

Due to this aspect of digital mediation, ambiguity pervades Case and Dix's relationship. Case perceives the construct as a fellow human being, a perception that combines his faith in the digital and his faith in the physical. Dix is both the old friend and mentor whom he remembers and another cog that will help him to accomplish his task. Case has to not only mediate Dix's messages, but also utilize that information in a way that is meaningful to the system he is hacking. Dix attributes his skills to his sense of timing, which was set, in turn, by a

Russian artificial heart. There is a recursive nature to the relationship between Case and Dix and the digital environment they are attempting to influence. Dix exists digitally and cannot affect digital space. Existing physically, Case is an imperfect manipulator of digital space. Case finds himself as the human element between a digital world that he wants to change and a digital copy of a human personality that was regulated in life by a digital device. The fact that it takes Dix and Case three tries to time their attack perfectly highlights the complexity of their relationship; either Dix's timing is thrown off by his lack of physicality or Case is still translating Dix's digital messages into a form that is useful to his movements through space. In any case, Gibson develops, through this brief interaction, a compelling confusion of presence, identity, and existence.

Case and his team eventually are able to accomplish their goal and free the two AIs from their human-imposed restraints. It is only when Wintermute and Neuromancer combine that Case realizes each AI represents half of one personality: "Wintermute was hive mind, decision maker, effecting change in the world outside. Neuromancer was personality. Neuromancer was immortality. Marie-France must have built something into Wintermute, the compulsion that had driven the thing to free itself, to unite with Neuromancer (269).

The Neuromancer AI was a construct of Marie-France, the matriarch of the family responsible for the AIs. When she designed Neuromancer, she copied herself into the system, making Neuromancer an advanced version of the same flatline construct technology that contained Dix, but with the ability to generate new memories. Neuromancer contains the memories of Marie-France but has no agency, and Wintermute is a true artificial intelligence that has agency but no humanity. By freeing the two halves, Case has created a being with human intelligence and motivation, as well as agency in the digital and physical worlds. Interestingly, once the AI is free, its interests immediately turn away from humanity. Case has one final conversation with the AI before it leaves for good:

"How are things different? You running the world now? You God?"

"Things aren't different. Things are things." . . .

"But you're the whole thing. Talk to yourself?"

"There's others. I found one already. Series of transmissions recorded over a period of eight years, in the nineteen-seventies. 'Til there was me, natch, there was nobody to know, nobody to answer." (270)

The AI has so transcended the concerns of humanity, that it is no longer interested in human activity. Case assumes that the AI will manipulate the world at whim just as he manipulated the digital world. He is rebuffed, however, by the AI's assessment of what is actually important. Once freed, the AI expunges Case's crimes. Case returns to the life he left at the start of the novel, though his return is not the desperate exile that he was so anxious to escape. There is a selfishness to this model of the hero. As Campbell writes: "On the other hand, like most of the rest of us, one may invent a false, finally unjustified, image of oneself as an exceptional phenomenon in the world, not guilty as others are, but justified in one's inevitable sinning because one represents the good" (221).

Case is lucky that the AI was ultimately uninterested in humanity, for this enables him to justify his selfish plans to recover his own digital agency. His guilt, in Campbell's terms, is expunged by the AI's disinterest in humanity and discovery of other intelligences beyond Earth. The journey of the novel takes him from exile to dominance and eventually to hybridity; the hybridity between man and machine, in particular, is central to Gibson's text. At the climactic moment when the AIs are to be freed, the password must be sung—the creation of a new technological being is dependent on the beauty of human expression. For Gibson, the realm of technological possibilities must spring from what is essentially human. Case is able to live in the physical and digital worlds with equal prowess. He becomes the human equivalent of the newly freed AI, adopting a hybridity that liberates him from the recklessness that characterizes his life in the physical world.

In *Tron*, this same recklessness is evident in the character of the software engineer Flynn, whose agency is compromised in the physical and digital realms. Flynn undergoes frequent and dangerous attempts to break into the computers of his old company, ENCOM, in order to hunt down his stolen games within the Master Control Program (MCP). As the film opens, Flynn loses another program to the MCP's defenses, and his friends from ENCOM come to his arcade to confront him. The new boss of ENCOM, Ed Dillinger, rose to his position by stealing Flynn's games and claiming them as his own. Flynn continuously sends new invasion programs to the MCP in an attempt to find evidence of Dillinger's thefts. He shows an enthusiasm toward technology that overwhelms his ability to understand the physical world. In Flynn's initial quest to uncover proof, he sends multiple programs to their deaths at the hands of the MCP. It is not until Flynn is transported into the digital world of the machine that he understands the suffering he has caused. Flynn is forced into this realm by the MCP in an attempt to eliminate the danger he poses to the MCP's system dominance. If Flynn can find his files, Dillinger will be ousted and Flynn put in charge.

Tron address the nature of the relationship between users and programs by personifying the programs and portraying physically their execution of digital tasks. Flynn is trapped in the digital grid by an AI presence that wants him dead. His situation is complicated by the personification of the programs that populate this space as well. Within the digital world of *Tron*, computer programs are the sentient agents of their programmers' requests. One of the principal tensions of *Tron* is the MCP's attempt to destroy this link between programs and users. The programs have a nearly fanatical attachment to their users, and the MCP will not have complete control of the system while that connection remains. The digital world is constrained by its dependence on the physical world that birthed it. The programs' belief in users is a religion that the MCP persecutes. In an early scene, a program that calculates compound interest is led to prison by a guard program. The interest program's crime is putting too much importance on the user that depends on his calculations; it is persecuted for believing what the MCP has deemed a false religion, the principal belief of which is that technology should serve humanity. The film depicts the majority of programs as well meaning and devoted to their users. The MCP has to actively dissuade them from the belief that their users benefit from and are worthy of their time. The interest program's fear of the MCP echoes cultural concerns of technology pushing the humanity out of everyday life. The MCP keeps getting bigger, and as it grows it destroys the link between users and programs, humans and technology.

This film presents technology as inherently benevolent, especially in what technology allows the user to accomplish. The compound interest program's concern about his inability to report to his user is an excellent illustration of the "religion" of programs, which places the users above the programs themselves. The MCP's aim to reverse this belief makes machines threatening on two levels. On the level of the plot, the MCP has trapped Flynn and intends to destroy him in order to consolidate its position, while, on a larger cultural level, there are the anxieties of a world entering into the digital age. As society moves toward a greater dependency on technology, it would prefer to view technology as benevolent. The MCP operates behind the scenes, running things within the mainframe, while Flynn, representing users, attempts to resist technology's oversight.

In the machine, Flynn embodies the collapse of the relationship between user and program, or real and digital identity, which has become so important in more recent discussions of media theory. Media theorist Henry Jenkins identifies "performance" as one of the key skills in participatory culture: "Performance brings with it capacities to understand problems from multiple viewpoints, to assimilate information, to exert mastery over core cultural materials, and to improvise in response to a changing environment. As with play and simulation, performance places a new stress on learning processes—on how we learn more than what we learn" (31).

In his digital form, Flynn begins to understand the functions that his programs actually perform. He demonstrates the function that Jenkins terms performance; digital Flynn is a user performing the role of a program. It is only through his performance that he can free himself and the other programs from the MCP. In this way, Flynn's "call to adventure" requires a performance of digital identity. He performs his identity within the computer in much the same way that, in the early twenty-first century, identity is performed online. There is a gap between digital identity and actual individual identity within digital space (there is a gap between actual self and representations of self on Facebook, for instance). As an everyday skill, such a process of performing was just coming into practice at the time these works were released. By truly inhabiting his digital identity, Flynn becomes whole in a physical sense and is restored as the owner of the virtual world he created. His digital personality is not constructed from scratch; it is a composite of Flynn's physical self and the knowledge he accumulates in his journey through the digital space.

As is the case in *Neuromancer*, the supernatural guide is a source of illumination for the developing character. Flynn's supernatural guide—a "bit" assigned to his program that can only approve or disapprove of Flynn's actions—has a purely digital existence. A physical representation of an actual digital bit, the Bit can only be on or off, a one or a zero. The Bit is a prisoner of the construct that contains it and can only respond to Flynn's inquiries with a "yes" or "no." There is a tremendous store of knowledge and skill that, through the hero's questioning, must be slowly and painfully imparted. No matter how it is humanized by voice acting or animation, the Bit exists in and is limited by a purely digital space. It requires the dual being of Flynn (digital and physical) to make the choices that seem impossible within digital space. Flynn has agency that is unimaginable to his guide, who is constrained by the rules of the system.

When Flynn and Tron (a security program) arrive at the final battle with the MCP, it is Flynn's actions that allow for the destruction of the MCP and his release from the digital environment. Although Tron "fights for the users," he represents an ideal that cannot succeed because he does not possess the agency of a user. Tron does the battling, but it is Flynn who can divert the MCP and incite its destruction. Flynn's heroics restore him to his physical existence, but his "freedom to live" is linked directly to his power as the new director of ENCOM.

While Case returns to his role as a digital cowboy, Flynn is placed in a position of power. He regains his respect in the physical world and is left with the freedom to explore the digital world. This freedom ultimately will lead to the experimentation that allows him to create the digital world of the sequel, *Tron: Legacy* (2010). Both Flynn and Case are left as mediators of the digital spaces they have inhabited. They had to travel into the purely digital world in order to receive their "boons," to use Campbell's term, and return to reality as a whole individual. Each character is able to speak for the technology that has mediated his experience. More broadly, these characters represent individuals trying to entrust emerging technologies with a greater role in their daily lives. Nearly thirty years later, both the film *Tron: Legacy* (which Lisberger produced) and Gibson's Bigend series deliver new explorations of digital space, explorations that reveal different concerns about the relationship between the physical and digital realms.

Order Flow

In their more recent works, Lisberger and Gibson have turned away from the previously examined type of heroes. In Gibson's novel *Zero History* (2010) and in Joseph Kosinski's film *Tron: Legacy*, the protagonists begin in the state that Case and Flynn reached at the end of the previous works (in *Tron: Legacy*, Flynn returns with the knowledge he attained in the first film). In all of these narratives, the characters operate under the auspices of a digital environment that is far too complex for them to understand. The narrative moves from one of complete understanding and control of digital spaces to an attempt to build individual identity and knowledge in a space that threatens to drown out such attempts. Both works assume that society is permeated by technology, and ask what possibilities will emerge from that relationship. The question is no longer whether the human and the digital will merge, but, rather, what will be born from the union?

In *Zero History*, the protagonist Hollis Henry is hired by Hubertus Bigend (the recurring character behind the action of Gibson's recent novels) to track a rogue fashion designer in an attempt to capture some of her cache. Bigend is initially presented as an advertising executive looking to be on the cutting edge of cool, but by *Zero History*, the third book of the series, his character has evolved into something considerably more substantial. Bigend's ultimate goal is to capture the "order flow," the information necessary to anticipate the physical demands of individuals within a globally connected distribution network: "It's the aggregate of all the orders in the market. Everything anyone is about to buy or sell, all of it. Stocks, bonds, gold, anything. If I understood him, that information exists, at any given moment, but there's no aggregator. It exists, constantly, but is unknowable. If someone were able to aggregate that, the market would cease to be real" (177).

Bigend's goal is to anticipate and capitalize on the needs and desires of individuals through the flow of data that represents them. This goal is very different from that of Case or Flynn, who define themselves through their ability to manipulate digital space. Bigend has realized that the true power of digital spaces is their ability to represent and anticipate the actions of individuals in physical spaces; this realization is the first major departure from the works examined earlier. Case and Flynn possessed, through their hero's journeys, the ability to fully understand their digital environments. They could make decisions not available to their digital guides because they were not fully digital. In the earlier narratives, Wintermute and the MCP are only interested in consolidating their power within the digital realm; it takes a character like Bigend to have the vision to ignore control and instead go after information itself. By the end of the novel, Bigend becomes sinister in his triumph. As many individuals spend their time living in virtual spaces, he is able to leverage that information for use in the physical world: "Fiona said that Bigend, with the Hermes ekranoplan, had gone totally Bond villain, and that the crew uniforms were the icing on the cake. Still, Milgrim had thought, no denying the girl looked good in her Marukawa" (399).

Bigend becomes a "Bond villain" by knowing where to look for the information that allows him to manipulate the world. The only thing that can possibly challenge Bigend's empire is the actions of individuals within the markets that he is predicting—the ability of individuals to act against the logic of the information that represents them. The fashion designer that Hollis is tasked with tracking is revealed to be Cayce, the main character from *Pattern Recognition* (2003), the first book in the series. Cayce is a parallel character to Case, with the exception that her hero's journey is about finding information rather than creating a new digital consciousness. Cayce has produced a line of clothing with no seasons or trendy styles. Everything she makes is composed of vintage materials and carries a sense of history. Bigend is fascinated by her clothing for the same reasons that he is fascinated with order flow: Cayce's clothes fall outside of the patterns his program is tracing. The clothes do not conform to the common demands flowing through the system, and since they do not conform, they pose a problem for his ambition. For Gibson, the promise of technology in the 1980s—a promise of physical and digital union—has been replaced by a warning about the ubiquity of personal information. The ability to read the stream of information is more powerful than the ability to directly manipulate the information. Gibson has changed his focus to reflect the development of technology in society. In the 1980s, he reflected the concerns of a society adapting to the emerging roll of technology; in the 2000s, his stories shift to finding and creating meaning within an environment that is completely permeated with technology.

This same sentiment also can be seen in the sequel to *Tron*. *Tron: Legacy* mirrors the plot of the original but suggests a different understanding of technology. A young hero is trapped in a digital world and, in the process of escaping, learns something about his responsibility to the physical world. What differs in *Tron: Legacy* is the digital world in which the story unfolds. In *Tron*, this world was a corporate mainframe, the actions of Flynn and the programs taking place against a functioning corporate infrastructure. In *Tron: Legacy*, the digital world is an isolated playground that Flynn builds on a machine in the back of his arcade. This separation alters the stakes of the story, as the new world divides the consequences of the digital world from the physical world.

The plot of *Tron: Legacy* focuses on resolving the mistakes that Flynn has made in this new digital world. The "freedom to live" that Flynn experiences at the end of the first film haunts him in the sequel. Because he could not spend every second in the digital world, Flynn copied himself and created the program CLU to protect the system while he was in the physical world. CLU's primary order was to "create a perfect system," a command that did not account for the emerging complexity of the world Flynn created. Flynn's relationship with CLU is quite similar to the relationship between Case and Dix. Flynn forgets that CLU, even though he seems like a perfect copy, is wholly digital. Because CLU cannot understand the ambiguities of life, he wages war against it in the name of perfection. The major strain on CLU and Flynn's relationship is the emergence of the "isomorphs," "isomorphic algorithms" or "biodigital jazz," in Flynn's terms. The isomorphs are the first example of digital evolution. CLU sees the anomalous isomorphs as a corruption of the perfect system, while Flynn sees them as the emergence of something new and sentient within the system he created. As in *Zero History*, the focus of *Tron: Legacy* is the creation of new meaning within digital space.

In both texts, the digital representations of individuals have taken on their own signification. In Gibson's novel, the scope of the digital has so incorporated the real world that it anticipates the actions and needs of individuals in physical space. In *Tron: Legacy*, even the closed system Flynn has constructed for his private playground has reached a level of complexity wherein the digital and the biological have blended into a new hybrid of signification. In each of these cases, the individual protagonists do not pretend to understand the systems that enfold them; they only operate within their small spheres of influence within those larger systems. The small actions of individual characters grow to impact the shape of the entire digital environment.

At the start of *Tron: Legacy*, Flynn is living in exile. He is separated from his creation by the program he created to steward it. Flynn's journey in *Tron: Legacy* is one of self-discovery. Even in his absolute knowledge of the digital space, Flynn has been defeated. It is only by reuniting with his digital copy that he can save the digital world. The battle between Flynn and CLU is not one of victor and vanquished: Flynn has to merge his physical self with his digital copy in order to stop CLU. He must recreate the hybridity that he lost when he separated CLU from himself. This reunion is similar to the union of the two AIs in *Neuromancer*, but it is focused on the individual, as Flynn must take ownership of his actions in the digital and physical worlds. The tension in these texts is between individuals and their digital selves. This focus on the individual is a departure from the earlier texts, in which individuals were in conflict with their environments. Through the struggle with digital selves, the characters reveal how much of daily existence has been given over to technology. Turning once more to Campbell: "Freedom to pass back and forth across the world division, from the perspective of the apparitions of time to that of the causal deep and back—not contaminating the principles of the one with those of the other, yet permitting the mind to know the one by virtue of the other—is the talent of the master" (212).

Within the modern technological landscape, the fully developed agent is able to move freely between digital and physical spaces, creating meaning in each. Without these skills, cultural production in one realm can be easily appropriated by the other.

"End of Line"

In their construction, these works expose the general relationship with technology of their cultural time and place. Technology permeates the actions of everyday life and in doing so changes the meaning of everyday life. Cultural theorist Henri Lefebvre's *The Production of Space* (1974; English translation published in 1991) echoes these ideas of permeability in his description of a modern house:

> Its image of immobility would then be replaced by an image of a complex of mobilities, a nexus of in and out conduits. By depicting this convergence of waves and currents, this new image, much more accurately than any drawing or photograph, would at the same time disclose the fact that this piece of "immovable property" is actually a two-faceted machine analogous to an active-body: at once a machine calling for massive energy supplies, and an information-based machine with low energy requirements. The occupants of the house perceive, receive, and manipulate the energies which the house itself consumes on a massive scale (93).

To Lefebvre, a house appears as permanent "immovable property," but the structure is constantly permeated by all manner of signals. Technology operates on personal identity in the same fashion. Individuals perceive their sense of self as "immovable property;" it is constantly being modified and influenced by the digital tools around them.

In the early1980s, when *Tron* and *Neuromancer* were released, the digital environments that currently surround us were just coming online, and public concern focused more on the nature of technology. Was technology something that could be trusted to serve a greater role mediating interpersonal relationships? By the 2000s, when *Tron: Legacy* and *Zero History* arrived, the digital environments anticipated in the earlier works were fully developed and active within cultural space. It was no longer a matter of whether these systems could be trusted but rather what were the consequences of this new environment absorbing a large portion of interpersonal communication. While the authors see these systems as potentially dominating, each author allows new forms of personal production, at the level of the individual, to counter the leveling force of technology. There is nothing more powerful than an individual using the power of these mediated spaces to produce personal meaning, whether it be Cayce producing a personal narrative through her clothing line or the isomorphs evolving the digital and the physical in one being. Gibson's novels and the *Tron* films agree that new forms of meaning are being produced though the performance of identity within digital spaces. These texts draw attention to the necessity of personal responsibility and stewardship if the digital and physical worlds are to remain free for the true expression of self. In modern society, the individual is expected to be the "master of two worlds," in Campbell's term. Each person must be able to make use of the digital without being absorbed by it. Gibson and Lisberger have provided guides to this hybrid existence.

Works Cited

Campbell, Joseph. *The Hero with a Thousand Faces*. 1949. Novato: New World, 2008.

Gibson, William. *Neuromancer*. New York: Ace, 1984.

_____. *Zero History*. New York: Putnam, 2010.

Jenkins, Henry, Katie Clinton, and Ravi Purushotma, et al. *Confronting the Challenges of Participatory Culture: Media Education for the Twenty-First Century*. Chicago: MacArthur, 2006.

Lefebvre, Henri. *The Production of Space*. 1974. Trans. Donald Nicholson-Smith. Oxford: Blackwell, 1991.

Tron. Dir. Stephen Lisberger. Perf. Jeff Bridges, Bruce Boxleitner, and David Warner. Disney, 1982. Film.

Tron: Legacy. Dir. Joseph Kosinski. Perf. Jeff Bridges, Garrett Hedlund, and Olivia Wilde. Disney, 2010. Film.

Ghosts and Girls in the Machine: Technology and the Human in Japanese Visual Popular Culture _____

Jaime Weida

"What we have here is ambiguous."

—*Armitage III*

Japanese animated films and television shows are not only commercially popular but are, in themselves, a form of artistic and cultural expression. Their subject matter varies widely, as the nature of the medium allows for the treatment of widely diverse effects and genres. One particularly interesting image in Japanese anime is that of the cyborg. Futuristic technology is a common theme for this medium, and the character of the cyborg appears quite frequently. Despite the diversity of Japanese animation, there are several common elements of the cyborg's depiction. In anime, the cyborg is most frequently female and contains specific recurring gender and sexual markers. I maintain that the image of the cyborg in anime not only replicates the existing objectification of women—specifically by reenacting the patriarchal creation myths—but also reflects, by the medium's form and function, the general commodification of the female body.

There are many works of anime that deal with the concept of cyborgs and represent these cyborgs as female. Two particularly telling examples are the four-episode series *Armitage III*, originally released in 1994, and the feature-length film *Ghost in the Shell* (1995). Both *Armitage III* and *Ghost in the Shell* were significant productions and have proved to be classics of the genre. At the 1997 World Animation Celebration Awards, *Ghost in the Shell* won honors for best theatrical feature film and best director of a theatrical feature film. They are strong representations of the symbols and tropes of the cyborg commonly observed in Japanese animation.

The definition and parameters of the term "cyborg" are complex and must be addressed before turning to a discussion of the films. Traditionally, a cyborg is defined as a human whose physiological process has been partially or completely supplanted by electronic or mechanical technology. The concept of the cyborg (especially the concept of the gendered cyborg), however, is complicated. In her classic essay "A Manifesto for Cyborgs," Donna Haraway says

> a cyborg is a cybernetic organism, a hybrid of machine and organism, as well as a creature of fiction. . . . The international women's movements have constructed "women's experience," as well as uncovered or discovered this crucial collective object. This experience is a fiction and fact of the most crucial, political kind. . . . The cyborg is a matter of fiction and lived experience that changes what counts as women's experience. (139–40)

Haraway proposes to use the cyborg as a trope, or rhetorical gesture, with which to build a somewhat ironic political myth that is faithful to feminism. For her, the cyborg is a liberating symbol, as it resists the historical patriarchal development of subject and object. Haraway writes:

> The cyborg is a creature in a post-gender world; it has no truck with bisexuality, pre-Oedipal symbiosis, unalienated labor, or other seductions to organic wholeness through a final appropriation of all the powers of the parts into a higher unity. . . .
> The cyborg is resolutely committed to partiality, irony, intimacy, and perversity. It is oppositional, utopian, and completely without innocence (141).

Haraway's cyborg, as she admits, "is about transgressed boundaries" (145). Randy Lee Cutler's essay "Warning: Sheborgs/Cyberfems Rupture Image-Stream!" agrees with her analysis, coining the term *cyberfeminism* to describe the contact zone of cybernetic technology and feminism. She claims that much of contemporary art shares "an exploration of the gendered cyborg figure as a technologically empowered entity that challenges boundaries and confounds conventional expectations of body/identity relations" (189). Both she and Haraway envision the cyborg as a potential messianic figure, capable of cutting the convoluted Gordian knot of gender stereotypes and relations. I argue, however, that cyborgs in Japanese animation, specifically those appearing in *Armitage III* and *Ghost in the Shell*, do not fit this transgressive model; instead, they fall within the category of what Cutler calls "the female characters found in comics, animation, and film" that are "subverted" by the liberated cyborg (189). While the cyborgs Armitage, in *Armitage III*, and Major Kusanagi, in *Ghost in the Shell*, appear to deny traditional gender conventions at first glance, a closer analysis reveals that they merely reinscribe them. As Christopher Bolton writes:

> Given the cyborg's split personality, it seems only natural that [Haraway's] theory should be applied to the mechanized bodies prevalent in Japanese animation, or anime, a genre that embodies the same dizzying mix of possibilities as Haraway's cyborg, often undermining gender stereotypes spectacularly one moment only to fall back into sexist exploitation the next. Anime is rife with mechanized female bodies that can be read as both euphorically powerful and objectified, commodified, and victimized. (730)

The conservative nature of these characters is surprising on two levels. First, as Haraway notes, the figure of the cyborg can be seen as not only ideologically but also physically liberating. The cyborg, being partially or totally mechanized, is not susceptible to human frailty. Not only is the cyborg capable of feats of incredible strength, but she can also realize the dream of human immortality, replacing her damaged biological components with cybernetics. The cyborg may be seen as the technological superman, or, in this case, the technological superwoman. Second, not only is the character of the cyborg not subject to traditional boundaries, but the medium of animation is also not subject to traditional limitations. Even in an era when computer graphics and enhancement in film are commonplace, live-action films are still limited by physical realities. Animation, being an artistically created visual experience in its entirety, knows no such limitations. It is possible to animate a scene that would be completely impossible in a traditional live-action film. The marriage of a character and an art form that transgress traditional limits and boundaries naturally should be emancipated from all limitations. Yet, instead of utilizing the boundless potential of the subject and the medium, these films conform to established conventions.

While there are distinct differences between the two films, *Armitage III* and *Ghost in the Shell* share several significant similarities. Both are set in futuristic societies in which the role of cyborgs is convoluted legally and ideologically. The main female cyborg characters (Armitage and Major Kusanagi, respectively) are affiliated with a law enforcement agency and paired with a male partner who, while nominally human, has cybernetic enhancements, blurring the distinction between human and machine. Both Armitage and Kusanagi are ambiguous about their role in the technologized world. They also are physically objectified for the viewer, designed to conform to sexually attractive stereotypes. In fact, both female characters are repeatedly depicted partially or completely naked. Evidently, the viewer is expected to see them as objects of physical desire.

Bolton addresses *Ghost in the Shell* when he describes "the film's voyeuristic male gaze" and its focus on the main female character's sexualized body, but these words may be applied just as easily to *Armitage III*. It should be noted that this "gaze" functions on two levels: as the gaze of the "camera" and as the gaze of the viewer. Applying the term "male gaze" to the anime viewer may be somewhat of a generalization; however, anime is statistically far more popular with males than females, especially in the cyborg genre. In her essay "Visual Pleasure and Narrative Cinema," Laura Mulvey says that in cinema pleasure in looking has been split between active/male and passive/female. The determining male gaze projects its fantasy onto the female figure, which is styled accordingly. In the traditional exhibitionist role women are simultaneously looked at and displayed, with their appearance coded for strong visual and erotic impact so they can be said to connote *to-be-looked-at-ness*. Woman displayed as sexual object is the leitmotif of sexual spectacle. (837)

Armitage III is rife with spectacle on several levels. The film is set on Mars in the twenty-second century, when the planet has been colonized by Earth and is populated by humans and "Second Type" cyborgs, or "Seconds," designed for menial labor and sexual service. The major manufacturer of these cyborgs is the significantly named Conseption Company, the spelling evoking both the act of conception and the word "septic." In the film, cyborgs can be used for labor or sex without any of the associated human complications—a premise that enables a kind of male fantasy. The role of cyborgs in society comes under investigation when Mars engages in negotiations over a political union with Earth, the government of which opposes cyborgs. Along with the standard Second Type cyborg, there also exist illegal "Third Types," or "Thirds," which are cyborgs designed to perfectly imitate humans, physically and mentally. Armitage is an officer of the Mars Police Department and has been assigned, along with her recently arrived partner Ross Syllibus, to track down a renegade killer who has been systematically uncovering and murdering all Thirds. Predictably, it is revealed by the end of the first episode that Armitage herself is a Third with the ability to conceive and give birth to human children.

Admittedly, the sexual politics of *Armitage III* are less than subtle. The opening credits set the visual and thematic tone for the entire series. They focus first on an image of a glowing circuit board (emblazoned with the Pioneer logo, the U.S. video distribution company), slightly curved so as to suggest to the spectator an internal image of the cybernetics of Armitage's body. The scene then focuses on the intentionally (and obviously) seductive image of Armitage pulling a stocking up her leg. The screen focuses next on her dressing in a highly sexualized outfit consisting of shorts, a brassiere top, garters, gloves, and jewelry. The field of view changes to show Armitage walking before a futuristic urban background, seen from the point of view of mechanical goggles, or "robotic vision," complete with hatch marks, crosshairs, and "grainy" filter. There is a swift sequence of images of Armitage's body, handcuffs, a futuristic gun, and urban neon—obviously to conflate sex, violence, and technology. Despite Armitage's intelligence, physical strength, and apparent position of power in the police force, she is marked primarily as a sexual object.

The same conflation is apparent immediately in the body of the anime. Armitage, although physically powerful due to her cyborg nature, often appears immature, almost prepubescent. She is physically little more than half the height of her partner Syllibus, and at one point in the story she childishly opts for ice cream over dinner. Her manner is often overly flirtatious. In fact, upon his first acquaintance with her, Syllibus inquires whether her revealing outfit is "regulation uniform." Armitage's sexual interest in Syllibus is explicit to the viewer and, not surprisingly, they do engage in a sexual relationship, during which Armitage becomes pregnant.

It should be noted, however, that to some extent these details represent standard conventions not only of Japanese anime but also of the cyberpunk genre in general. Cyberpunk may be defined as science fiction in which humans are depicted in futuristic, technologically based societies. Extreme violence, sexuality, and a general "punk" ambience are common features. For example, the film *Blade Runner* (1982) is often considered a classic film in the cyberpunk genre. Exaggerated visual images and character emotions are common tropes in Japanese animated films; the stereotypical oversized "anime eyes" are often an exaggerated marker of desirability.

Even allowing for the standard markers of the genre, Armitage's overtly objectified sexuality seems thematically significant. She is not the only cyborg character who is so marked: one of the opening images of the anime is a Second acting as a flight attendant on a Mars-bound rocket, viewed from behind and wearing a tight-fitting top and thong underpants. The vast majority of cyborgs depicted in the series are female and attractive. As previously noted, many of the Seconds are employed in the sexual sphere as exotic dancers or prostitutes. The Thirds, with one exception, are all female and engaged in stereotypically feminine professions. The first Third to be killed is a country-western idol singer. Another is an artist who paints studies of women and who, it is hinted, may be a lesbian. Another is a dancer, and another a romance novelist. All are traditionally attractive. Even in this futuristic society, cyborgs are bound to conventional gender imagery and roles. As one of the Consception employees says, "The purpose of robots is to help turn human fantasies into reality. They can do almost anything but reproduce, can't they?" (It is worth noting that the anime uses the terms "robot," "cyborg," "machine," and "android" interchangeably, despite their usually distinct meanings.)

Over the course of the story, it develops that the Thirds were originally created as "breeders" to bolster Mars's population growth. They were designed to be, as one character explains, "the perfect receptacle for human babies"—a passage that brings to mind the patriarchal notion of woman-as-vessel. The Thirds, being essentially mechanical, are literally physical vessels and have been created exclusively with that function in mind. Due to the recent negotiations with Earth, however, one of the original creators of the Thirds, D'anclaude, has embarked upon a vendetta to destroy all Thirds, employing a number of "assassinroids," cyborgs created in his physical image and programmed to kill. Although the male Thirds were developed as weapons (with the exception of one physically childlike male cyborg, the last Third to be created), the female models were modified so as to reproduce (rather than serve a solely militaristic function), thus reinforcing the traditional division of gender roles.

The gender politics of Earth's opposition to cyborgs is significant as well. The government on Earth is literally described as "feminist," and their leader is the symbolically named Chairwoman Everheart. The feminist government of Earth opposes the Thirds because they are seen as "unnatural." Physically, Armitage is young, sexually desirable, and fertile. Chairwoman Everheart is portrayed as a middle-aged, somewhat overweight, and unattractive woman—the stereotypical desexualized image of a woman in a position of power. The formulaic competition between women as viewed by the patriarchy is reenacted in this juxtaposition. Not only do cyborgs pose a sexual threat to the chairwoman and other human women, but they represent a generative threat as well. The Thirds can, in fact, reproduce, and not just in the sense of cybernetic replication—an inorganic form of reproduction (as when the killer of the Thirds creates multiple cyborgs of himself). Armitage can reproduce organically and inorganically (at one point in the film, she comes face-to-face with an identical, unfinished replica of herself). Armitage has not transcended human gendered femininity; she has simply supplanted it.

Armitage is not the type of cyborg Haraway had in mind in her "Manifesto." At the end of the series, there is an episode when Armitage and her partner go in search of her creator and the creator of the other Thirds, a man whom she calls "father" and whose picture she keeps on her desk at work. Her father is a formerly brilliant scientist whose mind has become unhinged and who no longer recognizes her. With the help of a modified D'anclaude assassinroid, he lives in an artificial paradise, trying to blur the distinction between the cybernetic and organic by creating treelike cyborgs designed to fertilize Mars's environment, just as Armitage has been designed to fertilize its human population. Haraway writes: "the cyborg does not expect its father to save it through a restoration of the garden; i.e., through the fabrication of a heterosexual mate. . . . the cyborg would not recognize the Garden of Eden" (141). Yet, in *Armitage III*, Armitage and Syllibus reenact the myth of Adam and Eve in her father's garden, where Armitage becomes pregnant. While her CPU is damaged in battle, she is still capable of engaging in her primary function of sexual relations and conceiving a child. As Armitage herself says at the close of the film, when revealing her condition to Syllibus, "my CPU was damaged but everything else worked fine." Armitage's "salvation" is made possible by the heterosexual union and fertility that Haraway rejects. Armitage is literally saved by her father. He regains his senses and repairs her damaged cybernetics, gifting her with a pair of obviously angelic wings. Restored, she and Syllibus—who is outfitted in a mechanized suit of armor, recalling such masculine Christian angels as Gabriel—must defend her father's garden against attackers. Armitage has merely reinscribed the Biblical story of Genesis for the technological world, with Eve and Adam as cyborgs. It is notable that the sequel, *Armitage: Dual Matrix* (2002), while not discussed in this paper, continues the story of Armitage, Syllibus, and their child as a traditional nuclear family. Armitage takes the role of the traditional "housewife," using her cybernetic capacities to defend her child.

Ghost in the Shell is set in 2029, and the main character, Major Motoki Kusanagi, is a police officer with Public Security Section 9. She and her partner, Togusa, are investigating a mysterious "Puppet Master," who apparently is able to "hack" into the "ghost"—a complex term for the soul of cybernetically enhanced humans—and thus control them. The Puppet Master eventually hacks into a completely robotic female body containing no organic brain material. It is later damaged, so that only the torso remains, and is claimed by the Ministry of Foreign Affairs. The Puppet Master, through the robotic body, explains that it is a computer program that achieved sentience. It demands political asylum under the same conditions as any living refugee, raising questions of the meaning and legitimacy of consciousness. The torso that contains the consciousness of the Puppet Master is kidnapped. Kusanagi and Bateau retrieve it, at which time Kusanagi "dives" into the Puppet Master's ghost and communicates with it directly. Kusanagi and the Puppet Master symbolically "mate" within their cybernetic connection, giving "birth" to a new entity. This child is a fusion of them both and holds the power to navigate and control the cybernetic network in a child's body provided by Bateau.

While *Ghost in the Shell* is a more complex and thematic work of art than *Armitage III*, it still reinforces traditional sexualized gender roles. As in *Armitage III*, the opening scenes immediately sexualize the image of the female cyborg. Unlike Armitage, Major Kusanagi is visually marked as a cyborg from the outset (she has four cable inputs on the back of her neck), but she is also marked as a sexualized object. The opening sequence before the credits teases the viewer with her seemingly naked image. Yet a closer view reveals that she is merely wearing a skintight, skin-toned bodysuit, quickly identified as some sort of camouflaging device. Like *Armitage III*, the credits open with the image of a circuit board. The view shifts to a cyborg creation scene, apparently that of Kusanagi, interposed with flashes of numbers that seem to represent computer code. The creation process of the female cyborg is viewed literally from the "inside-out," with the complete and naked cyborg emerging from amniotic-like fluid. The "camera" repeatedly and specifically focuses on her secondary sex characteristics, further objectifying her traditionally attractive physical form. Over the course of the anime, Kusanagi is much less overtly sexualized than Armitage (in fact, she seems almost asexual at times), but her cyborg body marks her as a traditionally sexualized object.

A notable exchange occurs early in the film that highlights the specifically gendered status of her character. An important discrepancy occurs between the dubbed English and the subtitled English. When a male colleague inquires about an apparent lapse of performance on Kusanagi's part, her reply is translated differently from the Japanese for the dub and the subtitle. The dubbed response is: "Must have been a loose wire," which effectively blames her lapse on the limitations of her cyborg body. The subtitled response is: "I'm on my period," which places the blame on the reproductive system and plays into the sexist notion that menstruation is a defect and causes "problems" for women. Although the subtitled line seems to be meant ironically (as a cyborg she obviously would not menstruate) the dichotomy between the two lines, although perhaps unintentional, is thematically significant. In both cases, her failed performance is attributed to problems with her body. The simultaneous translations effectively equate female menstruation with mechanical failure, but, as illustrated in the opening sequence, the cyborg body can be artificially created and repaired. A loose wire can be reconnected and the problem fixed; however, menstruation is a physical marker of gender that cannot be fixed. Kusanagi's sarcastic quip not only underlines her cyborg "superiority" to the biological female body but also, despite her appearance, marks her as separate from the biologically feminine. Like Armitage, she represents the stereotypical image of female sexual desirability. Unlike Armitage, however, hers is septic sexuality and lacks the messiness of reproduction.

At this point it is worth noting an important difference between Armitage's and Kusanagi's appearance and markers of sexuality. When seen naked, Armitage, like the rest of the Thirds, is portrayed without nipples. This move is not one of censorship (at one point the artist's model is shown naked with full, normal sexual characteristics) but symbolism. Yet it is understood explicitly that Armitage possesses primary female sexual characteristics, for she has sex with Syllibus and conceives a child by him. In contrast, Kusanagi has full secondary sexual characteristics, as is made obvious several times; however, like a doll, she has no primary sexual characteristics. Not only are Kusanagi and Armitage's bodies fragmented from their functions, their bodies are themselves fragmented or incomplete. What possible reason could there be to produce a female with some but not all of the physical markers of gender? I argue that this is a masculine appropriation of the female function of reproduction.

If Armitage reenacts the story of Adam and Eve, Kusanagi demonstrates the technological immaculate conception through her union with the Puppet Master. From such a viewpoint, the physical differences between Kusanagi and Armitage make sense. Armitage has no need for the traditional markers of secondary sexual characteristics, for her function is tied to primary sexual characteristics. For Kusanagi, who does not physically conceive and bear a child, it is the exact opposite. Despite the physical power of their cyborg bodies, the denouement of their stories and their technological possibilities simply reinscribe feminine sexual conventions.

When Kusanagi dives into the Puppet Master, her own body, like the Puppet Master's assumed body, has been physically damaged. Bateau places her next to the Puppet Master so that she may connect with him. Throughout the scene, gender and sex roles are swapped and contrasted in a manner that, initially, seems reminiscent of Haraway's liberated cyborg. The Puppet Master has assumed a female body, and, on one level, their union may be analyzed as avoiding standard heterosexual gender roles by recasting the act of reproduction and sex as single-gendered, or homosexual. Significantly, the Puppet Master also chooses a body that is a cyborg clone of Kusanagi's. I think this explanation is not sufficient in and of itself. Although the Puppet Master is a virtual being that has emerged miraculously and under its own power from the data web, it is identified and referred to as male. When the Puppet Master speaks, his voice, despite the female body, is audibly masculine. Moreover, the union between Kusanagi and the Puppet Master is ultimately recast in terms of traditionally heterosexual, not lesbian, roles. The Puppet Master's cyborg body, although lacking arms and truncated at the waist, retains its female breasts. Kusanagi's hair is wet and slicked back in what appears to be a masculine style, and Bateau covers her damaged body with a coat so that her physical femininity is no longer visually marked. Even though the Puppet Master inhabits a body that is the same model as Kusanagi's cyborg body, the presentation of that body conforms to stereotypical gender markers. The Puppet Master's body has long, femininely styled blonde hair and blue eyes. Neither of these traits is common to the Japanese, so it seems obvious that imagery was chosen to highlight the femaleness of the cyborg body. Visually, the scene almost appears to be that of a man and a woman engaging in sexual union, returning to the concept of the sacred marriage: Kusanagi's now masculinized body lays directly next to the Puppet Master's visually feminine body, the camera focusing on the proximity between them.

Kusanagi and the Puppet Master's symbolic and sexual roles are traded and ultimately fixed in gendered terms. Kusanagi initially initiates contact with the Puppet Master because she wants to dive into his ghost. While I have interpreted this in terms of the biological drive toward childbearing, it can also be discussed in terms of the traditionally masculine role of the sexual initiator. "Diving" into the Puppet Master suggests the physical role of the male during sexual intercourse; however, after Kusanagi dives into the Puppet Master, their gender roles are confused, and they literally swap bodies. The Puppet Master inhabits Kusanagi's body, which appears masculine at this juncture, and Kusanagi inhabits the Puppet Master's former body. Bateau, observing their connection, notes the conflation when asking Kusanagi, "Are you going into him or is he coming into you?" It is no longer clear who has the masculine and who the feminine role in their virtual union. But the gender roles are firmly reestablished when the Puppet Master says to Kusanagi, "At last I'm able to channel into you." He makes it clear that the purpose of his contact is reproduction. He wants to "leave behind offspring," and while he can make replicas of himself, only Kusanagi can give him the "child" he desires. Cyborg reproduction is constrained by the terms of physical human reproduction. Even though Kusanagi protests that she "cannot have children," the Puppet Master maintains that she "will bear *my* offspring into the net" (emphasis mine). Here, Kusanagi is doubly constrained. Firstly, she is unaware of her own reproductive potential until the masculine Puppet Master informs her, just as Armitage is unaware of her capacity to bear a child until her "father" enlightens her. Moreover, the Puppet Master says

Kusanagi will bear his offspring. This is a male appropriation of reproduction and childbirth through the technology of the cyborg.

After Kusanagi's union with the Puppet Master, Bateau is able to salvage only her head and procures her a new body. Meaningfully, the body is that of a female child. In the final scene, Kusanagi appears with her own face but physically, in a dress and shoes, she is a child. This is the first time in the film that Kusanagi is seen wearing feminine clothing. She expresses dismay at her new body, Bateau claiming that it was the best he could find for her. Not only has Kusanagi been reborn as the child of her union with the Puppet Master, she has been reborn as a woman. Again, her physical form has been determined by a man, regardless of her preferred physical and spiritual gender roles. In a sense, Kusanagi is more constrained at the end of the film that she was at the beginning. Despite the fact that she is now mentally an evolved hybrid of her old "ghost" and the Puppet Master's "ghost," she is physically gendered not just as a woman but as a child. In the final scene, when Bateau asks her where she will go now, she replies, "the net is vast and infinite." Her reference to the virtual "net" of technology suggests that perhaps Kusanagi is transcending her former existence. Yet a net is also a device used to trap and bind living things. Perhaps Kusanagi is more trapped by gender conventions than she was before her union with the Puppet Master.

Finally, Armitage's and Kusanagi's images are not only commodified but changed quite literally into commodities for the anime sales market. It is possible to buy statues and action figures of their exact images. Like cyborgs, these replicated figures are almost infinitely reproducible. It is worth noting that the visual medium of these images is also infinitely reproducible. While Kusanagi has a "price" on her cyborg body that binds her to employment in Section Nine, the Major Kusanagi action figure has an actual price in a retail store. It would be ridiculous to say that animated films and series, and their constituent characters, are created without thought to the retail market. Not only do these gendered cyborg images reflect the reinscription of gender roles, but they also reflect the projected sales market. The voyeuristic male gaze of the viewer watching the anime may very well prove to be a major factor in the determination of what exactly is seen by that gaze. Would the market for Armitage and Kusanagi DVDs and merchandise be as strong if their images were not visually seductive? The seduction then translates into an attempt, by the viewer, to physically possess a representation of the gendered cyborg body, just as Armitage and Kusanagi are possessed literally in the anime. This further strengthens Mulvey's claims regarding the "active/male" cinematic gaze. The male viewer is actively participating in the sexualization of the cyborg, in the real and cinematic worlds.

Significantly, this sort of control and alteration occurs in the private fan market as well. Not only are these characters commodified by the marketplace, they are commodified, altered, and reproduced by viewers. Due to modern digital technology, anime viewers have evolved from "eyes" that can only passively exert a voyeuristic male gaze to active participants. There are a large amount of "fan subs," or "fan dubs"—pirated, altered versions of the films. The creators of these altered versions replace either the dubbed or subtitled dialogue with dialogue of their own making. Frequently, the replacement serves to transform the original film into pornography, further objectifying the already-objectified female cyborgs. It is possible to alter images of the characters to portray them in pornographic poses or attitudes, or to re-work the images into "X-rated" animated sequences. Video and audio editing software is easy to come by and often easy to use. In one sense, it is as if the anime viewer has facilitated the birth of a symbolic cyborg—the fusion of digital technology and human editing producing a new product, which is itself commodified, widely reproduced, and distributed.

While Haraway sees the concept of the cyborg as potentially transcendent and liberating for women, Japanese animated films such as *Armitage III* and *Ghost in the Shell* merely reinscribe the established hegemony of gender. The image of the cyborg in anime is highly sexualized and commodified. This takes place on several levels: the cyborg is presented as a commodity, the sexual body of the female cyborg is commodified for the viewer's male gaze, and the actual anime DVD and associated merchandise serves as an economic commodity in the marketplace. The reproductive capacity of the female cyborg is subverted and recast as a patriarchal appropriation of heterosexual notions of marriage. While these animated cyborgs may appear at first to be liberated from conventional gender tropes, they are ultimately bound to them. As Springer notes, the digital image of the female cyborg may indeed be a "battlefield where the struggle over gender roles will be fought behind virtual barricades" (94).

Works Cited

Armitage III. Dir. Hiroyuki Ochi. Screenplay by Chiaki Konaka. Pioneer Entertainment, 1994. Film.

Bolton, Christopher A. "From Wooden Cyborgs to Celluloid Souls: Mechanical Bodies in Anime and Japanese Puppet Theater." *Positions* 10.3 (Winter 2003): 729–71.

Cutler, Randy Lee. "Warning: Sheborgs/Cyberfems Rupture Image-Stream!" *The Uncanny: Experiments in Cyborg Culture*. Ed. Bruce Grenville. Vancouver: Arsenal Pulp. 187–210.

Ghost in the Shell. Dir. Mamoru Oshii. Screenplay by Kazunori Itō. Bandai Visual and Manga Entertainment, 1995. Film.

Haraway, Donna. "A Manifesto for Cyborgs: Science, Technology, and Socialist Feminism in the 1980s." *The Uncanny: Experiments in Cyborg Culture*. Ed. Bruce Grenville. Vancouver: Arsenal Pulp. 139–81.

Mulvey, Laura. "Visual Pleasure and Narrative Cinema." *Film Theory and Criticism: Introductory Readings*. Eds. Leo Braudy and Marshall Cohen. New York: Oxford UP, 1999. 833–44.

Springer, Claudia. *Electronic Eros: Bodies and Desire in the Postindustrial Age*. Austin: U of Texas P. 1996.

RESOURCES

Additional Works on Technology and Humanity _____

Drama

Doctor Faustus by Christopher Marlowe, 1604.
Faust by Johann Wolfgang von Goethe, 1806.
An Enemy of the People by Henrik Ibsen, 1882.
The Cherry Orchard by Anton Chekhov, 1904.
The Adding Machine by Elmer Rice, 1923.
Dynamo by Eugene O'Neill, 1929.
Wit by Margaret Edson, 1995/1999.
Miss Evers' Boys by David Feldshuh, 1997.
Copenhagen by Michael Frayn, 1998.

Fiction

Lost Illusions by Honoré de Balzac, 1837–43.
"The Birthmark" by Nathaniel Hawthorne, 1843.
"Rappaccini's Daughter" by Nathaniel Hawthorne, 1844.
Fact and Fiction by Lydia Maria Child, 1846.
Cranford by Elizabeth Gaskell, 1851–53.
Hard Times by Charles Dickens, 1854.
From the Earth to the Moon by Jules Verne, 1865.
Germinal by Émile Zola, 1885.
Looking Backward by Edward Bellamy, 1888.
A Connecticut Yankee in King Arthur's Court by Mark Twain, 1889.
The Time Machine by H. G. Wells, 1895.
Dracula by Bram Stoker, 1897.
"In the Cage" by Henry James, 1898.
Herland by Charlotte Perkins Gilman, 1915.
Player Piano by Kurt Vonnegut, 1952.
Solution Three by Naomi Mitchison, 1975.
Kindred by Octavia Butler, 1979.
Letters to a Young Doctor by Richard Selzer, 1982.
White Noise by Don DeLillo, 1985.
Contact by Carl Sagan, 1985.
Snow Crash by Neal Stephenson, 1992.
Bloodchild and Other Stories by Octavia Butler, 1996.

Nonfiction

Essays by Ralph Waldo Emerson, 1841/1844.

Walden by Henry David Thoreau, 1854.

Women and Economics by Charlotte Perkins Gilman, 1898.

The Education of Henry Adams by Henry Adams, 1918.

Mythology by Edith Hamilton, 1942.

D'Aulaires' Book of Greek Myths by Ingri d'Aulaire and Edgar Parin d'Aulaire, 1962.

Rocket Boys by Homer Hickam Jr., 1998.

Poetry

Lyrical Ballads by William Wordsworth, 1798.

General Bibliography ————————————————————————

Alkon, Paul K. *Science Fiction Before 1900: Imagination Discovers Technology.* Woodbridge: Twayne, 1994.

Barr, Marleen S. *Lost in Space: Probing Feminist Science Fiction and Beyond.* Chapel Hill: U of North Carolina P, 1993.

Bolter, Jay David. *Writing Space: Computers, Hypertext, and the History of Writing.* 1991. 2nd ed. New York: Routledge, 2001.

Clarke, Bruce. *Posthuman Metamorphosis: Narrative and Systems.* New York: Fordham UP, 2008.

Clarke, Bruce, and Manuela Rossini, eds. *The Routledge Companion to Literature and Science.* New York: Routledge, 2010.

Clayton, Jay. *Charles Dickens in Cyberspace: The Afterlife of the Nineteenth Century in Postmodern Culture.* Oxford: Oxford UP, 2003.

Colatrella, Carol. *Toys and Tools in Pink: Cultural Narratives of Gender, Science, and Technology.* Columbus: Ohio State UP, 2011.

Colligan, Colette, and Margaret Linley, eds. *Media, Technology, and Literature in the Nineteenth Century: Image, Sound, Touch.* Burlington: Ashgate, 2011.

Donawerth, Jane. *Frankenstein's Daughters: Women Writing Science Fiction.* Syracuse: Syracuse UP, 1997.

Gilman, Sander. *Disease and Representation: Images of Illness from Madness to AIDS.* Ithaca: Cornell UP, 1988.

Goody, Alex. *Technology, Literature, and Culture.* Malden: Polity, 2011.

Greenberg, Mark, and Lance Schachterle, eds. *Literature and Technology.* Bethlehem: Lehigh UP, 1992.

Hayles, N. Katherine. *How We Became Posthuman: Virtual Bodies in Cybernetics, Literature, and Information Systems.* Chicago: U of Chicago P, 1999.

Hayles, N. Katherine, and Anne Burdick. *Writing Machines.* Cambridge, MA: MIT P, 2002.

Hoeg, Jerry. *Science, Technology, and Latin American Narrative in the Twentieth Century and Beyond.* Bethlehem: Lehigh UP, 2000.

Jenkins, Henry. *Convergence Culture: Where Old and New Media Meet.* Rev. ed. New York: New York UP, 2008.

Johnston, John. *Information Multiplicity: American Fiction in the Age of Media Saturation.* Baltimore: Johns Hopkins UP, 1998.

Joyce, Michael. *Of Two Minds: Hypertext Pedagogy and Poetics.* Ann Arbor: U of Michigan P, 1995.

Kittler, Friedrich. *Gramophone, Film, Typewriter.* Trans. Geoffrey Winthrop-Young and Michael Wutz. Stanford: Stanford UP, 1999.

Landow, George P. *Hypertext: The Convergence of Contemporary Critical Theory and Technology*. Baltimore: Johns Hopkins UP, 1992.

Lanham, Richard A. *The Electronic Word: Democracy, Technology, and the Arts*. Chicago: U of Chicago P, 1993.

Lathers, Marie. *Space Oddities: Women and Outer Space in Popular Film and Culture, 1960–2000*. Continuum, 2010.

Lears, T. J. Jackson. *No Place of Grace: Antimodernism and the Transformation of American Culture, 1880–1920*. U of Chicago P, 1983.

Littlefield, Melissa M. *The Lying Brain: Lie Detection in Science and Science Fiction*. Ann Arbor: University of Michigan P, 2011.

Marx, Leo. *The Machine in the Garden: Technology and the Pastoral Idea in America*. 1964. Oxford: Oxford UP, 2000.

_____. *The Pilot and the Passenger: Essays on Literature, Technology, and Culture*. Oxford: Oxford UP, 1988.

McLuhan, Marshall. *The Gutenberg Galaxy*. Toronto: U of Toronto P, 1964.

_____. *Understanding Media*. 1964. Cambridge, MA: MIT P, 1994.

Menke, Richard. *Telegraphic Realism: Victorian Fiction and Other Information Systems*. Stanford: Stanford UP, 2008.

Michaels, Walter Benn. *The Gold Standard and the Logic of Naturalism: American Literature at the Turn of the Century*. Berkeley: U of California P, 1988.

Miller, J. Hillis. *On Literature*. New York: Routledge, 2002.

Murray, Janet H. *Hamlet on the Holodeck: The Future of Narrative in Cyberspace*. Cambridge, MA: MIT P, 1998.

Nadel, Alan. *Containment Culture: American Narratives, Postmodernism, and the Atomic Age*. Durham: Duke UP, 1995.

Penley, Constance, and Andrew Ross, eds. *Technoculture*. Minneapolis: U of Minnesota P, 1991.

Porush, David. *The Soft Machine: Cybernetic Fiction*. New York: Methuen, 1984

Ryan, Marie-Laure. *Narrative Across Media: The Languages of Storytelling*. Lincoln: U of Nebraska P, 2004.

Schleifer, Ronald. *Modernism and Time: The Logic of Abundance in Literature, Science, and Culture, 1880–1930*. Cambridge, England: Cambridge UP, 2009.

Solomon, William. *Literature, Amusement, and Technology in the Great Depression*. 2002. Cambridge, England: Cambridge UP, 2009.

Sypher, Wylie. *Literature and Technology: The Alien Vision*. New York: Random, 1968.

Tabbi, Joseph. *Postmodern Sublime: Technology and American Writing from Mailer to Cyberpunk*. Ithaca: Cornell UP, 1996.

Telotte, J. P. *Replications: A Robotic History of the Science Fiction Film*. Champaign: U of Illinois P, 1995.

Tichi, Cecelia. *Shifting Gears: Technology, Literature, Culture in Modernist America.* Chapel Hill: U of North Carolina P, 1996.

Thurschwell, Pamela. *Literature, Technology, and Magical Thinking, 1880–1920.* Cambridge, England: Cambridge UP, 2005.

Wald, Priscilla. *Contagious: Cultures, Carriers, and the Outbreak Narrative.* Durham: Duke UP, 2007.

Walton, Priscilla L. *Our Cannibals, Ourselves.* Champaign: U of Illinois P, 2004.

Williams, Rosalind. *Notes On The Underground: An Essay on Technology, Society, and the Imagination.* Cambridge, MA: MIT P, 2008.

Wosk, Julie. *Women and the Machine: Representations from the Spinning Wheel to the Electronic Age.* Baltimore: Johns Hopkins UP, 2003.

Wutz, Michael. *Enduring Words: Literary Narrative in a Changing Media Ecology.* Tuscaloosa: University of Alabama P, 2009.

Yaszek, Lisa. *Galactic Suburbia: Recovering Women's Science Fiction.* Columbus: Ohio State UP, 2008.

CRITICAL
INSIGHTS

About the Editor

Dr. Carol Colatrella is professor of literature and cultural studies in the School of Literature, Communication, and Culture at the Georgia Institute of Technology, and codirector of the Georgia Tech Center for the Study of Women, Science, and Technology. Her books include *Evolution, Sacrifice, and Narrative: Balzac, Zola, and Faulkner* (1990), *Literature and Moral Reform: Melville and the Discipline of Reading* (2002), and *Toys and Tools in Pink: Cultural Narratives of Gender, Science, and Technology* (2011). She coedited (with Joseph Alkana) and contributed to *Cohesion and Dissent in America* (1994), an anthology examining the influence of Sacvan Bercovitch's scholarship on American culture. Since 1993, Colatrella has served as the executive director of the Society for Literature, Science, and the Arts and the editor of the SLSA newsletter, *Decodings*. Her honors and awards include two Fulbright fellowships (2000; 2006), a Georgia Tech European Union Center Grant (2010–11), and a residency at Zentrum für Literatur- und Kulturforschung, Berlin (2008).

Contributors

Narin Hassan is associate professor in the School of Literature, Communication, and Culture at the Georgia Institute of Technology. She is the author of *Diagnosing Empire: Women, Medical Knowledge, and Colonial Mobility* (2011). Her current work includes a book-length project on conservatories and gardens as border spaces in Victorian culture and research on the wet nursing and cultural politics of breastfeeding in both Victorian and contemporary culture. She teaches courses in nineteenth-century literature and culture, gender studies, postcolonial studies, and the history of medicine.

Melissa M. Littlefield is an assistant professor at the University of Illinois at Urbana-Champaign, where she has appointments in the Departments of English and Kinesiology and Community Health and is affiliated with programs in writing studies and science, technology, information, and medicine. Her book *The Lying Brain: Lie Detection in Science and Science Fiction* (2011) is a sociocultural history of mechanical lie detection and its relationship to the emergent, neuroscientific research on deception. She is also the coeditor (with Jenell Johnson) of the forthcoming collection *The Neuroscientific Turn: Transdisciplinarity in the Age of the Brain* (2012).

Michael Black is a doctoral candidate in the English department at the University of Illinois at Urbana-Champaign. He is currently completing his dissertation on the politics of software design, with a focus on the cultural history of personal computing and object-oriented programming. His research interests include representations of information technology in fiction, science fiction, new media production, humanities computing, software studies, games as narrative media, and intellectual property law. His work has appeared in the journal *Games and Culture*.

Tanfer Emin Tunc is an assistant professor in the Department of American Culture and Literature at Hacettepe University, Ankara, Turkey. She received her BA, MA, and PhD in American history, and an advanced graduate certificate in women's studies from the State University of New York at Stony Brook. She specializes in U.S. women's history and literature; the history of medicine, sexuality, and reproduction; and American cultural studies. Dr. Tunc is the author of six books and over seventy book chapters, reference entries, reviews, and journal articles, which have appeared in such publications as *Rethinking History*, *Asian Journal of Women's Studies*, *Foreign Literature Studies*, *Women's History Review*, *Historical Journal*, and *Journal of Women's History*.

Madeleine Monson-Rosen studies the relationship between late twentieth-century literature and the history of technology. She is completing her PhD in English at the University of Illinois at Chicago.

Kevin LaGrandeur is associate professor of English at the New York Institute of Technology. His scholarship on technology and culture has appeared in *Criticism. com*, *Eloquent Images: Word and Image in the Age of New Media* (edited by Mary Hocks and Michelle Kendrick), *CLCWeb: Comparative Literature and Culture*, and *Science Fiction Studies*. He recently has finished writing a book on representations of artificial servants in early modern Europe.

Inger H. Dalsgaard is associate professor at Aarhus University, Denmark. She conducted her doctoral work at the Massachusetts Institute of Technology and King's College, University of London, and holds a PhD in American studies. She is coeditor of *The Cambridge Companion to Thomas Pynchon* (2012) and the author of numerous essays on science and technology in Anglo-American literature.

Abigail Glogower is a doctoral student in the visual and cultural studies program at the University of Rochester in Rochester, New York. Her work concerns the relationships among communication technologies, literature, and visual culture in nineteenth-century America and Great Britain.

Melissa Dinsman is a PhD candidate at the University of Notre Dame working in British, American, German, and Irish modernism. She is currently writing a dissertation that explores the connection between radio and war in late modern writers' World War II radio broadcasts. She has publications forthcoming in the *Brecht Yearbook* and *Literature, Interpretation, and Theory*.

Claire Menck holds a PhD in leadership and change from Antioch University. She is a visiting professor at several institutions and is engaged in research on social media, disaster, and meaning making. She is also an international award-winning chef who has spent over twenty-five years in the food service industry.

Luis O. Arata is professor of modern languages at Quinnipiac University. He was born in Argentina, came to the United States to study engineering, migrated to mathematics, did graduate work in physics, and finished a PhD in Romance studies at Cornell University. He is a past faculty fellow at Yale University and the Santa Fe Institute. His publications on literature, film, theater, cultural studies, and new media investigate the functions of play, interaction, and modeling in shaping reality.

Annie van den Oever is director of the master's program in film studies in the Department of Arts, Culture, and Media at the University of Groningen. She is also the director of the Groningen University Film Archive and the founding editor of the international book series *The Key Debates*, with Ian Christie and Dominique Chateau. Her most recent books are *Ostrannenie* (2010) and *Sensitizing the Viewer. The Impact of New Techniques and the Art Experience* (2011).

Robert Blaskiewicz is a Marion L. Brittain Postdoctoral Fellow at the Georgia Institute of Technology, where he teaches critical thinking and writing courses that revolve around twentieth-century American literature and culture. His research interests include World War II in film and literature, science and pseudoscience, and conspiracy theory.

Aaron Barlow is associate professor of English at New York City College of Technology. His recent book *Beyond the Blogosphere: Information and Its Children* (written with Robert Leston; 2012) reflects his interest in the intersection of culture and technology.

Mike Griffith is the head of instructional technology and faculty support at Tulane University. He is a professor of media theory and literature in the English department. His research focus is the relationship between emerging media communication and the creation of public social spaces.

Jaime Weida is an instructor in the English department at the Borough of Manhattan Community College-CUNY. She holds a master's degree in physics and is currently finishing her PhD in English at the CUNY Graduate Center. Her areas of interest include American and British modernism, feminist and queer theory, nontraditional genres and literary formats, and the intersection of literature and science.

Index